# Software for Educational Computing

A General-Purpose Driver for Computer-Assisted Instruction, Interrogation and System Simulation ('MACAID')

By

**K. Ahmed, PhD**

Systems Manager, Computation Services Unit,
McMaster University Medical School, Hamilton, Ontario

**D. Ingram, PhD**

Senior Lecturer in Medical Physics and Computing,
St Bartholomew's Hospital Medical College, London

*and*

**C. J. Dickinson, DM**

Professor of Medicine in the University of London, at
St Bartholomew's Hospital Medical College, London

Published by
MTP Press Limited
Falcon House
Lancaster, England



**British Library Cataloguing in Publication Data**

Ahmed, K
Software for educational computing.
1. MACAID (Computer programs)
I. Title II. Ingram, David
III. Dickinson, C J
371.39′445 LB1028.5

ISBN 0-85200-359-5



Printed in Great Britain by
Clark Constable Ltd, Edinburgh

# Contents

## APPENDICES

# Preface

Our goal in this book is to introduce a new and complete system of computer-aided instruction and interrogation which for quick reference we have called 'MACAID'. It is a fully portable system which can be run on virtually any computer in the world today, providing it has a FORTRAN compiler and provides for direct-access of a text file. The precompiled standard Driver reads and acts on a standard format of text file. The Driver can interpret a wide variety of responses including numeric and numeric range, character, keyword and keyword combinations using dictionaries, and multiple choice 'yes/no' or graded responses. Provision is made for cursor control of the user's visual display unit, for keeping count of scores and totals, for setting flags, and for conditional branching. Selected answers can be entered on an answer file for subsequent analysis.

Many of these facilities are available in other systems, but MACAID has the added advantage of being compatible with all standard FORTRAN subroutines, which can be called at will during execution, and which can be operated according to commands in a text file. A comprehensive on-line Editor is part of the system, as is a checking and frame-renumbering facility. These features make it possible to mount computational subroutines and simulation models within a framework of interrogative text which can easily be written and edited by someone with no computer expertise at all. To this end we have planned the main body of the book (Parts 2 and 3) to describe the file system and the Driver in ordinary (i.e. 'non-computer') language, but in the Appendices to supply a programmer implementing the system with a complete FORTRAN program of the standard Driver, a table of FORTRAN symbol names, and with examples of a directory of text files and FORTRAN supervisor program.

Part 1 of the book comprises a review of current systems of computer-aided instruction and interrogation, and also contains a model text exercise which takes MACAID through all its paces. The dialogue is given in full opposite the relevant parts of the text file, and two illustrative FORTRAN subroutines are called up by the Driver during the course of the exercise (these are listed in full in the Appendix).

We hope that for those entering the exciting field of computer-assisted instruction that MACAID may prove to be a simple and satisfactory system capable of answering all their needs: we hope that those already experienced in the field will find that MACAID has sufficiently comprehensive features to enable it at least to contribute to the much-needed standardization which all would agree should be our ultimate goal and which would pave the way to widespread implementation of the system on microprocessors. To this end we shall continue to welcome comments and suggestions from users.

# Acknowledgements

Although the development of MACAID has proceeded in many places, McMaster University has been its geographical centre, and we are specially grateful for the computer services provided us there and for the help of Don Gilchrist. We have also extensively used the London University computer services to develop medical teaching exercises using MACAID, and we are particularly grateful to the staff of Queen Mary College Computer Centre for providing excellent time-sharing services for teaching purposes.

We are also most grateful to Eileen Tinlin for typing the many manuscript revisions.

Khursheed Ahmed

Computation Services Unit,
McMaster University Medical Centre,
Main Street West,
Hamilton, Ontario, L8N 3Z5,
Canada

David Ingram
John Dickinson

Department of Medicine,
St Bartholomew's Hospital Medical College,
West Smithfield,
London EC1A 7BE,
England.

# Part 1
# Review of interrogative systems – the design and objectives of MACAID

# 1
# Introduction – computer-aided instructional and interrogative programs; the need for standardization; linking text and scientific computation

The past decade has brought considerable advances in the design of interactive computer terminals, which are now easy and convenient to use. For various reasons, especially the cost of computer 'hardware' (such as arithmetic processors, short- and long-term memory devices, printers, tape readers, disc drives and visual display units) international standards and conventions were adopted to make different types of equipment mutually compatible. The design of supporting 'software' (i.e. compilers, programs, data-bases) is of equal importance for the successful development of interactive systems. The cost of software, being related to general salary levels, now tends to dominate the economics of a complete system. This trend will continue (USA Congress OTA, 1979). With the spectacular and continuing fall in the price of computer hardware, particularly of solid state devices, and the increased power available, emphasis has shifted to the more efficient writing of programs and the adoption of standard software systems and programs which can be transferred readily between machines.

By a somewhat indirect route, which we shall explain later, we became interested in the design of software for computer-assisted instruction and assessment. A similar type of software is required in systems for interviewing people – for example in preliminary interviews or surveys of medical patients. Wider and more economical use of such systems requires not only that the software is 'portable' (i.e. usable on a large variety of different computers), but also that it allows teachers, designers and other staff not proficient in computing to write and develop instructional material, interviews or tests to meet their individual needs. There is much duplication of effort in programming such systems. The creative activity of working out and introducing educational material, for example, tends to take second place to solving the banal technical problems of man/machine interaction, since the foundations of the software must be laid before any material can be used. Very good educational material is often developed around the constraints of badly designed local driving software written in an idiosyncratic manner which is often highly 'machine-dependent'. (By 'machine-dependent' we do not just imply machine code programming – which is as great a waste of human effort as is the continued handsetting of type for newspapers and books – but also the use of non-standard languages, and local dialects of the more common languages.)

Many educational programs containing text material have been written in FORTRAN. This makes the programs portable, but anyone with even slight knowledge of this useful scientific language knows that it is clumsy and inconvenient for handling text material, either input or output. As we shall discuss more fully in the next chapter, more flexible systems often need a non-standard language and a 'dedicated' machine (i.e. a computer which can be used for one or only a few related purposes).

The objectives of this book are two:

(1) To describe, and to propose as an international standard, a simple format of interrogative text and text control instructions which can be interpreted by a master program, or 'Driver', capable of handling uncompiled text and compiled scientific subroutines concomitantly and flexibly.
(2) To provide a standard FORTRAN version of the proposed Driver which can run on virtually any computer at present available.

Although we anticipate that many readers who study this book will be chiefly interested in the second objective – thus saving themselves the huge labour and expense of writing their own software, we regard the first objective as the more important. Although FORTRAN shows little sign of becoming a dead language, it will certainly become one eventually, or evolve out of recognition. Therefore, the FORTRAN driver structure is described in considerable detail, and commented on fully, so that it could be rewritten in other languages such as APL, Pascal or BASIC. Any Driver could then run any text file. If an instructor wanted, for example, a program to teach acid–base physiology to medical students, he would need only to beg, borrow or buy a text file written by experts, perhaps accompanied by a short computational subroutine to do any necessary arithmetic. His own Driver would make the program at once operational on his own computer. If an instructor has written an interrogative program of which he is proud, and which he would like to make widely available to others, he could write it in standard text form knowing that all over the world fellow instructors could at once run the program on their own computers, within minutes of receiving the text on magnetic tape or floppy disc.

Perhaps we shall be unsuccessful in persuading others that our system is the best. In that event, we hope to provoke sufficient interest to encourage agreement on some more satisfactory international standard. In any case, providing that the system acquires enough users, it will become worthwhile to write translation programs to and from other systems such as COURSE-WRITER, TUTOR and PILOT.

It is remarkable that computer-aided instruction has so little fulfilled its initial promise. In many institutions, especially in the USA, it has been relegated to the bottom of the league table in the allocation of student and faculty time and resources. Thus, the use of computers in teaching institutions has been mainly confined to sophisticated scientific and technological research. Despite the predictions of the sixties, there has not been large-scale and effective use of computers in the classroom and for self-guided learning. A few centres have capitalized on these developments, but most have not. This is surprising, because a tool as versatile as the modern digital computer, especially when provided with several 'time-sharing' (i.e. simultaneously active) peripheral interactive terminals, is capable of establishing a one-to-one dialogue with a student at all levels from elementary teaching to highly sophisticated simulation exercises.

The costs have in the past been prohibitive; and students as well as teachers are generally conservative. Furthermore, there has been little exchange of ideas between instructors and users. Even wealthy institutions have usually not found it worthwhile to invest in and take advantage of many excellent instructional computer programs developed elsewhere, because of the difficulties of adapting them to the local computer. In addition, although it is technically easy for many separate institutions to share the use of a single large computer facility, the telephone 'connect time' necessary is expensive, and typically accounts for half the running costs (Forman *et al.*, 1979).

Neither the 'high-level' languages FORTRAN or BASIC (both using easily comprehensible semi-grammatical English) were designed for programmed interrogation and instruction. Although they offer good facilities for mathematical computation, they are clumsy and inconvenient when called upon to process or display text. These limitations were recognized long ago, and a host of 'authoring' languages (i.e. languages suitable for creating, editing and running text files) have been developed in the past decade. Well known examples include COURSEWRITER, TUTOR, AIDS, IDA, PILOT, NATAL 74 and MIL; but in general these need elaborate implementation on a dedicated computer, sometimes even with special hardware.

Increasingly, local needs will be met by the burgeoning microprocessor revolution, providing inexpensive local 'intelligent' terminals (i.e. terminals incorporating a miniaturized computer). Just as the audio-tape cassette and the 2″ square slide are now standard, so we would envisage that text material for interactive computers should likewise become standard. A standard form of Driver and text file can provide the analogue of standard musical notation. Just as a piano piece can be played on a million different pianos or transcribed for other instruments, it ought to be possible for interrogative programs to be run on anyone's computer.

A longer term aim, which would be realized if the proposed system was accepted as a standard, would be the implementation of the master Driver in 'firmware' (pre-programmed silicon chips, with 'read-only' memory, i.e.

with a standard and unalterable mode of operation). It seems desirable, in order to prevent wasteful mistakes, to initiate discussion about needs and standards. We hope to do this by means of this book.

## Linking text material with mathematical computation

By 1970, McMaster University in Canada had an IBM 1130 in the Department of Epidemiology and Biostatistics, and this was made available at weekends and in evenings to the first small class of 20 medical students. Most students became familiar with the console, and learnt how to load a deck of cards and run programs interactively. At around the same time, University College Hospital Medical School in London acquired a small PDP8 and small interactive programs were introduced for student teaching. In 1970 the availability of the McMaster computer, and the lack (at that time) of any facilities for class experiments on animals, prompted one of us, with other colleagues at McMaster, to develop a simulation model for teaching elementary systemic haemodynamics (Dickinson, Sackett and Goldsmith, 1973). This was made available to students, working either alone or in small groups, studying problems in basic or applied physiology, and making use of the model to examine problems. The model (later christened 'MacMan') had a modest success and was later translated to many computer systems elsewhere. Later other physiological models were developed, in London (England) and in Hamilton (Ontario). These included systemic circulation, body fluids and kidneys (Dickinson and Shephard, 1972), human respiration and gas transport (Dickinson, 1977), pharmacokinetics (Bloch, Sweeney, Ahmed, Dickinson and Ingram, 1980) and cardiorespiratory aspects of the neonate (Dickinson, Allen, Ingram and Sinclair, 1980). Many others are being written.

From the first we were trying to avoid duplication of modelling effort between different centres, and for this reason chose to write all the models in standard FORTRAN IV, so as to make them fully portable. We can claim some success for this policy, insofar that the 'Mac' family of models has been successfully set up at more than 100 medical schools and universities throughout the world, and the programs are in regular and increasing use in many undergraduate and postgraduate courses.

Alongside the models, we were also developing more conventional computer self-teaching systems for clinical and preclinical use, using various simple question-and-answer devices. In some cases we wrote the text of these ourselves, using mainly either the FORTRAN IV or BASIC languages. In other cases, we obtained tried and tested programs from other people, and set them up on various interactive systems, which were used at both medical schools from 1971 onwards. Our programs were also adapted to other systems. For example, the original systemic haemodynamic model mentioned above was translated into MUMPS by members of Dr Octo Barnett's department at the Massachusetts General Hospital, but this model began to approach the limit of computing capacity available with the MUMPS language, which is not designed for this type of application. The model has also been successfully translated into BASIC in several institutions.

Extensive instructional text material cannot be handled in the FORTRAN language using compiled text. The storage requirements would be huge for each program, and there would be a total lack of flexibility. Editing a single word of text would be a major exercise requiring recompilation each time. The BASIC language is not much better, but for different reasons, especially lack of standardization, slow arithmetic and the existence of numerous machine-dependent features. Nonetheless, we persevered, as no doubt many others have done, in the attempt to devise a system which would be at the same time convenient and fully portable (by being written in a standard language).

To examine the possibilities of using a file of uncompiled text material whose printing was controlled by a FORTRAN master Driver we began, in 1972, by trying to translate a MUMPS program, written by Dr Edward P. Hoffer, designed to teach the principles of cardiopulmonary resuscitation. This program contained more than 800 lines of text (each line extending as far as possible towards a full 72-column width). The original concept was simple – to give each line of text a sequential number and to write a Driver program which could distinguish between a line of text and a line which contained instructions for the transfer of control to some other part of the program. This was all right until one wanted to delete or insert lines in the file. If this was to be done, each single line of control transfer instruction had to be rewritten, so that the transfer addresses were correct. The need to maintain flexibility meant that the Driver program had to read every line of the text file, and to store the address of each numbered frame in a large integer array before the text could be run. When a particular line or frame of text was needed, a special search to find the number could be conducted reasonably quickly, moving the pointer to and fro according to whether the line number was greater or less than the specified line number. More than two-thirds of the numbers were not needed, since in most cases several lines of text were always read as a single block, and never needed separately.

All over the world, in the last 5–10 years, people in other universities, colleges, schools, and commercial undertakings have been grappling with this same problem, and have gone through much the same sequence of trials, errors and amendments. The standard form of text and Driver we have developed during this same period is much simpler and far more flexible than our original though it retains the original design of sequentially numbered frames and binary search. To speed up operation, a directory of control line addresses has now been made part of the text file.

In 1976 we realized that, although a scientific computing language such as FORTRAN is a clumsy vehicle for any kind of text handling, it was possible to envisage a Driver compiled from a master program calling up not only text, but also, as a subroutine, any compiled subprogram written in the same language. We then realized the possibilities of making complex mathematical simulation programs such as our 'Mac' series of physiological models accessible to a Driver. It was easy to arrange for control instructions to a subroutine to be written within the text file, and executed on demand. By this means it was possible to branch freely between text and model, to preprogram various experiments for illustrative purposes, and to envisage almost unlimited possibilities of combining the enormous power and flexibility of high-level scientific languages such as FORTRAN with interrogative text material. So far we have only just begun to develop this technique, but we can already foresee its almost unlimited capabilities. Virtually without modification the system may be used to control graph plotting routines, for example, and to capitalize on different types of output device. Innumerable examples could be given of useful software capabilities which become available with such a system.

All this can be achieved on almost all computers, using standard FORTRAN language, standard terminal equipment, and standard file storage capabilities.

In the next chapter we shall list all the tasks that have been set or envisaged for different types of interactive system, describe the main published work, indicate the advantages and shortcomings of current systems, and then derive the desirable characteristics of a simple but comprehensive scheme.

The remainder of the book will describe the system we have devised to meet these objectives.

## SUMMARY

The main barrier to the productive use of computers in computer-aided interrogation and instruction is the dearth of good, well-tested and portable software (i.e. programs). Within and between universities, the large size of such computer programs, and the extensive documentation which is needed to make them generally useful, impede or prevent free translation, and lead to wasteful duplication of effort. In particular, it is difficult to combine the scientific computational strength of high-level languages such as FORTRAN with the efficient handling of text material in question and answer form.

This book will review the software currently available in published form, and describe a proposed flexible standard system which is capable of simultaneously handling text and scientific computation.

# 2
# Classification of interrogative programs – survey of current systems in the medical field; objectives and capabilities of 'MACAID'

We shall start by considering the two extremes – the 'super system' and the 'amateur effort'. The 'super' system will have taken very many man years to develop. It therefore represents an enormous commercial investment. Examples which spring to mind are the PLATO teaching system and the MUMPS system for hospital record keeping and computer-aided instruction. By contrast, the 'amateur effort' is usually made by a university department or a small commercial organization, whose software is developed for a few specific purposes. This will have taken perhaps a few hundred man hours or days to develop, and may have some commercial value which can be realized; but direct profit from software sales is not usually the main motive behind such systems.

The 'super system' is a costly commercial product and in most cases will be beyond the means of teaching institutions, even if the appropriate computer is available to run it. Unfortunately, 'amateur efforts' are also usually non-transferable, though for different reasons. Universities throughout the world are fertile beds for the growth and development of amateur efforts. The members of a university staff might be expected to include some able and imaginative systems designers. Such men and women are likely to be less pressed for time than their colleagues in industry, and their designs might reflect this, by being more economical and better thought out. However it is very rare for university departments to publish and thus to make available to others software they have developed for themselves. The main drawback is the lack of a suitable forum. Computer packages such as the NAG library of numerical algorithms and the SPSS statistical package have achieved widescale use after emerging from their university environment into the commercial world of software marketing. The functions of these types of system are well defined and documented and the user usually only wishes to incorporate them in his own work as 'black boxes' to perform a particular job of processing or analysis.

Traditionally all forms of scientific knowledge and technique are rapidly and efficiently spread across the world through the medium of scientific papers in learned journals. The system works extremely well for fundamental advances in knowledge, which can usually be rapidly and economically disseminated by such means. Unfortunately, it works extremely badly in disseminating useful and original computer software. Rigorous experimental scientists find this not surprising, since many, probably most, regard mathematical analysis and model building (which nowadays usually involves a sophisticated computer analysis) as an intellectually second-rate activity. However, there are numerous examples in which the only way to test a hypothesis is by some sort of model building. Notable examples include the test of structural consistency of the DNA double helix model by Watson and Crick, and the mathematical model to explain the propagation of the nerve impulse by Hodgkin and Huxley. Much modern work in fundamental particle physics, especially as applied to astrophysics, and in understanding the behaviour of gases and liquids depends crucially on the use of computers as truly creative tools, without which further progress would be impossible. Scientific papers these days abound with descriptions of mathematical analyses of systems in the real world. This is especially true in biology.

The authors of papers describing such work ('A Computer Analysis of . . .' is a frequent component of the title of such papers) commonly give only the sketchiest account of their computer solution. Sometimes this is unnecessary if it is explicit in the mathematical equations describing the system. More commonly in the case of complex systems the description is not specific enough to enable others to reproduce it. The only way in which complex mathematical models can be properly assessed is to provide other scientists with the wherewithal to recreate in their own computers an image of the hypothesis and its mathematical analysis. This could provide a highly efficient way of allowing other scientists to test the analysis, by putting the model to work on problems which perhaps the originators had not envisaged, to see how well it stood up to rigorous testing.

A few years ago one of us took a portable piece of software (a computer model of human respiration – Dickinson, 1977) to Dr Arthur Guyton's Department of Physiology and Biophysics in Jackson, Mississippi, where it was rapidly tested out by a large number of physiologists on time-sharing terminals connected to a central computer. This interesting and entertaining experience led Dr Tom Coleman, who collaborated with Guyton in his massive and comprehensive computer analysis of circulation and body fluids (Guyton, Coleman and Grainger, 1972), to suggest that an international physiological conference of the future might be organized rather along the lines of a chess match between rival chess-playing computer programs. Each protagonist who claimed that he understood the way a system worked might bring a program along, set it up and challenge the rival protagonists to prove it wrong, in a proper Popperian manner.

At present, only one barrier stands in the way of such an exercise. Most system analyses are very far from portable, and few are formulated in sufficient depth to examine adequately a large range of simulated experiments. Most journal editors cannot allot enough space for programs to be published in full, and many programs are anyway written in whole or in part in a non-transferable manner and need the authors' machine to run them. Therefore, all over the world great effort is being spent in duplicating modelling work which has been published only in sketch form. It is almost impossible to test most of these simulations and analyses rigorously.

So far we have only mentioned scientific programs. Indeed, it is perhaps presumptious to refer to in the same breath, or to treat as analogous a general purpose interrogative program with no scientific pretentions at all. Our justification is that many of the same problems of communication and the same resultant duplication of effort afflict programs designed to help in using computers for interrogation, instruction and assessment, and in linking them with more interesting simulation models. We shall review in this chapter some of the published accounts in scientific and educational journals of systems designed to do these things in the medical field. It is enough to say at this point that there have been very few and so far inadequate attempts to standardize what, in principle, is a simple exercise in computer programming. Published accounts of the use of computers for interrogative and instructional purposes are usually sketchy in the extreme. Although the authors usually offer to send the program to interested parties, most recipients have found the effort of translation, disentangling the machine-dependent features and understanding the program logic too formidable a task, so that the program lies gathering dust on the shelves. Meantime, the recipient designs his own equally idiosyncratic system to do the same job.

A good summary of the desirable features of generally useful software was given by Helppi *et al.* (1977) in a review of published programs for analysing and interpreting the human electrocardiogram. In their analysis of published programs for doing this, the authors found none which satisfied all their criteria, which were:

(1) The program must be in a language and format acceptable to a majority of computers. 'Arguments for the elegance of ALGOL, power of APL, flexibility of PL/1, or efficiency of Assembler are overshadowed by the fact that FORTRAN IV, without the frills that manufacturers add, is the only acceptable language for a portable program, due to its general availability and well-defined standards'.
(2) The distribution medium should be 9-track, 800 bpi magnetic tape (1600 would now be specified) with EBCDIC coding.
(3) Machine-dependent FORTRAN coding should not be used.
(4) Built-in test features should be provided, especially trace options and error checks.
(5) Design should be modular with one routine performing each specific function.
(6) Documentation should be adequate, the program well commented, and the function of all subroutines described.

(7) The distributor should supply enough test cases, with all relevant results, to allow the implementor to test all parts of the program.

Similar considerations apply to computer-assisted interrogation programs. To be readily transferable, a system must be designed from the start with that objective in mind.

It might be argued that the range of applications needed is so wide that it is impracticable to attempt standardization of supporting software. Our experience, confirmed by many others, suggests that there are many common features provided by supporting software for this type of system and thus there seems wide scope for beneficial collaboration. The first benefit of standardization will derive from elimination of the necessity to write basic interactive software. The flexibility required for acceptable use is such that typically several man years of effort might have to be expended here and the end-product might well not be very good if the programmer is inexperienced in the field. The second benefit will derive from the possibility of wider dissemination of material written, for example, for medical interviews and computer-assisted learning. Even granting that local requirements must be catered for, it will often be easier to start with someone else's attempt at the problem as an initial guide, and to build upon it.

## Survey of current systems

Over the past 20 years a large number of groups have explored the application of the computer as an educational resource. It has often been used to present information to students individually and selectively according to the speed at which each works and the understanding each shows in response to questions asked. In medicine it has been used in a more exciting way to simulate complex systems with which the student may experiment, and to represent a clinical encounter or interview in which the computer provides clinical details at the behest of the student interviewer. Such systems can help to develop specific skills of control or reasoning. Similar systems have been applied to formal assessment of student performance and to automation of interviews, as, for example, eliciting a basic medical history from a clinic patient.

We will concentrate here on medical applications, in themselves an exceptionally diverse group. By the use of selected examples, we shall show first the range of complexity (in educational terms) of the systems so far developed, and secondly the different approaches used to design systems to meet these objectives. Although the examples are from the field of medicine, most have counterparts in other fields.

For a full description of medical educational systems in North America the reader should consult the book edited by Deland (1978) which is the most comprehensive survey so far published. For a general introductory guide to educational computing and the issues it raises, the reader will find a concise account by Rushby (1979). The use of systems for assessment purposes is reviewed by Senior (1976) and in a survey compiled for the USA Congress Office of Technology Assessment (1979).

### *Case studies in general practice*

Murray (1979) and colleagues at Glasgow University have developed a series of exercises for clinical students which discuss details of presentation, diagnosis, treatment and long-term management as appropriate for typical illnesses encountered in general practice. Students work at visual display terminals and at each stage alternative decisions which might be made are displayed. Students, who usually work in small groups, are invited to rank each alternative investigation or management decision on a 5-point scale of advisability or likelihood where 1 indicates that the option *must not* be adopted, 2, 3 or 4 that it *should not, could*, or *should* be adopted and 5 that it *must* be adopted. The student's responses to all the suggested options are compared with grades which represent values agreed by a panel of practitioners. If options graded 'must not do' and 'must do' are not correctly identified, a warning is given and the student asked to try again. Gradings for other options are accepted if accurate to within $\pm 1$, otherwise a feedback message is again generated. The material is presented as a linear sequence of frames of information and questioning without branching logic. Student responses may be stored for subsequent analysis.

### *The 'CASE' system*

The acronym stands for 'Computer-aided simulation of the clinical encounter'. The system has been developed by Harless, Drennon, Marxer *et al.* (1971) at the University of Illinois College of Medicine and subsequently at the Ohio State University School of Medicine. The system aims to simulate a clinical encounter where the student assumes the role of physician and the computer that of a patient. After an introductory description of the patient, the student uses the terminal keyboard to type questions, request laboratory tests and determine any findings on physical examination. No clues or cues are given and questions and answers are all given in free text. Once the student feels he has sufficient information, he proceeds to a section where he enters his diagnosis and suggested treatment.

Finally the system provides the student with a list of the health problems in the case being dealt with, suggested management of these, a list of critical items of information considered essential for the diagnosis and treatment of the patient. The student is also rated in terms of the extent to which this information was elicited and how efficiently.

### *Computer-assisted instruction for guiding clinical decision-making*

Warner, Woolley and Kane (1974) have described a system which was designed to teach problem-solving behaviour associated with history-taking. The system uses a model of clinical decision making based on Bayesian conditional probability. A disease is selected at random from the set for which probabilistic information is known and a representative simulated case generated using this information. The student is then told the age and sex of the patient and the 'primary complaint' – related to the highest probability symptom in the disease. The system then lists possible diagnoses and the student is asked to choose the most likely one using the information thus far available. He is graded according to the choice he makes. He is also asked to choose from among questions he might ask or tests he might request and graded according to the relative discriminating power of these. The program cycles through a succession of choices of probable diagnosis and elicitation of further confirmatory evidence at each stage.

### *A simulation and instructional system for teaching diagnosis and treatment of clinical conditions*

Aida, Minamikawa, Takai *et al.* (1977) have described a system where the student is presented with a simulation of a patient with congestive heart failure. Using traditional question and answer frames the student is taught how to diagnose the condition and is then left to treat the simulated subject. By selection from options, the student is presented with detailed information on clinical history, test results and previous therapy. X-rays and ECGs are also available using slide projection. At any stage the student may select a diagnosis from among a list offered. Treatment includes restriction of activity, restriction of fluid and salt intake and administration of cardiac glycosides. The therapy chosen is applied to a mathematical description of the drug kinetics. A record is maintained of the student's efforts and these are graded according to the degree of effective control which would be predicted by the model.

### *Automated medical interviews*

Gottlieb *et al.* (1972) have developed systems for the automation of medical interviews. The computer can perform complex logical decisions to control the questioning. The decision to pursue further or ignore a line of questioning is made according to the presence or absence of certain responses as specified by the specialist who defined the form of interview. All patient responses have to be in numerical form.

A cheap microprocessor-based system for conducting medical interviews has been developed by Evans *et al.* at the National Physical Laboratory, near London. The patient uses a normal display unit linked to a four-function keyboard which he uses to indicate 'yes', 'no', 'don't know' or 'don't understand' in response to the questions. The interview is constructed as a mainly linear selection of questions with the sequence at each stage dependent on the immediately preceding answer, although some branching is also used. When the patient presses the fourth ('don't understand') button further explanation of the question is given and there can be several alternative ways of expressing the question which will be used in rotation on each successive encounter with that particular part of the questionnaire. The information elicited during the interview is summarized on a printer for subsequent use by the doctor. Clinical experience with these types of systems to date has been summarized by Lucas, Mullin, Crean *et al.* (1977).

### *Models of fluid and electrolyte balance*

The most computationally sophisticated forms of system within our field of interest are those which embody dynamic models of aspects of patient physiology which are then used as simulations which the student may use to learn about prescribing treatment. These programs include the models of haemodynamics, fluid and electrolyte balance, respiration and pharmacokinetics which we have developed over the past 9 years and distributed to centres around the world (p. 6). The FLUIDMOD system (Deland, Winters, Dell and Zuckerman, 1972) developed at the RAND corporation and UCLA is of this kind also. The student works at a graphics console. To tackle a problem he must first understand the nature of the imbalances in water and electrolyte concentrations which in acute illness may not be correctly controlled by normal homeostatic mechanisms. Treatment then consists of giving or withholding various therapeutic fluids. The aim of the system is to allow the student to learn experimentally rather than just using time-tested rules-of-thumb and in this way to develop a more refined sense of what constitutes optimal therapy in individual situations. Where the student is in doubt or makes an error the program includes instructional material to assist him. It also permits institution of treatment according to normal clinical patterns and supplies information in the form of the usual laboratory and nursing reports.

## **Approaches taken to the design of software**

The systems which have been described are implemented using a diversity of programming techniques and hardware. As a first step in discussing these we will summarize the main features displayed in varying degrees by all of the systems.

### (1) *Display of text or graphic information to the user*

With most output devices all information is normally printed sequentially at the console. With alphanumeric and graphic display units, information can often be directed to appear anywhere on the screen. Displays differ greatly in the features they provide, e.g. character size, selective video inversion, cursor positioning, and selective brightening of screen contents. These features and the software needed to activate them are highly specific to different manufacturers' equipment. Virtually all visual displays can be used in 'roll' mode to allow writing of sequential text on the screen, exactly as text is displayed by typewriter.

For most purposes it is desirable to control the positioning of information on a screen. Certain regions may be designated for information of a particular kind. This type of display, for example, is used for a time-dependent simulation of management of common emergencies (Murray, 1977). Information about changes in the patient's condition and reporting of laboratory results appears asynchronously with dialogue, during a student's management of the case, according to passage of simulated time. The information appears in a 'window' on the screen reserved for this purpose and would probably cause confusion if presented in the main flow of dialogue between student and system.

A flexible system should be capable of controlling external devices, e.g. an addressable random-access slide projector. It may need to present more of the environment than an operator's visual field, as in the case of a flight simulator which physically tilts the pilot trainee in accordance with his physical movements of the simulated controls, or when the program is controlling an animated manikin to train anaesthetists (Abrahamson, Denson and Wolf, 1969).

### (2) *Accepting information from the user*

The sophistication of software and hardware varies between the simple function keys of the MICKIE system to software processing free text input, attempting interpretation of misspelt words and determining the meaning of the text with reference to large lists of synonyms and qualifiers relating to concepts recognized by the system. Voice recognition and touch sensitive screens have also been used. All of these are conceived in one way or another as more realistic or easier to use than typing at a keyboard. There is no likelihood of universal agreement as to which constitutes the best approach since it will depend largely on the context of use.

### (3) *Branching logic to control presentation of material or response of the system to the user*

Some of the systems have the ability to generate selective feedback to the user, but cannot branch selectively within the material presented. Others branch conditionally upon current user input, but have no means for remembering previous responses and acting upon them conditionally at a later time. Some have the ability to act on input 'globally', i.e. by altering course at any time in the interaction on recognizing universally defined keywords. In this type of system the user has no impression of a predefined logic.

### (4) *Grading of student performance; tracing of users' responses for subsequent analysis*

The marking of multiple choice questionnaires is commonly done using computers. Grading students according to their performance in more complex educational programs is more difficult. Certain systems attempt to assess a student's understanding of key concepts, to keep a tally of student performance and guide attempts to remedy errors. At another level the CASE system has been applied by the American National Board of (Medical) Examiners to the assessment of clinical competence for the purpose of specialist recertification (USA Congress OTA, 1979). Here the criteria are much debated because of the difficult balance between efficiency in diagnosis and avoidance of undue risk through failure to investigate. By saving all responses, a complete retrospective assessment can be made of a physician's performance.

### (5) *Linkage of instructional exercises with large banks of information*

It is usually considered more satisfactory to use real than invented clinical data for instructional exercises. This presupposes that banks of clinical data are available in a readily compatible form. Such considerations favour certain types of software, e.g. the MUMPS system discussed below, which provide for construction and manipulation of banks of data. The ATS system (Weber and Wagamen, 1972) is also being developed along these lines using the APL language.

### (6) *Aids for authors developing material*

These vary from purely off-line writing of exercises which demand from the author some programming skill, to very extensive aids for on-line development. The more versatile the system used, the greater the skills required of the author. A special development program may be provided to interrogate the user and perform the coding of the exercise automatically from his requests. The DEC system DECAL adopts this approach. TUTOR has a system called QWRITER for building a fairly restricted type of branching questionnaire and for the CASE system a program called GENESYS (Harless, Drennon, Marxer *et al.*, 1973) allows an author to specify details of a patient and then prepare a COURSEWRITER III program which implements the details. With all these systems it is necessary for a programmer to test the simulation exhaustively and build in further details of other subject responses in order for the free format enquiry procedure to work effectively in practice.

Few systems have the facility for on-line editing of material intermixed with running the exercise itself.

### (7) *Linkage of interactive sequences with extensive computational procedures*

The FLUIDMOD system, the MGH Bayesian diagnostic aid systems and our own exercises in clinical physiological problems all depend on flexible interactive dialogue combined with extensive computations. Ideally, we want the possibility for developing flexible text exercises and the availability of efficient computation.

It would take a lot of space to discuss fully the technical issues involved in implementing systems using general purpose programming languages, such as BASIC and FORTRAN, the use of so-called 'Author' languages which have been designed specifically for the purpose of enabling non-specialists to write material for educational computing exercises, and the use of text interpreters or 'drivers'. Our aim here is not to survey the field exhaustively, since many reviews (e.g. Deland, 1978) have already done this, but to list the practical options which faced us.

## Author languages versus general purpose languages

The features required of an author language are still widely debated, and many compete for acceptance, e.g. TUTOR, STAF, LAL, COURSEWRITER. These languages vary in their flexibility. TUTOR, used for the PLATO system (Seidel and Rubin, 1975), has extensive facilities for graphical display and interaction, computation and free text input, but it may require several months of use to master all the facilities. PLATO may be used in a restricted mode for straightforward free-structured interactive sequences. Each system has its adherents and certainly for material which uses a good deal of interactive dialogue, the effort involved in programming the system will be much less than for a general purpose language such as BASIC or FORTRAN. If the material is compiled ('condensed' in the case of TUTOR) then it cannot be edited without subsequent recompilation and this is a considerable disadvantage when working through and debugging instructional material. In addition because the languages are not widely used, few new entrants to the field will have access to machines which use them. As Rushby (1979) has pointed out, the usual route into the field is through use of spare capacity on an existing system. Although there is sometimes the possibility of renting PLATO terminals or implementing other author languages, the costs associated with these cannot often be justified at the outset of a project.

PLATO is a tremendously impressive piece of engineering which is said to be capable of supporting 1000 or more interactive users at once on a CDC 7600 computer, providing that few are simultaneously performing substantial calculations. In terms of the facilities it offers it is without rival, but for many of the needs we have discussed its rental costs clearly outweigh benefit.

The CASE systems have been built up around the COURSEWRITER language, available at present on IBM systems and transferred by private enterprise to some others. The CASE programs have been translated into TUTOR without much reported difficulty and there seems little doubt that such transfers are possible with varying amounts of programmer intervention or purely by machine-program translation. Translation is more usually inhibited by problems of running machine-dependent features, e.g. graphics displays on systems which do not have sufficiently sophisticated hardware.

## Text interpreters

A widely used technique has been the separation of the software for controlling the dialogue with the user from the specification and generation of material which constitutes the particular lesson, interview or text. Such systems have generally been designed as interpreters with the material stored sequentially and organized into a series of frames. The material may be stored in binary form or as text records on some backing storage device such as a disc. A coding scheme is adopted for the different types of frame and a 'driver' program or interpreter reads the file and acts on the code it encounters in the frames, according to the responses from the user. A simple text interpreter is, for example, used in the 'MICKIE' microprocessor interviewing system (Summerville, Evans, Pobgee and Bevan, 1979).

A more sophisticated system is the AIDS driver developed at Massachusetts General Hospital (MGH) by Svedlow, Barnett, Grossman and Souder (1972). This has been used for teaching programs which reference a complex data-base of diagnostic information and for interviews where simple calculations are required as well as question and answer. The AIDS system has been built around the MUMPS language developed originally at MGH and designed principally as a language suitable for structuring a complex data-base, storing and retrieving information. Although more MUMPS systems are appearing, there is a restriction on portability of software since few are currently on the market. The need to mix text input and output with large amounts of arithmetic, e.g. in linking a simulation program to a computer-assisted learning exercise, still dictates the use of FORTRAN if wide-scale portability is desired. More advanced languages such as Pascal may achieve widespread use in time and would be suitable also, particularly since many Pascal compilers allow COMMON stores and compatibility with FORTRAN subroutines. The idea of mixing languages, e.g. using a MUMPS section for data-base manipulation and a FORTRAN section for arithmetic is attractive, but its implementation on one computer would probably not help with transfer to other machines since linkage between modules coded using different languages is largely dependent upon programming conventions unique to a particular machine's software.

## OUTLINE DESCRIPTION OF A PROPOSED STANDARD SYSTEM (MACAID)

The system which we shall describe in this book was baptized 'MACAID' the *M*c*M*a*ster *C*omputer-*A*ided *I*nstructional *D*river. We later noted that 'AID' could also spell the initial letters of our surnames. We propose to use 'MACAID' throughout the book simply as a quick shorthand. The system has continuously evolved since 1972 when the earliest version was written. Since then it has shuttled to and fro between England and Canada, on numerous magnetic tapes, and each of us has worked extensively on developing and improving it over a period of 7 years. Much of the development has been in fits and starts, and there has been a continuing process of progressive improvement. We have tried very hard when introducing new features, giving greater flexibility and convenience, to avoid making the structure either of the file, or of the Driver itself, too complicated, lest the exercise should become self-defeating. We believe that the structure of the control instructions is as unambiguous and at the same time as simple as it can reasonably be made.

The system has been applied successfully and without difficulty to some 20 diverse clinical and physiological tests, including some linked with physiological models. We have not encountered problems with execution errors or text editing with the present version of the Driver, and thus we feel that the time is now ripe to introduce and describe the system to give others the opportunities of testing it further since we believe that it reconciles in a new way various different objectives. Its portability has already been demonstrated on a large number of different computers, and it fulfils all the criteria of Helppi *et al.* (1977) (listed on p. 11) for a portable program.

As we shall describe more fully in Part 2, the text file comprises a sequence of fixed-length (72-character) control and text lines, which are addressed by direct-access using the precompiled Driver program. The line records are contiguous, and expansion or deletion of a file is a slow process which involves sequentially copying all the records distal to a deletion or addition. This is less economical in file storage space than would be a variable-length set of text lines, distributed in many different parts of a disc memory. However, we believe that with the rapidly increasing availability of very large and decreasingly expensive file stores of many different kinds, extreme economy of file storage is becoming less and less necessary. There are many advantages to be gained by the simple file structure used by MACAID, because complexities of machine-dependent data-base manipulation are avoided. Although a MACAID text is slightly less convenient to edit than a text written in AIDS or COURSEWRITER, for example, we believe that the unlimited computational facilities available with MACAID, its versatility and the ultimately stable nature of most established text programs for instruction and interrogation give it on balance an advantage over most other systems.

We have concentrated on providing a kernel of widely used facilities. Other special needs can be satisfied by adding FORTRAN subroutines which can be called from the Driver under the control of instructions stored in special frames on the text file. Arithmetic other than simple scoring, keeping a running total and setting and testing of flags for conditional branching logic is performed outside the main Driver.

## Design objectives of MACAID

It would be untruthful to pretend that the development of MACAID proceeded by logical stages, starting with the agreed definition of a number of objectives, followed by the construction of a program to achieve them. As the system has evolved, it has in the process become more comprehensive and at the same time simpler and more economical in construction, and also more economical in storage requirements, and faster to run.

The system we have developed has the following features:

(i) The text material is split into frames, each occupying any number of card-image format records on a disc file. This file is addressed by the Driver as a direct-access file. The first record of each frame contains codes starting with an asterisk which define the frame type, and frame number. Then follow three numbers giving display instructions, scoring information and type of input expected, if any, and how to interpret it; and finally the frame to branch to next. The frame types implemented are listed in Table 2.1 (see opposite).

There is no maximum length of file, but manipulations of files for individual exercises exceeding 1000 lines in total length is rather clumsy, and such files are more efficiently coded by a master index which first identifies a

**Table 2.1 Frame types in use**

| | |
|---|---|
| A(nswer) | prints text on output (answer) file. |
| B(egin) | points to directory of frame addresses and indicates the frame number where driver should start interpreting file; always first line of the text file. |
| D(ictionary) | defines dictionary of key-words and numeric values to be associated with these; used with Q frames (see below). |
| E(nd) | prints text and instructs the Driver to exit from an exercise. |
| F(lag) | prints text and sets internal flag to some specified integer value, or according to the current score. |
| G(lobal) | defines global commands entered by operator which are to be recognized at any time; defines for each of these a frame number to branch to; always 2nd line of the text file. |
| I(f) | prints text and branches conditionally on flag setting. |
| M(arking) | prints one or several multiple choice questions; receives input (either as yes/no/? or numeric values); gives feedback and grades as specified for wrong answers. |
| Q(uestion) | prints text; receives and processes input, recognizes numeric values, ranges of values, text strings, or combinations of strings defined in a dictionary frame. |
| R(eturn) | prints text and returns control to previous frame. |
| S(ubroutine) | calls user-defined subroutines, to which information can be passed from the text line(s) which follow the control line of the frame. |
| T(ext) | prints text. |
| (Z) | logic is user-definable to allow for features not covered by the above frame types). |

sequence of text lines by means of line numbers defining the beginning and end, and then passes control to the master Driver to allow the user to branch to and fro within the designated portion of the file (Appendices IV and V give practical examples of such master indexes).

The text file comprises control lines and text, together with a control line directory giving the driver information about line location. Control lines in most cases occupy just one line of the file, but in the case of complex control instructions, any number of continuation lines are allowed. Dictionaries can likewise occupy any number of continuation lines. Text for printing can be associated with any type of control line or lines (except those specifying the use of special FORTRAN subroutines). The whole group of lines comprising the control line(s) plus the associated text constitutes a 'frame'.

(ii) Global key words may be defined in an initial frame and all subsequent user input is first checked for a match with the key words. These can be used for accessing information asynchronously with the flow of logic in the main dialogue. This facility allows, for example, the option to make test results available according to a system timer. Also a user could ask for his score at any time by typing 'score' or list dictionary key words by typing 'list'.

(iii) A comprehensive Editor is available to any user signing on with a certain password. This allows him to create a text file from scratch, modify and delete lines, insert lines, renumber all frames within the file and check for duplicate frame numbers and incorrect codes. A restricted Edit and Trace facility (not allowing any writing on the text file) is available at all times.

(iv) Simple scoring of user performance is provided – for example, deducting marks for wrong answers starting from an initial score of 100. There is also a running total kept which can be added to by individual frames, to simulate, for example, the passage of time or accumulated financial costs. Branching can be made conditional upon the current value of the running total or score. More sophisticated assessments and computations may, of course, be obtained using the subroutine facility.

(v) All or selected parts of a user's input may be stored on a disc file for subsequent analysis of performance of possible relevance to designers of the material or, in the case of patient interrogation, to record patients' answers. Free text entries may be solicited and stored on an answer file. Headings or other text material can also be entered from the text file on to the answer file.

(vi) Cursor control of a visual display unit or control of external devices is provided for in all frame types.

By way of introduction to MACAID, the next chapter contains a short illustrative text exercise which employs most of the facilities available in the system. The reader who wishes to get the quickest possible idea of the capabilities of MACAID can examine the dialogue in the next chapter. This includes two computational subroutines which are called by the Driver from instructions in the text file.

## SUMMARY

It is possible to classify interrogative computer programs, whether to be used for teaching, testing or guiding practice according to several different categories. These involve the structure of the program, and its capacity to branch and to group questions; its capacity to accept various types of alphanumeric keyboard entry, prompted or unprompted; the type of output (whether visual, auditory or tactile), availability of cursor control and graphics; capacity for on-line error messages and corrections; speed of operation; associated mathematical capabilities; authoring and editing capabilities (especially on-line); portability of software, and machine-dependence.

The main features of MACAID (the proposed standard system of text and driver) are described, by way of introduction to the illustrative text exercise in the next chapter.

# 3
# Illustrative interrogative and model simulating test program using MACAID

The purpose of this chapter, which comprises an illustrative interrogation and the text from which it was run, is to take 'MACAID' through its paces and to demonstrate virtually all its features. A close study of the dialogue between a user and a MACAID controlled computer provides a quick and efficient way of examining the system's capabilities.

The structure of the program will be described in full in Parts 2 and 3 of the book. As mentioned in the previous chapter, the text material is split into 'frames', each occupying any number of records in a rapidly accessible file. The Driver addresses this file by 'direct-access', i.e. each line is sequentially numbered and can be accessed directly without reading the whole file. The first record of each frame starts with an asterisk in the first column position, and contains codes which define the frame type, frame number, display instructions, scoring information, type of input expected (if any), how to interpret it, and finally the frame to branch to next. Any text, if present, follows the control line or lines. Comment lines, preceded by '*C' and placed before the control line are provided to help in following the sequence of questions and answers.

The control line (or lines) of each frame contains, in left-to-right sequence the following information:

(a) A letter (in column 2) defining the type of operation to be performed.

(b) A unique frame number, by which the frame is referenced.

(c) A 'display control' number (the 1st control line parameter) by which the cursor of a screen display is controlled, or external devices controlled.

(d) A 2nd or 'score' parameter, used either to subtract the designated number of points from a running score, or (if positive) to control other operations.

(e) A 3rd or 'add' parameter, used in some frames to augment a running total, or to supply the Driver with certain control information.

(f) One or more addresses, to which control passes unconditionally (in the case of one address) or conditionally (in the case of multiple addresses).

The first line of the file is a *B(egin) line, which gives the number of the starting frame, and also tells the driver where to find the 'directory' (a list of 'addresses' or line numbers of each of the numbered control frames of the text file). The text file ends with a double asterisk **, followed by the directory.

Global key words are defined in the second or *G(lobal) line of the file, and all user input is first checked for a match with these. This facility can be used for accessing information asynchronously with the flow of logic in the main dialogue. For example, a user might ask for his score at any time by typing 'SCORE', or stop at any time by typing 'STOP'. The following text contains both these global commands.

An illustrative nonsense text exercise is printed in full here, on the right hand pages opposite the dialogue between operator and computer, so that the operation of the system can be compared with the lines of the text file which at each stage control it. Subprograms 4 and 5, called by the text exercise, are given in full in Appendix III in the form of FORTRAN subroutines.

As well as illustrating virtually all features of MACAID the text exercise which follows can be used as a test when MACAID is implemented on any computer for the first time. For this purpose it is supplied, together with the standard FORTRAN Driver program, when a magnetic tape containing the program is obtained from the authors (p. 178).

```
TO START, TYPE   GO   , THEN PRESS *RETURN* KEY
?GO
TYPE  1  FOR THE HEWLETT-PACKARD TERMINALS,
TYPE  2  FOR ALL OTHER VISUAL DISPLAY UNITS,
OTHERWISE JUST PRESS THE *RETURN* KEY
?_
PLEASE TYPE TODAY*S DATE LIKE THIS.. 12/10/79 ..THEN PRESS *RETURN*
?_12/1/80
NOW YOUR DATE OF BIRTH, IN SIMILAR FORMAT, PLEASE
?_1/2/27
PLEASE TYPE YOUR NAME, THEN AGAIN PRESS THE 'RETURN' KEY
?_DICKINSON, C.J.
 WHAT IS YOUR SEX? - TYPE M OR F AND PRESS 'RETURN' KEY AGAIN
?_WHY?
PLEASE TRY AGAIN
?_WHAT?
PLEASE TRY AGAIN
?_M
NOW PLEASE GIVE ME YOUR ADDRESS - PRESS RETURN KEY AT THE END OF
EACH LINE, AND TWICE AT THE END
?_ST.BARTHOLOMEW'S HOSPITAL MEDICAL COLLEGE,
?_WEST SMITHFIELD,
?_LONDON EC1A 7BE,
?_ENGLAND.
?_
 THANK YOU.
 ARE YOU READY TO PROCEED?
?_N
```

```
TEST PROGRAMME


*B    1  396

*G 'SCORE',300 'STOP'2001
TEST EXERCISE INCORPORATING VIRTUALLY ALL FEATURES OF 'MACAID'
(NORMALLY COMMENT LINES REQUIRE A *C TO IDENTIFY THEM, BUT IF THEY
 IMMEDIATELY FOLLOW THE *G FRAME, THIS IS NOT NEEDED)

*C NEXT *A FRAME WRITES HEADING ONTO ANSWER FILE
*A1 0 0 0 2
DATE

*C NEXT *T FRAME HAS NO TEXT.  ITS ONLY FUNCTION HERE IS TO CLEAR SCREEN
*C AND SET CURSOR TO TOP LEFT OF SCREEN (IF AN APPROPRIATELY
*C CONTROLLABLE VISUAL DISPLAY UNIT IS AVAILABLE) -
*C DISPLAY PARAMETER TO CODE THIS INSTRUCTION = 2000.  3RD ('ADD')
*C PARAMETER (=-1) IS AN INSTRUCTION TO PROCEED WITHOUT PROMPTING
*T2 2000 0 -1 3

*C *S FRAME CALLS SUBROUTINE #4 (3RD PARAMETER=4), WHICH ASKS FOR THE
*C DATE OF BIRTH AND TODAY'S DATE, AND COMPUTES AGE. DISPLAY PARAMETER=1
*C INSTRUCTS SUBROUTINE 4 TO INSERT DATE ON LINE 1 AT THE END OF THE
*C DIRECTORY, IN THE SPARE FILE SPACE.  THE 2ND '4' IS THE EXIT ADDRESS
*S3 1 0 4 4

*C THE NEXT *A FRAME READS THE 1-LINE SUBROUTINE ANSWER, STORED ON
*C LINE 1 OF THE SPARE END-OF-FILE SPACE AND WRITES IT INTO THE ANSWER
*C FILE.  THIS NOW HAS TODAY'S DATE, ENTERED BY SUBROUTINE  #4
*A4 1 0 1 5

*C INSERT ANOTHER HEADING ONTO THE ANSWER FILE
*A5 0 0 0 6
NAME, SEX, AGE AND ADDRESS

*C NEXT QUESTION CAN BE SATISFIED BY ANY ANSWER ('').
*C SCORE PARAMETER (=2) IS AN INSTRUCTION TO RECORD THE ANSWER GIVEN
*C ON THE OUTPUT FILE
*Q6 0 2 0 ''7
PLEASE TYPE YOUR NAME, THEN AGAIN PRESS THE 'RETURN' KEY

*C CONVENTIONAL FORM OF A *QUESTION FRAME, WITH ALTERNATIVE ANSWERS
*C (NOTE THAT SPACES AND COMMAS ARE OPTIONAL)
*Q7 0 0 0 'M',10   'F' 8 'WOM'8
 WHAT IS YOUR SEX? - TYPE M OR F AND PRESS 'RETURN' KEY AGAIN

*C IF ANSWER INDICATES FEMALE SEX, SET FLAG TO 2, FOR USE LATER
*F 8 0 0 2 9

*C WRITE ANSWER (IN FULL) ONTO ANSWER FILE
*A 9 0 0 0 11
  FEMALE

*C IF ANSWER INDICATES MALE, LEAVE FLAG UNCHANGED AND JUST WRITE
*C ANSWER (IN FULL) ONTO ANSWER FILE
*A10 0 0 0 11
  MALE

*C WRITE AGE (COMPUTED BY SUBROUTINE #4 AND STORED) ONTO ANSWER FILE
*A11 2 0 1 12

*C NEXT *TEXT FRAME CLEARS THE SCREEN AGAIN AND INVITES THE ENTRY OF
*C FREE TEXT, TO BE WRITTEN ONTO ANSWER FILE ('SCORE' PARAMETER = 2)
*T12 2000 2 0 13
NOW PLEASE GIVE ME YOUR ADDRESS - PRESS RETURN KEY AT THE END OF
EACH LINE, AND TWICE AT THE END

*C NEXT *T FRAME TURNS ON ADDER (3RD OR 'ADD' PARAMETER =-6)
*T13 0 0 -6 15
 THANK YOU.

*C STANDARD FORM OF *QUESTION FRAME
*Q15 2000 0 0 'Y'30 '',20
 ARE YOU READY TO PROCEED?
```

```
 IS THIS BECAUSE YOU ARE UNCERTAIN OF YOUR ABILITY? (ANSWER
'YES', 'NO', 'DON'T KNOW', OR 'EXPLAIN')
?_E
 I WANTED JUST TO CHECK THAT YOU WERE REALLY READY TO GO BEFORE
 WE STARTED - I HOPE WE ARE NOW!
PRESS *RETURN*
?_
 ARE YOU READY TO PROCEED?
?_Y
 RIGHT - LET'S GO
 NOW FOR SOME GENERAL KNOWLEDGE QUESTIONS. I SHALL PUT THESE IN THE FORM
 OF A MULTIPLE-CHOICE QUESTION, TO WHICH YOU SHOULD ANSWER 'YES' OR 'NO'.
PRESS *RETURN*
?_
 WHICH OF THE FOLLOWING STATEMENTS ARE TRUE?
1.NEW YORK IS THE CAPITAL OF THE USA
2.MICHELANGELO PAINTED THE 'MONA LISA'
3.97 IS A PRIME NUMBER
4.ELECTRONS ARE POSITIVELY CHARGED
5.THE OPERA 'MARRIAGE OF FIGARO' WAS WRITTEN BY ROSSINI
6.SOCRATES WAS THE DISCIPLE OF PLATO
 TYPE YOUR ANSWERS ACROSS A LINE, E.G.YYNN?Y - THEN PRESS RETURN KEY
TYPE RESPONSES FOR EACH QUESTION ALONG A LINE
?_YYNXY
INCOMPLETE ANSWER
TYPE RESPONSES FOR EACH QUESTION ALONG A LINE
?_YYNNXN
 FOR QUESTIONS -> 1 2 3 4 5 6
IS THIS RIGHT? -> Y Y N N ? N ?_NO
PLEASE ANSWER AGAIN FOR EACH OF THE 6 STATEMENTS OR QUESTIONS
 WHICH OF THE FOLLOWING STATEMENTS ARE TRUE?
1.NEW YORK IS THE CAPITAL OF THE USA
2.MICHELANGELO PAINTED THE 'MONA LISA'
3.97 IS A PRIME NUMBER
4.ELECTRONS ARE POSITIVELY CHARGED
5.THE OPERA 'MARRIAGE OF FIGARO' WAS WRITTEN BY ROSSINI
6.SOCRATES WAS THE DISCIPLE OF PLATO
 TYPE YOUR ANSWERS ACROSS A LINE, E.G.YYNN?Y - THEN PRESS RETURN KEY
TYPE RESPONSES FOR EACH QUESTION ALONG A LINE
?_YYNNXY
 FOR QUESTIONS -> 1 2 3 4 5 6
IS THIS RIGHT? -> Y Y N N ? Y ?_Y
Q.1
 WASHINGTON (D.C.) IS THE CAPITAL OF THE USA
PRESS *RETURN*
?_
Q.2
 IT WAS INDEED A FAMOUS ITALIAN, BUT HE WAS CALLED LEONARDO!
PRESS *RETURN*
?_
Q.3
YOU CAN'T DIVIDE 97 EXACTLY BY ANY SMALLER NUMBER, THEREFORE IT IS PRIME
PRESS *RETURN*
?_
```

```
TEST PROGRAMME
CONTINUED

*C NEXT FRAME IS A SIMPLE FORM OF *MARKING FRAME, USING 1 QUESTION
*C WITH 4 ALTERNATIVE ANSWERS (3RD PARAMETER =14). 'YES' IS CODED=1,
*C 'NO'=0, 'E'=3 AND ANY OTHER ANSWER AT ALL IS CODED=2.
*C NOTE THAT DISPLAY PARAMETER ('3400') CONTROLS CLEARING OF SCREEN
*C BELOW TEXT DISPLAY POINT, AND POSITION OF CORRECTIVE MESSAGES
*M20 3400 0 14 30, 0 25 26 27
 IS THIS BECAUSE YOU ARE UNCERTAIN OF YOUR ABILITY? (ANSWER
'YES', 'NO', 'DON'T KNOW', OR 'EXPLAIN')
 -     -     -             -

*C *RETURN FRAME, PROVIDING MESSAGE AND RETURN OF CONTROL
*C TO THE PRECEDING *M FRAME
*C NOTE THAT NO CONTROL PARAMETERS HAVE BEEN USED.  THE DISPLAY IS
*C PREDETERMINED BY THE *MARKING FRAME (#20) ABOVE.  SINCE THERE IS
*C ONLY 1 QUESTION, CONTROL IS TRANSFERRED TO THE EXIT ADDRESS(=30)
*R25
 TAKE HEART - LOTS OF STUPID PEOPLE HAVE DONE THIS TEST!

*C A *TEXT (OR ANY FRAME APART FROM *RETURN) TRANSFERS CONTROL OUT OF
*C THE *MARKING FRAME ABOVE
*T26 0 0 0 30
 I THINK THAT IF YOU DON'T KNOW WHY YOU ARE NOT READY TO PROCEED
 WE HAD BETTER PROCEED NONETHELESS!

*C 2ND ('SCORE') PARAMETER = 1 MEANS THAT THE ANSWER FILE WILL RECORD
*C THAT THE USER ACCESSED FRAME #27, I.E. THAT HE HAD MADE A REQUEST
*C TO 'EXPLAIN'
*T27 0 1 0 15
 I WANTED JUST TO CHECK THAT YOU WERE REALLY READY TO GO BEFORE
 WE STARTED - I HOPE WE ARE NOW!

*C WHEN 3RD PARAMETER =0 IN A *TEXT FRAME, PROGRAM WILL ASK FOR A
*C PROMPT (E.G. 'PRESS RETURN') BEFORE PROCEEDING.
*C WHEN IT IS '-1' (AS HERE) PROGRAM PROCEEDS AT ONCE WITHOUT PROMPTING
*T30 2000 0 -1 60
 RIGHT - LET'S GO

*C TURN ON SCORER ('SCORE' PARAMETER=6)
*T60 1000 6 0  70
 NOW FOR SOME GENERAL KNOWLEDGE QUESTIONS. I SHALL PUT THESE IN THE FORM
 OF A MULTIPLE-CHOICE QUESTION, TO WHICH YOU SHOULD ANSWER 'YES' OR 'NO'

*C A MORE COMPLEX TYPE OF MULTIPLE CHOICE *MARKING FRAME.  THE 3RD
*C PARAMETER (=62) INDICATES 6 QUESTIONS, WITH 2 ALTERNATIVES FOR EACH
*C (YES/NO). NOTE THAT THE INFORMATION RUNS ONTO A CONTINUATION (+) LINE
*C (OPTIONAL COMMAS SEPARATE OUT RESPONSE CODES FOR EACH QUESTION)
*C  OPTIONAL)
*M70 2500 0 62 100, 0 75,0 76,77 0,0 78, 0 79,
+0 80
 WHICH OF THE FOLLOWING STATEMENTS ARE TRUE?
1.NEW YORK IS THE CAPITAL OF THE USA
2.MICHELANGELO PAINTED THE 'MONA LISA'
3.97 IS A PRIME NUMBER
4.ELECTRONS ARE POSITIVELY CHARGED
5.THE OPERA 'MARRIAGE OF FIGARO' WAS WRITTEN BY ROSSINI
6.SOCRATES WAS THE DISCIPLE OF PLATO
 TYPE YOUR ANSWERS ACROSS A LINE, E.G.YYNN?Y - THEN PRESS RETURN KEY

*C NOTE THAT A *RETURN FRAME MAY HAVE A 'SCORE' PARAMETER
*C AND ALSO (AS IN THIS CASE) A 3RD ('ADD') PARAMETER.  THE LATTER
*C WILL BE USED TO KEEP A CHECK ON THE NUMBER OF WRONG ANSWERS.  THE
*C FRAME MUST BE GIVEN A 'DISPLAY' PARAMETER, EVEN THOUGH IT
*C WILL NOT NORMALLY BE USED - (IN SUCCEEDING *R FRAMES, THIS IS 0).
*C IT ALSO, OF COURSE, NEEDS A (2ND) DUMMY 'SCORE' PARAMETER (=0)
*R75 0 0 1
 WASHINGTON (D.C.) IS THE CAPITAL OF THE USA

*R76 0 0 1
 IT WAS INDEED A FAMOUS ITALIAN, BUT HE WAS CALLED LEONARDO!

*R77 0 0 1
YOU CAN'T DIVIDE 97 EXACTLY BY ANY SMALLER NUMBER, THEREFORE IT IS PRIME
```

```
Q.5
 ROSSINI WROTE 'THE BARBER OF SEVILLE' (WHICH HAS SOME OF THE SAME
 CHARACTERS) BUT IT WAS MOZART WHO WROTE 'THE MARRIAGE OF FIGARO'
PRESS *RETURN*
?_
Q.6
 THIS IS THE WRONG WAY ROUND - PLATO WAS THE DISCIPLE OF SOCRATES
PRESS *RETURN*
?_

 I WILL NOW ADD UP THE WRONG AND INDETERMINATE ANSWERS!
PRESENT TOTAL IS      5.0
 I'M AFRAID THAT MADE BETWEEN 3 AND 5 ERRORS - THIS IS NOT VERY GOOD
PRESS *RETURN*
?_
WRONG ANSWERS IN A MARKING FRAME SUBTRACT 2 FROM SCORE AUTOMATICALLY;
INDETERMINATE ANSWERS SUTRACT ONE MARK AUTOMATICALLY
WOULD YOU LIKE TO KNOW YOUR SCORE?  TYPE 1 FOR YES, 2 FOR NO
?_YES
PLEASE TRY AGAIN
?_I WOULD
PLEASE TRY AGAIN
?_YES
WOULD YOU LIKE TO KNOW YOUR SCORE?  TYPE 1 FOR YES, 2 FOR NO
?_1
YOUR SCORE IS  91

(I HOPE THIS IS CORRECT)
NOW FOR A LITTLE GEOGRAPHY!
PRESS *RETURN*
?_
 TRAVELLING DUE WEST FROM MANHATTAN, WHICH 3 STATES, IN ORDER, WOULD YOU
 PASS AFTER LEAVING NEW YORK STATE? (TYPE 'HINTS' TO GET HINTS)
?_WAS IT HAWAII?
YOU ARE TRYING TO MAKE A FOOL OF ME! I SHALL DEDUCT 50 MARKS AT ONCE
 TRAVELLING DUE WEST FROM MANHATTAN, WHICH 3 STATES, IN ORDER, WOULD YOU
 PASS AFTER LEAVING NEW YORK STATE? (TYPE 'HINTS' TO GET HINTS)
?_PENNSY, THEN OHIO?
```

```
TEST PROGRAMME
CONTINUED

*R78 0 0 1
ELECTRONS ARE NEGATIVELY CHARGED - YOU WERE THINKING OF POSITRONS

*R79 0 0 1
 ROSSINI WROTE 'THE BARBER OF SEVILLE' (WHICH HAS SOME OF THE SAME
 CHARACTERS) BUT IT WAS MOZART WHO WROTE 'THE MARRIAGE OF FIGARO'

*R80 0 0 1
 THIS IS THE WRONG WAY ROUND - PLATO WAS THE DISCIPLE OF SOCRATES

*C 3RD ('ADD') PARAMETER (=-7) PRINTS THE SUM TOTAL OF WRONG ANSWERS.
*C NOTE THAT A BLANK LINE OF TEXT IS SIMPLY TRANSCRIBED AS SUCH
*T100 2000 0 -7 104

 I WILL NOW ADD UP THE WRONG AND INDETERMINATE ANSWERS!

*C FURTHER HEADING WRITTEN ON ANSWER FILE
*A104 0 0 0 105
GENERAL KNOWLEDGE - TOTAL ERRORS

*C 3RD ('ADD') PARAMETER =-2 IS AN INSTRUCTION TO PRINT 'SUM(TOTAL)' (OF
*C WRONG ANSWERS) ONTO OUTPUT FILE
*A105 0 0 -2 106

*C INSERT FURTHER HEADING ONTO ANSWER FILE
*A106 0 0 0  107
GEOGRAPHY - SCORE

*C EXAMPLE OF A *QUESTION FRAME WHICH WILL TAKE ITS (NUMERICAL)
*C ANSWER FROM THE 'SUM(TOTAL)' REGISTER   (2ND PARAMETER =-2)
*C NOTE THAT '()' WILL BE SATISFIED BY ANY NUMERICAL ANSWER.
*Q107 0 0 -2 (0,.99)110 (.99,2)120 (2,5)130 (),140

*C RESPONSES CONDTIONAL ON COUNT OF WRONG OR INDETERMINATE ANSWERS
*T110 0 0 0 160
 VERY GOOD - YOU GOT EVERYTHING RIGHT

*T120 0 0 0 160
 NOT TOO BAD - BUT THERE ARE A FEW GAPS IN YOUR KNOWLEDGE

*C NOTE THAT THE MESSAGE BELOW WAS ISSUED IF THE NUMBER OF ERRORS
*C COUNTED BY THE *Q FRAME ABOVE WAS MORE THAN 2 AND NOT MORE THAN 5
*T130 0 0 0 160
 I'M AFRAID THAT MADE BETWEEN 3 AND 5 ERRORS - THIS IS NOT VERY GOOD

*T140 0 0 0 160
 I SHALL HAVE TO GRADE YOU AS ALMOST INCREDIBLY IGNORANT!

*C 3RD ('ADD') PARAMETER = -6 RESETS THE ADDER AND SETS 'SUM' TO ZERO
*T160 2000 0 -6 170
WRONG ANSWERS IN A MARKING FRAME SUBTRACT 2 FROM SCORE AUTOMATICALLY;
INDETERMINATE ANSWERS SUTRACT ONE MARK AUTOMATICALLY

*Q170 3400 0  0 (1)180 (2)185
WOULD YOU LIKE TO KNOW YOUR SCORE?  TYPE 1 FOR YES, 2 FOR NO

*C 'SCORE' PARAMETER (=7) PRINTS THE SCORE; 3RD PARAMETER =1 STARTS
*C COUNT OF THE NUMBER OF REQUESTS FOR THE SCORE
*T180 0 7 1 185
(I HOPE THIS IS CORRECT)

*T185 0 0 0 190
NOW FOR A LITTLE GEOGRAPHY!

*C *QUESTION FRAME USING DICTIONARY #1 TO FIND INDENTIFYING NUMBERS OF
*C VARIOUS KEYWORDS, WHOSE CORRECTNESS AND ORDER IS CHECKED.  N.B. TWO
*C CONTINUATION LINES USED. 3RD PARAMETER = 1 SAYS 'USE DICTIONARY #1'
*Q190 2300 0 1 <1+2+3>191 <1+3+2>192 <2+1+3>192
+ <1+2>193 <4>194 <2+3>197
+ <5>195 <6>196 <1>198 <2>198 <3>198 'HIN'199
 TRAVELLING DUE WEST FROM MANHATTAN, WHICH 3 STATES, IN ORDER, WOULD YOU
 PASS AFTER LEAVING NEW YORK STATE? (TYPE 'HINTS' TO GET HINTS)
```

```
 YOU HAVE FORGOTTEN NEW JERSEY - AN EASY MISTAKE TO MAKE
 TRAVELLING DUE WEST FROM MANHATTAN, WHICH 3 STATES, IN ORDER, WOULD YOU
 PASS AFTER LEAVING NEW YORK STATE? (TYPE 'HINTS' TO GET HINTS)
?_NEW JERSEY, THEN OHIO, THEN PENNSYLVANIA?
RIGHT STATES - WRONG ORDER!
 TRAVELLING DUE WEST FROM MANHATTAN, WHICH 3 STATES, IN ORDER, WOULD YOU
 PASS AFTER LEAVING NEW YORK STATE? (TYPE 'HINTS' TO GET HINTS)
?_HINTS
THE STATES AROUND INCLUDE NEW JERSEY, MARYLAND, OHIO, PENNSYLVANIA,
MASSACHUSETTS, AND VIRGINIA.  CHOOSE 3 FROM THESE!
 TRAVELLING DUE WEST FROM MANHATTAN, WHICH 3 STATES, IN ORDER, WOULD YOU
 PASS AFTER LEAVING NEW YORK STATE? (TYPE 'HINTS' TO GET HINTS)
?_NEW JERSEY, THEN PENNSY THEN OHIO?
 ABSOLUTELY RIGHT!
PRESS *RETURN*
?_
 WHEN I AM MARKING DIFFICULT GEOGRAPHY TESTS, I MARK YOU ACCORDING
 TO YOUR DEGREE OF IGNORANCE.  WOULD YOU LIKE TO KNOW YOUR SCORE NOW?
?_YES
YOUR SCORE IS  36

 YOU MIGHT LIKE TO NOTE THAT YOU CAN GET YOUR SCORE ANY TIME YOU LIKE
 BY JUST TYPING 'SCORE' AND PRESSING THE 'RETURN' KEY.
PRESS *RETURN*
?_
I SHALL NOW DEMONSTRATE THE USE OF THE 'GRADING' SYSTEM. PLEASE
NOTE THAT WE HAVE A MAXIMUM OF 5 GRADES AVAILABLE, WHICH CAN BE
TAKEN TO INDICATE:
```

```
TEST PROGRAMME
CONTINUED

*C THIS IS DICTIONARY #1, USED IN CONNECTION WITH THE *Q FRAME ABOVE
*C NOTE THAT THIS MAY ALSO HAVE CONTINUATION LINES.
*C (UP TO 18 NUMBERED DICTIONARIES ARE ALLOWED.  THEY CAN BE PLACED
*C ANYWHERE IN THE FILE (AFTER LINE 2) BUT MUST BE IN SEQUENTIAL
*C ORDER OF REFERENCE NUMBER.  NOTE ALSO THAT COMMAS AND
*C SPACES ARE OPTIONAL IN *DICTIONARY FRAMES)
*D 1      'JERS',1 'PEN' 2 'OHIO'3 'IND'4 'ILL'4 'VIRG'5 'KENT'5
+ 'MARY'5 'HAWA'6

*C TRANSFERS CONTROL
*T191 0 0 0 200
 ABSOLUTELY RIGHT!

*C ALL OTHER *RETURN FRAMES WHICH FOLLOW DO NOT TRANSFER CONTROL,
*C BUT GIVE CORRECTIVE MESSAGES, AND DEDUCT VARIOUS MARKS FROM THE
*C SCORE, DEPENDING ON THE SEVERITY OF THE MISTAKE MADE
*R192 0 -1
RIGHT STATES - WRONG ORDER!

*R193 0 -2
 THE FIRST TWO ARE RIGHT, BUT I NEED ANOTHER

*R194 0 -4
 TOO FAR WEST!

*R195 0 -3
 TOO FAR SOUTH

*R196 0 -50
YOU ARE TRYING TO MAKE A FOOL OF ME! I SHALL DEDUCT 50 MARKS AT ONCE

*R197 0 -3
 YOU HAVE FORGOTTEN NEW JERSEY - AN EASY MISTAKE TO MAKE

*R198 0 -2
YOU HAVE ONE RIGHT, AT LEAST!  TRY AGAIN, OR ASK FOR 'HINTS'

*R199 0 -1
THE STATES AROUND INCLUDE NEW JERSEY, MARYLAND, OHIO, PENNSYLVANIA,
MASSACHUSETTS, AND VIRGINIA.  CHOOSE 3 FROM THESE!

*C 3RD 'ADD' PARAMETER =-1 MEANS 'PROCEED AT ONCE, NO PROMPT'
*T200 2000 0 -1 201
 WHEN I AM MARKING DIFFICULT GEOGRAPHY TESTS, I MARK YOU ACCORDING
 TO YOUR DEGREE OF IGNORANCE.  WOULD YOU LIKE TO KNOW YOUR SCORE NOW?

*Q201 0 0 0 'Y'205 'AFFIRMATIVE'205 'I WOULD'205 'SCORE',205
+ 'N'305

*C PRINT SCORE ('SCORE' PARAMETER = 7)
*T205 0 7 0  305
 YOU MIGHT LIKE TO NOTE THAT YOU CAN GET YOUR SCORE ANY TIME YOU LIKE
 BY JUST TYPING 'SCORE' AND PRESSING THE 'RETURN' KEY.

*C NEXT FRAME IS UNCONNECTED WITH THE FLOW OF TEXT, BUT IS SIMPLY
*C USED AS A GLOBAL INSTRUCTION TO PRINT THE SCORE ('SCORE' PARAMETER
*C =7), AND THEN TO RETURN CONTROL TO THE CALLING FRAME.
*C (THE 2ND (*GLOBAL) LINE OF THE FILE CONTAINS "'SCORE',300").
*C THE 3RD ('ADD') PARAMETER (=1) COUNTS NUMBER OF REQUESTS FOR 'SCORE'
*R300 0 7 1

*C WRITE PRESENT SCORE ON ANSWER FILE (3RD PARAMETER = -1)
*A305 0 0 -1 510

*C WRITE HEADING ON ANSWER FILE
*A510 0 0 0 520
HUMANITARIAN EXERCISE

*T520 2000 0 -1 530
I SHALL NOW DEMONSTRATE THE USE OF THE 'GRADING' SYSTEM. PLEASE
NOTE THAT WE HAVE A MAXIMUM OF 5 GRADES AVAILABLE, WHICH CAN BE
TAKEN TO INDICATE:
```

```
 0 = MUST NOT DO
 1 = MIGHT DO
 2 = SHOULD SOMETIMES DO
 3 = SHOULD DO MOST OF THE TIME
 4 = MUST DO
PRESS *RETURN*
?_
 I AM GOING TO GIVE YOU A HUMANITARIAN TEST.  GIVE GRADES AS FOLLOWS:
 0 = MUST NOT DO
 1 = MIGHT DO
 2 = SHOULD SOMETIMES DO
 3 = SHOULD DO MOST OF THE TIME
 4 = MUST DO
....OK - HERE IS THE QUESTION:
PRESS *RETURN*
?_
 IF YOU WERE DRIVING ALONG A DESERTED COUNTRY HIGHWAY AND
 YOU SAW A CAR SLEWED OFF THE ROAD, WITH A FRONT WING BUCKLED AGAINST A
 TREE, HOW WOULD YOU GRADE THE FOLLOWING COURSES OF ACTION?
1. STOP THE MOTOR;
2. GET OUT, AND LOOK TO SEE IF ANYONE WAS INJURED;
3. IF NO-ONE IS IN SIGHT, IMMEDIATELY GET BACK AND DRIVE ON
  -   GRADE EACH QUESTION ON THE SCALE 0-1-2-3-4,  EG. 042
TYPE RESPONSES FOR EACH QUESTION ALONG A LINE
?_041
 FOR QUESTIONS -> 1 2 3
IS THIS RIGHT? -> 0 4 1 ?_N
PLEASE ANSWER AGAIN FOR EACH OF THE 3 STATEMENTS OR QUESTIONS
TYPE RESPONSES FOR EACH QUESTION ALONG A LINE
?_042
 FOR QUESTIONS -> 1 2 3
IS THIS RIGHT? -> 0 4 2 ?_Y
Q.2 ACCEPTABLE - THOUGH MY GRADE WOULD BE SLIGHTLY  LOWER
PRESS *RETURN*
?_
Q.3
 TO HANG AROUND AT ALL IN SUCH A SITUATION IS MOST UNWISE!
PRESS *RETURN*
?_

NOW FOR A HISTORY QUESTION:
PRESS *RETURN*
?_
WHO WAS THE BRITISH PRIME MINISTER AT THE OUTBREAK OF THE 1939-45
WAR - THE ONE WHO ACTUALLY DECLARED WAR WITH GERMANY?
?_I DON'T KNOW!
I WOULD SUGGEST YOU TYPE 'HINTS' TO GET SOME SUGGESTIONS!
WHO WAS THE BRITISH PRIME MINISTER AT THE OUTBREAK OF THE 1939-45
WAR - THE ONE WHO ACTUALLY DECLARED WAR WITH GERMANY?
?_HINTS
SOME BRITISH PRIME MINISTERS TO CONSIDER ARE LLOYD GEORGE,
MACDONALD, BALDWIN, CHURCHILL AND CHAMBERLAIN
WHO WAS THE BRITISH PRIME MINISTER AT THE OUTBREAK OF THE 1939-45
WAR - THE ONE WHO ACTUALLY DECLARED WAR WITH GERMANY?
?_CHURCHILL?
YOU ARE ONE OUT IN TIME SEQUENCE...
WHO WAS THE BRITISH PRIME MINISTER AT THE OUTBREAK OF THE 1939-45
WAR - THE ONE WHO ACTUALLY DECLARED WAR WITH GERMANY?
?_CHAMBERLAIN
 CORRECT!
 NOW I SHALL ADD UP YOUR SCORE AND GRADE YOU ON THE PRECEDING
 EXERCISES - LEAVING OUT YOUR HUMANITARIAN ASSESSMENT!

PRESS *RETURN*
?_
```

```
TEST PROGRAMME
CONTINUED

*T530 0 0 0 540
 0 = MUST NOT DO
 1 = MIGHT DO
 2 = SHOULD SOMETIMES DO
 3 = SHOULD DO MOST OF THE TIME
 4 = MUST DO

*C SWITCH OFF SCORER ('SCORE' PARAMETER = 3), BECAUSE ALL *MARKING
*C FRAMES, SUCH AS #552 WHICH FOLLOWS, MAKE AUTOMATIC ADJUSTMENTS TO
*C THE SCORE, UNLESS THE SCORER IS SWITCHED OFF.
*C NOTE THAT NEXT *TEXT FRAME USES THE TEXT OF ANOTHER (THE PREVIOUS
*C *TEXT FRAME), EMBEDDED IN ITS OWN TEXT ('/USE 530')
*T540 2000 3 0  552
 I AM GOING TO GIVE YOU A HUMANITARIAN TEST.  GIVE GRADES AS FOLLOWS:
/USE 530
....OK - HERE IS THE QUESTION:

*C *MARKING FRAME WITH 3 QUESTIONS, 5 GRADES (3RD PARAMETER = '35').
*C ACCEPTABLE, THOUGH NOT QUITE CORRECT GRADES, ARE '-1' POSITIONS.
*C THE 2ND('SCORE') PARAMETER (=2) INSTRUCTS THE DRIVER TO RECORD THE
*C FRAME NUMBER AND A USER'S CONFIRMED ENTRY ON THE ANSWER FILE
*M552 2500 2 35 580,  0 555 555 555 555, 560 560 -1 0 -1,
+ 570 570 570 570 0
 IF YOU WERE DRIVING ALONG A DESERTED COUNTRY HIGHWAY AND
 YOU SAW A CAR SLEWED OFF THE ROAD, WITH A FRONT WING BUCKLED AGAINST A
 TREE, HOW WOULD YOU GRADE THE FOLLOWING COURSES OF ACTION?
1. STOP THE MOTOR;
2. GET OUT, AND LOOK TO SEE IF ANYONE WAS INJURED;
3. IF NO-ONE IS IN SIGHT, IMMEDIATELY GET BACK AND DRIVE ON
  -   GRADE EACH QUESTION ON THE SCALE 0-1-2-3-4,  EG. 042

*R555
 IT IS VERY UNWISE TO STOP THE MOTOR IN SUCH A SITUATION
 SINCE THIS MAY PERHAPS BE SET UP FOR SOME CRIME - BE
 PREPARED TO GET AWAY

*R560
 MOST OF THE TIME YOU SHOULD STOP, TO SEE IF ANYONE NEEDS HELP; BUT IT
 IS UNREASONABLE TO SAY YOU SHOULD ALWAYS INVESTIGATE

*R570
 TO HANG AROUND AT ALL IN SUCH A SITUATION IS MOST UNWISE!

*C TURN ON SCORER AGAIN ('SCORE' PARAMETER =4)
*T580 0 4 0 581

NOW FOR A HISTORY QUESTION:

*C *QUESTION FRAME USING ANOTHER DICTIONARY (#2)
*Q581 2300 0 2 <1>590 <2417>584 <3>584 'H'582 ''583
WHO WAS THE BRITISH PRIME MINISTER AT THE OUTBREAK OF THE 1939-45
WAR - THE ONE WHO ACTUALLY DECLARED WAR WITH GERMANY?

*C DICTIONARY #2 - THOUGH PLACED IMMEDIATELY AFTER THE RELEVANT
*C *QUESTION FRAME, THIS COULD HAVE BEEN PUT ANYWHERE IN THE FILE,
*C AS LONG AS IT WAS AFTER DICTIONARY #1
*D 2 'CHAMBER'1 'CHURCHILL'2417 'BALDWIN'3

*R582 0 -2
SOME BRITISH PRIME MINISTERS TO CONSIDER ARE LLOYD GEORGE,
MACDONALD, BALDWIN, CHURCHILL AND CHAMBERLAIN

*R583 0 -4
I WOULD SUGGEST YOU TYPE 'HINTS' TO GET SOME SUGGESTIONS!

*R584 0 -3
YOU ARE ONE OUT IN TIME SEQUENCE...

*T590 2000 0 0 600
 CORRECT!
 NOW I SHALL ADD UP YOUR SCORE AND GRADE YOU ON THE PRECEDING
 EXERCISES - LEAVING OUT YOUR HUMANITARIAN ASSESSMENT!
```

```
YOUR SCORE IS  27

 YOU ARE REALLY AN EXTRAORDINARILY IGNORANT
 MAN
PRESS *RETURN*
?_
 NOW I AM GOING TO TEACH YOU THE PRINCIPLES OF GRAPHS, AND GIVE
 YOU THE CHANCE OF PLOTTING SOME OF YOUR OWN.   HOWEVER, IF YOU WANT
 TO STOP ANYTIME, YOU CAN JUST TYPE IN 'STOP'. UNLESS YOU
 TELL ME TO STOP, I SHALL PROCEED!
PRESS *RETURN*
?_
 ARE YOU READY TO PROCEED?
?_Y
I SHALL NOW PLOT A SIMPLE GRAPH OF Y AGAINST X...   Y=5X
```

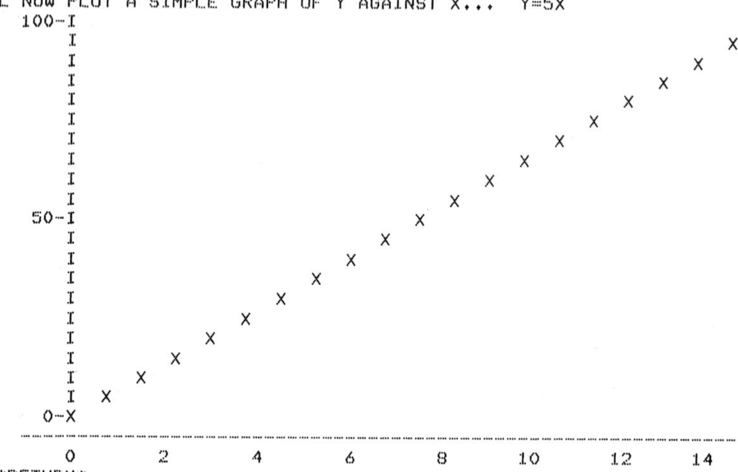


```
PRESS *RETURN*
?_
I CAN PLOT ANY SIMILAR GRAPH FOR YOU, USING THE FOLLOWING EXPRESSION:

                                 (4)   ... I.E. TO THE POWER OF (4)
          Y= (1) + (2)X + (3)X
PRESS *RETURN*
?_
 NOW TRY OUT VARIOUS GRAPHS FOR YOURSELF, CHANGING FACTORS (1),(2),(3)
 AND (4) TO PRODUCE VARIOUS SHAPES.  TO START WITH, I SHALL SET EACH OF
 THE FACTORS 1,2,3 AND 4 TO ZERO, SO THAT THE RESULT WILL JUST BE A FLAT
 LINE.  IF YOU ASK FOR '1.CHANGE' YOU CAN THEN CHANGE ANY OR ALL OF THE
 4 FACTORS TO ANY VALUE, + OR -.    I SHALL KNOW YOU UNDERSTAND WHEN
 YOU HAVE PLOTTED A CURVE STARTING AT Y=40, GOING UP, THEN DOWN TO CROSS
 THE X-AXIS AT X=12.  WHEN FINISHED, DO '3.STORE' AND LEAVE IT FOR ME TO
 LOOK AT.   I HOPE ALL GOES WELL!
PRESS *RETURN*
?_
```

```
TEST PROGRAMME
CONTINUED

*C FUNCTION OF THIS FRAME IS JUST TO PRINT THE SCORE - NO TEXT
*C IS ASSOCIATED WITH IT ('SCORE' PARAMETER=7)
*T600 0 7 -1 1000

*C EXAMPLE OF A *QUESTION FRAME WHICH TAKES AS ITS ANSWER THE TOTAL
*C SCORE (NORMALLY BETWEEN 0 AND 100). '()' MATCHES ANY NUMBER AND IS
*C A SIMPLE WAY TO COVER ALL POSSIBLE NUMERICAL VALUES
*Q1000 0 0 -1 (0,75)1010 (75,90),1020 ()1030

*T1010 0 0 -1 1050
 YOU ARE REALLY AN EXTRAORDINARILY IGNORANT

*C THIS FRAME TEXT WOULD BE PRINTED IF THE SCORE HAD BEEN MORE THAN
*C 75 AND NOT MORE THAN 90
*T1020 0 0 0 1500
 YOU ARE COMPETENT BUT NOT EXCELLENT

*T1030 0 0 -1 1050
 YOU SEEM TO BE A VERY ABLE AND KNOWLEDGEABLE

*C THE *IF FRAME WHICH FOLLOWS USES THE PREVIOUSLY SET VALUE OF
*C 'FLAG' (DETERMINED BY SEX) TO PRINT NEXT LINE.
*C SINCE NO HALT IN THE DIALOGUE IS NEEDED HERE, THE 3RD ('ADD')
*C PARAMETER IS SET TO -1
*I1050 0 0 -1 1060 1070

*T1060 0 0 0 1500
 MAN

*T1070 0 0 0  1500
 WOMAN

*C PRINT HEADING ON ANSWER FILE
*A1500 0 0 0 1501
NUMBER OF REQUESTS FOR 'SCORE':

*C PRINT SUM TOTAL ON ANSWER FILE ('ADD' PARAMETER = -2)
*A1501 0 0 -2 1600

*C NOTE INVITATION TO TYPE A GLOBAL KEWORD ('STOP') PREVIOUSLY
*C SUPPLIED TO THE PROGRAM BY THE 2ND *G(LOBAL) FRAME LINE, WHICH
*C CONTAINS THE GLOBAL INSTRUCTION 'STOP'2001
*T1600 2000 0 0 1601
 NOW I AM GOING TO TEACH YOU THE PRINCIPLES OF GRAPHS, AND GIVE
 YOU THE CHANCE OF PLOTTING SOME OF YOUR OWN.   HOWEVER, IF YOU WANT
 TO STOP ANYTIME, YOU CAN JUST TYPE IN 'STOP'. UNLESS YOU
 TELL ME TO STOP, I SHALL PROCEED!

*C THIS FRAME USES PREVIOUS TEXT FRAME, BUT THE 'YES/NO' TYPE QUESTION
*C IS THIS TIME POSED AS A *MARKING FRAME, WHICH IS POSSIBLE SINCE
*C 'Y' CODES AS 1, AND 'N' AS 0(ZERO).  SINCE THERE IS 1 QUESTION
*C WITH 2 ALTERNATIVES, THE 3RD PARAMETER IS '12'.
*M 1601 3400 0 12 1700, 1699 0
/USE 15

*T1699 0 0 0 1700
/USE 26

*C CLEAR SCREEN AND SET CURSOR TOP LEFT
*T1700 2000 0 -1 1710
I SHALL NOW PLOT A SIMPLE GRAPH OF Y AGAINST X...  Y=5X

*C NEXT FRAME CALLS SUBROUTINE #5 AND SENDS INSTRUCTIONS
*C TO CALL THE MODEL UP WITHOUT PRINTING ANYTHING (0), MAKE CHANGES(/1),
*C AND THEN CHANGE FACTOR 2(/2) TO A VALUE OF 5(/5), THEN
*C 'CONTINUE' (/2) AND FINALLY 'STOP'(/4).
*C THIS INSTRUCTS THE SUBROUTINE AUTOMATICALLY TO PRINT A GRAPH OF Y=5X
*S1710 0 0 5 1720
0/1/2/5/2/4

*C INSERT PAUSE FOR PROMPT (3RD PARAMETER = 0)
*T1720 0 0 0 1730
```

```
DO YOU WANT TO..1.CHANGE, 2.PLOT THE GRAPH, 3.STORE THE GRAPH, 4.STOP
?_1
TYPE NUMBER OF FACTORS (1-4) TO CHANGE
?_1 2 3 4
FACTOR 1 (CURRENT VALUE=    0.0), SPECIFY NEW VALUE
?_40
FACTOR 2 (CURRENT VALUE=    0.0), SPECIFY NEW VALUE
?_12
FACTOR 3 (CURRENT VALUE=    0.0), SPECIFY NEW VALUE
?_1
FACTOR 4 (CURRENT VALUE=    0.0), SPECIFY NEW VALUE
?_2
DO YOU WANT TO..1.CHANGE, 2.PLOT THE GRAPH, 3.STORE THE GRAPH, 4.STOP
?_2
        100-I          X
            I
            I
            I      X
            I
            I
            I
            I   X
            I
            I
         50-I X
            I
            X
            I
            I
            I
            I
            I
            I
            I
          0-I
     ------------------------------------------------------------------
            0       2       4       6       8       10      12      14
DO YOU WANT TO..1.CHANGE, 2.PLOT THE GRAPH, 3.STORE THE GRAPH, 4.STOP
?_1/3/-1/2
        100-I
            I
            I
            I
            I
            I                 X  X
            I          X  X         X
            I       X                  X
            I    X                        X
            I
         50-I X                              X
            I
            X
            I                                   X
            I
            I                                      X
            I
            I
            I                                         X
            I
          0-I
     ------------------------------------------------------------------
            0       2       4       6       8       10      12      14
DO YOU WANT TO..1.CHANGE, 2.PLOT THE GRAPH, 3.STORE THE GRAPH, 4.STOP
?_3
*** GRAPH NOW STORED
DO YOU WANT TO..1.CHANGE, 2.PLOT THE GRAPH, 3.STORE THE GRAPH, 4.STOP
?_4
WHAT WAS YOUR VALUE FOR FACTOR 3?
?_-1
A GOOD ESTIMATE - CONGRATULATIONS!
PRESS *RETURN*
?_
THAT IS THE END.  THANK YOU FOR YOUR COOPERATION.
IF YOU HAVE ANY COMMENTS, PLEASE TYPE THEM IN NOW, AND PRESS
 *RETURN* KEY TWICE
?_NO COMMENTS, THANKS
?_
THANK YOU
```

```
TEST PROGRAMME
CONTINUED


*C CLEAR SCREEN AGAIN AND RESET CURSOR
*T1730 2000 0 0  1740
I CAN PLOT ANY SIMILAR GRAPH FOR YOU, USING THE FOLLOWING EXPRESSION:

                                          (4)   ... I.E. TO THE POWER OF (4)
            Y= (1) + (2)X + (3)X

*T1740 0 0 0 1750
 NOW TRY OUT VARIOUS GRAPHS FOR YOURSELF, CHANGING FACTORS (1),(2),(3)
 AND (4) TO PRODUCE VARIOUS SHAPES.  TO START WITH, I SHALL SET EACH OF
 THE FACTORS 1,2,3 AND 4 TO ZERO, SO THAT THE RESULT WILL JUST BE A FLAT
 LINE.  IF YOU ASK FOR '1.CHANGE' YOU CAN THEN CHANGE ANY OR ALL OF THE
 4 FACTORS TO ANY VALUE, + OR -.   I SHALL KNOW YOU UNDERSTAND WHEN
 YOU HAVE PLOTTED A CURVE STARTING AT Y=40, GOING UP, THEN DOWN TO CROSS
 THE X-AXIS AT X=12.  WHEN FINISHED, DO '3.STORE' AND LEAVE IT FOR ME TO
 LOOK AT.   I HOPE ALL GOES WELL!

*C WRITE HEADING ON ANSWER FILE
*A1750 0 0 0 1760
GRAPH PLOTTING EXERCISE

*C CALL UP SUBROUTINE #5 AND ENTER (1) AND AWAIT USER'S INSTRUCTIONS
*C WHICH MAY INCLUDE THE STORAGE OF A GRAPH, AS PROOF OF THE
*C USER'S UNDERSTANDING.  NO DISPLAY INSTRUCTION IS NEEDED BECAUSE
*C THE SUBROUTINE WRITES THE FINAL GRAPH DIRECTLY TO THE ANSWER FILE
*S1760 0 0 5 1775
1

*C NUMERIC RANGE QUESTION
*Q1775 2300 2 0 (-3.5,-.01)1780 ''1785
WHAT WAS YOUR VALUE FOR FACTOR 3?

*T1780 0 0 0 1790
A GOOD ESTIMATE - CONGRATULATIONS!

*T 1785 0 0 0 1790
IT HAS TO BE NEGATIVE, AND NOT TOO BIG - AROUND -2 IS CORRECT

*C ANSWER FILE HEADING
*A1790 0 0 0 2000
FINAL COMMENTS

*C FINAL COMMENTS - FREE TEXT ENTRY PROMPTED BY 2ND PARAMETER = 2.
*C NOTE THAT "*RETURN*" IN THE LAST TEXT LINE HAS TO BE INDENTED
*C BY 1 SPACE TO PREVENT THE TEXT LINE BEING TREATED AS A CONTROL LINE
*T2000 2000 2 0 2001
THAT IS THE END.  THANK YOU FOR YOUR COOPERATION.
IF YOU HAVE ANY COMMENTS, PLEASE TYPE THEM IN NOW, AND PRESS
 *RETURN* KEY TWICE

*C FINAL FRAME
*E2001
THANK YOU


**
  96     2
 300     2    1     7    2    14    3    19    4    23    5    25    6    30    7    34
   8    37    9    39   10    43   11    46   12    49   13    53   15    56   20    63
  25    72   26    76   27    82   30    88   60    91   70    99   75   115   76   117
  77   119   78   121   79   123   80   126  100   130  104   134  105   138  106   140
 107   145  110   147  120   149  130   153  140   155  160   158  170   161  180   165
 185   167  190   172  191   186  192   191  193   193  194   195  195   197  196   199
 197   201  198   203  199   205  200   209  201   212  205   215  300   223  305   225
 510   227  520   229  530   233  540   244  552   252  555   261  560   265  570   268
 580   271  581   275  582   282  583   285  584   287  590   289  600   2961000   300
1010   3011020    3051030    3071050    3131060    3141070    3161500    3191501   322
1600   3261601    3351699    3371700    3401710    3471720    3501730    3521740   357
1750   3671760    3731775    3761780    3781785    3801790    3832000    3882001   393
  183   281     0     0     0     0     0     0     0     0     0     0     0     0
          12/1/80
          AGE 52
```

# Part 2
# The MACAID text file

# 4
# The text file; frames and control lines; processing a frame

## Components of the text file

The main body of the text is held on a direct (or random) access file, which consists of a number of 72-character lines in a stack exactly equivalent to a deck of IBM cards. Indeed, before cards were superseded by magnetic tape, the back-up card image text file would have actually been stored on a deck of cards, as in Figure 4.1 (overleaf).

The text file has four essential and various optional components. The essential parts are:

(1) The *B(egin) line, which is the first line of any text file, and gives setting up information to the Driver (Figure 4.1).
(2) The text file itself, of any length (i.e. of any number of individual lines) – this would normally comprise the bulk of the file.
(3) An 'end-of-text' line, marking the end of the text file, and the beginning of the 'directory'.
(4) A 'directory' of addresses, which tells the master Driver program where to find each separate piece of text or control information (Figure 4.1).

At the end of the directory, which on average occupies roughly 4% of the total length of an entire file, there may be a few spare, empty lines. This is a desirable convenience, to give some flexibility in expanding the text. This area can also be used as a workspace for intermediate storage of numerical values and characters.

We should emphasize, for those who are not familiar with the method of 'direct access' of a file that although the Driver program is written in a high-level language and has to be precompiled and loaded into the computer before it can be used, the text file remains at all times in a card image form. At the present day, the file would normally be held on a rapidly revolving magnetic disc, somewhat analogous to a gramophone record, from which information is extracted by placing a needle on it at different locations. On a dedicated microprocessor system the text file might be on a 'floppy disc'. If

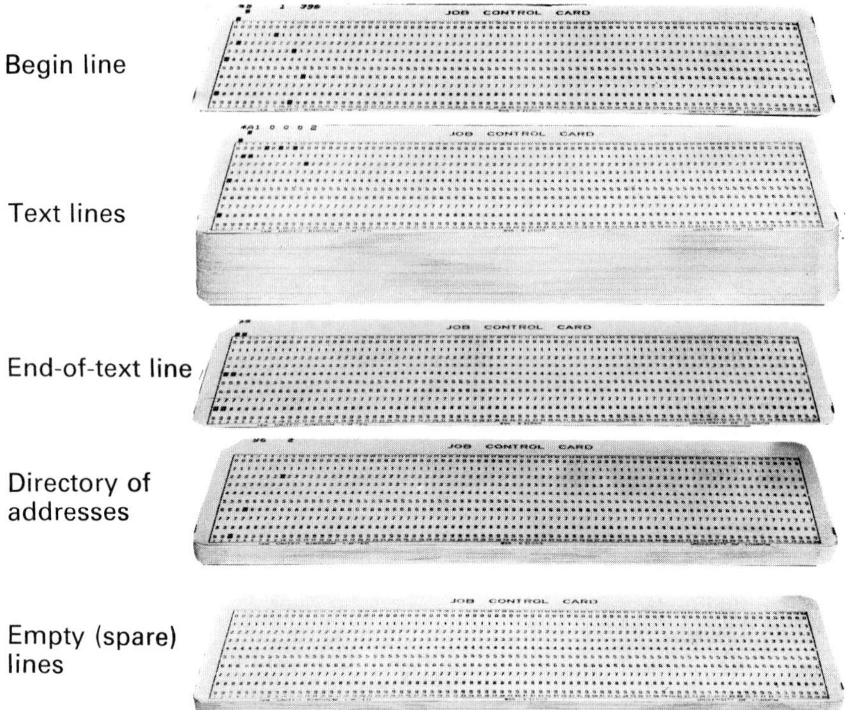


**Figure 4.1** Semi-diagrammatic illustration of the structure of a text file showing the fixed-length consecutive lines, with a *B(egin) line, text frames, **(end-of-text) line, frame directory, and spare (empty) lines to allow file expansion

large non-rotating information storage devices are available, the text file will obviously be stored upon such a system. All that is needed is the facility to be able to read from and write upon any individual line of the file, by giving the READ or WRITE unit the line address.

A file whose structure is as described above, i.e. consisting of uniform-length lines whose text is filled to column 72 by blanks, as needed, is potentially wasteful of space. In practical terms, the actual space necessary to store a text file as a 72-column direct access file is about one-third greater than that needed to store the same file in condensed form, i.e. with the end of each line of text or control information being shown by a 'carriage return/line feed' code. However, the difficulties of constructing a directory giving information about line location in a file whose lines are of unequal length are formidable for a system which is portable and is designed to allow on-line editing. They seem not worth the relatively slight waste of file storage space.

As described above, and illustrated in the model text exercise in the last chapter (p. 25) the frames are sequentially (though not necessarily evenly) numbered. This apparent limitation on flexibility and expansion can be overcome by placing extra frames at the end of the file (preserving sequential numbering of frames) or more radically by using the renumbering facility, described in Chapter 11, before running the program. There is no limitation to branching, to circular logical structures, or to the number of lines in a text file, but there is a limit to the number of control lines which can be handled, since this depends on the size of main memory available to the Driver. If the core size is large, the number of control lines which can be handled is likewise large.

## The control line 'directory'

This is the index to the whole file. If a specified (numbered) frame is requested, the Driver locates the correct line of the text file by a simple binary search procedure, using the information in the directory. The directory itself comprises three parts (Figure 4.2):

```
**
  96     2
   0     2    1     7    2    14    3    19    4    23    5    25    6    30    7    34
   8    37    9    39   10    43   11    46   12    49   13    53   15    56   20    63
  25    72   26    76   27    82   30    88   60    91   70    99   75   115   76   117
  77   119   78   121   79   123   80   126  100   130  104   134  105   138  106   140
 107   145  110   147  120   149  130   153  140   155  160   158  170   161  180   165
 185   167  190   172  191   186  192   191  193   193  194   195  195   197  196   199
 197   201  198   203  199   205  200   209  201   212  205   215  300   223  305   225
 510   227  520   229  530   233  540   244  552   252  555   261  560   265  570   268
 580   271  581   275  582   282  583   285  584   287  590   289  600   2961000   300
1010   3011020    3051030    3071050    3131060    3141070    3161500    3191501   322
1600   3261601    3351699    3371700    3401710    3471720    3501730    3521740   357
1750   3671760    3731775    3761780    3781785    3801790    3832000    3882001   393
  183   281     0    0     0    0     0    0     0    0     0    0     0    0
```

**Figure 4.2** Typical frame directory, taken from the illustrative text exercise of Chapter 3. Note that it follows immediately after the '**' end-of-text line (see text)

(1) The first line (which follows the end-of-text double asterisk line – see above) gives the total number of frames, and the total number of dictionaries (96 and 2, in the example).

(2) Line two to the penultimate line comprises pairs of numbers, the first of each pair being the frame number, and the second the 'address' or location of that frame.

(3) The last line gives the addresses of any dictionaries used (183 and 281 in the example).

All three parts of the directory are made automatically by the Driver, on command – the user needs only allocate the necessary space for it at the end of the file.

## Components of a 'frame'

A frame has one essential component and two optional components. The essential part is the 'control line'. This is specified by an initial asterisk (in column 1 of the card image), a code letter (in column 2) and a frame number. Then follow three control instruction numbers, and an exit address or table of addresses. The control line may be preceded by one or more (optional) 'comment' lines and it may itself run on to any number of continuation control lines. It may, but need not necessarily, be followed by one or more lines of 'text', each line consisting of up to 72 characters of any variety. The only limitation on text characters is that the 1st character of a text line must not be an asterisk (*), a slash (/) or a plus (+). These symbols are reserved for control lines. Lower case letters can be used freely.

The following example of a simple complete frame is taken from the illustrative text exercise of the last chapter:

```
*C CLEAR SCREEN, RESET CURSOR, TURN ON SCORER ('SCORE' PARAMETER=6)
*T60 2000 6 0  70
 I AM GOING TO ASK YOU SOME GENERAL KNOWLEDGE QUESTIONS.    I SHALL
 PUT THESE IN THE FORM OF A 'MULTIPLE-CHOICE' TYPE OF QUESTION, TO WHICH
 YOU SHOULD ANSWER 'YES' OR 'NO' ..
```

The structure of a frame may be thought of, as before, as cards in a stack (Figure 4.3). The first line, beginning '*C' is a comment line. The next line, beginning '*T' is the control line of frame #60. The final integer of the control line ('70') is the number of the next frame. The next three lines comprise the text belonging to that frame.

To summarize:

A *comment line* uniquely begins '*C';

A *control line* begins with '*' followed by a letter other than 'C';

*Text material* comprises any line or lines *not* beginning with '*', '/' or '+' in column 1. (A text author wanting to start a line with one of these symbols

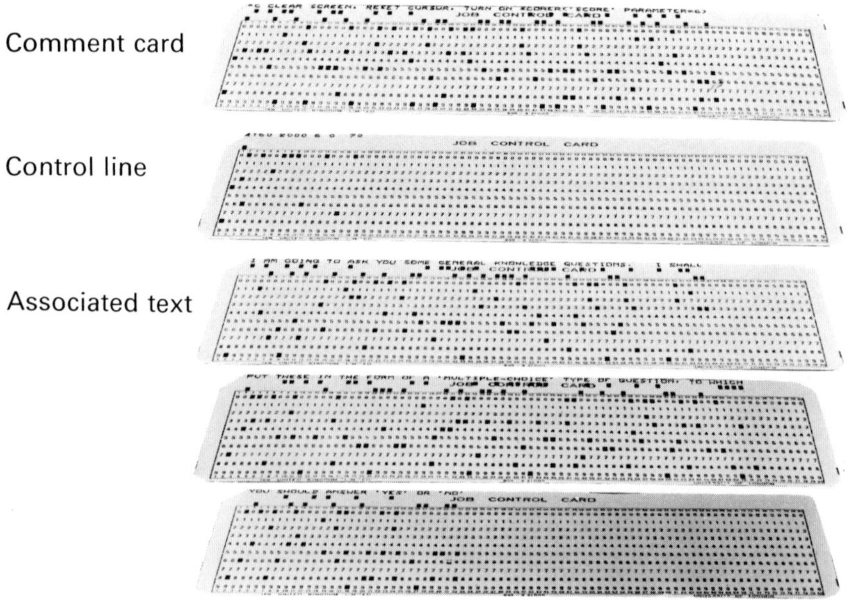


**Figure 4.3** Semi-diagrammatic illustration of the structure of a typical frame (see text). Note that all lines are of fixed, standard length. Comment line(s) precede, and text line(s) follow the *-control line

should indent it by one space, e.g. see frame 2000 from the illustrative text exercise in Chapter 3.)

## Structure of a control line

There are three indispensable components of a control line.

(1) An asterisk in column 1 (marking a control line).
(2) A letter, which must be A, B, E, F, G, I, M, Q, R, S or T, in column 2 (identifying the frame 'type').
(3) A unique frame reference number (which must be a positive integer greater than the number of the preceding frame, and less than that of the following frame).

An example of a frame with a control line of minimal size, taken from the illustrative text exercise in the last chapter could be:

```
*R570
 TO HANG ABOUT AT ALL IN SUCH A SITUATION IS MOST UNWISE!
```

Obviously a frame with no exit or transfer address can do nothing except return to the calling frame after its message has been printed. Normally the last number in a line of control instructions, e.g. '70' in the previous example:

```
*T60 1000 6 0  70
```

is the exit address. For frames offering conditional branching depending on a user's input or upon accumulated scores or totals, there may be more than one exit address. The control line of a frame asking a 'YES/NO' type of question might be (as in the illustrative text exercise in the last chapter)

```
*Q15 2000 0 0 'Y'30 '',20
 ARE YOU READY TO PROCEED?
```

Control is transferred to frame #30 if the user's answer is 'Y' or 'YES' and to frame #20 if the answer is 'NO' (or anything not beginning 'Y').

In this frame there are three other numbers between the frame number (15) and the exit addresses (30 and 20). These three numbers (2000, 0, 0) are, in order.

(1) The 1st, or 'display' parameter (controlling structured screen display and external devices; 0 = no display instructions, 2000 = clear screen).
(2) The 2nd, or 'score' parameter (modifying the running score, and also doing other tasks; 0 = no score instructions or score change).
(3) The 3rd, or 'add' parameter (concerned with the running total, and also supplying other information to the Driver; 0 = no special instuctions except a dialogue pause).

All numbers, including the frame number, are read in 'free format', from left to right, i.e. they can be anywhere on a line providing that one space is present between each number. The following control lines are legal and allowable, and all will be acted upon in identical manner:

```
*T60 2000 6 0 70
*T 60   2000    6    0     70
*TEXT 60 2000 6 0 70
*T60 2000 6 0 70 ****************************************************
```

In the case of the last example, the remaining unused part of the 72-character control line is filled with asterisks instead of blanks. In control lines, *an asterisk marks the end of the control information.* Asterisks, which are optional, have two functions. First they can be used to divide up the text neatly into frames, so that the boundary between one frame of text and the next frame is visible at a glance when reading through a file. Secondly, in the case of those frames with conditional addresses (e.g. the *Q(uestion) frame – see p. 51) an asterisk economizes on execution time by stopping the search of a control line for a match with user input.

The following lines would be illegal:

| | |
|---|---|
| `T60 2000 6 0 70` | ('*' missing in column 1 – the line would be treated as part of the text of the preceding frame) |
| ` *T60 2000 6 0 70` | ('*T' beginning in column 2, not in 1 – again would be treated as text) |
| `* T60 2000 6 0 70` | ('space' in column 2 – the 'T' in column 3 would not be recognized – this frame would be illegal and would stop the Driver) |

A control line without an exit address would return control to the preceding frame, and (except in special circumstances) would create a loop, e.g.

```
*T60 0 0 0 70
*T70
```

As long as the asterisk is in column 1 and the frame type letter in column 2, the free format input (which does not need a 'free format read' facility to be available on the computer's compiler) allows complete freedom of spacing.

The following is an example (from the last chapter's text file) illustrating a sequence of text frames, each accessing the next:

```
*T26 0 0 -1 30
 I THINK THAT IF YOU DON'T KNOW WHY YOU ARE NOT READY TO PROCEED
 WE HAD BETTER PROCEED NONETHELESS!
*T30 2000 0 -1 60
 RIGHT - LET'S GO
*T60 1000 6 0  70
 NOW FOR SOME GENERAL KNOWLEDGE QUESTIONS. I SHALL PUT THESE IN THE FORM
 OF A MULTIPLE-CHOICE QUESTION, TO WHICH YOU SHOULD ANSWER 'YES' OR 'NO'
```

### Reading of the text file by the Driver

In ordinary use, when no changes are being made to the text itself, the Driver first reads the *B(egin) line. To avoid the Driver having to read the whole file, the *B line contains the address of the first line of the directory

(Figure 4.1), i.e. the number of lines down the file at which it may be found. In the illustrative text exercise in the last chapter, the *B line is line 1, and the text occupies lines 2 to 394, so that the *B frame carries the figure '396' to tell the Driver that the directory starts at line 396. The Driver then reads the directory by 'direct-access' (i.e. a process in which it reads specified and numbered lines starting at line 396, and copies into its 'core' (short-term memory) a list of the control addresses for the particular exercise. For normal purposes, a maximum of 250 separate line addresses is allowed for the text file, though if lots of storage is available the directory could be any size, by enlarging the storage array.

## Processing of a frame

When the master Driver has been given a specified frame number (usually by a previous frame, or by the *B(egin) frame if the exercise is only just starting), it locates the line number, using a binary search on the directory of frame addresses already stored in memory. (This is possible because all the frames are in ascending numerical order and the corresponding index numbers are also in ascending order.)

First, the Driver reads the whole control line into memory, then records (and checks) the frame type (denoted by the letter in column 2). The 1st ('display') and 2nd ('score') parameters are then read and acted upon as described in Chapters 7 and 8. Then the Driver prints on the output terminal or console the whole text (if any) of the frame, each line in succession until a line is encountered with an asterisk (*) in column 1. This marks the comment or control line of the next frame, and hence the end of the current frame. The Driver then reads the 3rd ('add') parameter, and acts upon it appropriately (as will be described in later chapters). After processing any input, the Driver reads the appropriate exit address and locates the control line of the next frame. The whole process is then repeated.

## SUMMARY

The structure of a directly and randomly accessible text file is described. The standard MACAID file uses 72-column card image lines, the first of which is a *B(egin) line, followed by text, followed by a text-terminating line, and followed finally by a directory or index by means of which individual frames can be located.

The choice of a rigid and slightly wasteful storage system for text is justified by considerations of portability, flexibility and convenience.

The text consists of 'frames' which have a control line of numerical instructions, and (optionally) preceding 'comment' lines and associated text (printed at the terminal).

The general structure of a control line is described. It must have a designating type letter and frame number, and normally has at least three control instruction numbers in addition to an exit address.

In processing a frame, the first two control parameters are read, then any text is printed, and finally the rest of the control information is read and acted upon.

# 5
# Numbered, executable frames; duplicate text

In this chapter we shall describe the standard general purpose frames – *T(ext), *R(eturn), *F(lag), *I(f), *E(nd), *Q(uestion) and *M(arking), and the use of duplicate text.

## The T(ext) frame

This has already been exemplified in the last chapter. Its main function is to print text, but it can be used for other purposes. The three parameters concerned with structured screen display, scoring, and keeping a running total are acted upon whether or not any text is printed. For example, the *T frame #1720 in the illustrative exercise in Chapter 3:

```
*T1720 0 0 0 1730
```

contains no text and has the sole function of supplying the 3rd parameter ('0') which instructs the Driver to pause at this point and await a prompt (e.g. 'PRESS *RETURN*'). Frame #60 from the same exercise does contain some text, but its three control parameters (2000,6,0)

```
*T60 2000 6 0  70
```

not only request a pause (3rd parameter = 0), but also instruct the Driver to clear the screen of a visual display unit and position the cursor at top left (1st parameter = 2000), and to reset the scorer to 100 and switch it on (2nd parameter = 6). These parameters will be described fully in Chapters 7 and 8.

## Duplicate text

Any text line of a *T(ext) frame, or indeed any text line of any type of frame except the *A(nswer) frame, may be replaced by an instruction to use text from somewhere else in the file. For example, in the illustrative text exercise in the last chapter frames 15 and 1601 are as follows:

```
*Q15 2000 0 0 'Y'30 '',20
 ARE YOU READY TO PROCEED?


*M 1601 3400 0 12 1700, 1699 0
/USE 15
```

When frame #1601 is acted upon, the text of frame #15 is printed. The '/USE N' instruction can even be placed midway through text, as exemplified by frames 530 and 540:

```
*T530 0 0 0 540
 0 = MUST NOT DO
 1 = MIGHT DO
 2 = SHOULD SOMETIMES DO
 3 = SHOULD DO MOST OF THE TIME
 4 = MUST DO

*T540 2000 3 0  552
 I AM GOING TO GIVE YOU A HUMANITARIAN TEST.  GIVE GRADES AS FOLLOWS:
/USE 530
....OK - HERE IS THE QUESTION:
```

The corresponding dialogue with the user is shown on the page opposite this part of the illustrative text file (p. 32). The only limitation on this facility is that the whole frame text is necessarily displayed by '/USE N'. Two or more '/USE N' text instructions can be used in a single frame if desired.

It is essential that the slash (/) is the first character of the line, and that the 2nd character is 'U'. All the following would work:

```
/USE 530
/USE530
/U 530
/U530
/USE FRAME 530
```

but the following would not, and would simply be treated as ordinary text:

```
/ USE 530
 /USE 530
/PLEASE USE 530
```

| | |
|---|---|
| `/ USE 530` | ('U' not in 2nd column) |
| ` /USE 530` | ('/' not in 1st column) |
| `/PLEASE USE 530` | ('U' not in 2nd column) |

## The R(eturn) frame

This frame is generally similar to the *T(ext) frame, except that it has no exit address, and after the text is printed, and the score and add parameter (if present) have been acted upon, control returns to the calling frame. The following examples from the Chapter 3 illustrative exercise show typical *R(eturn) frames:

```
*R570
 TO HANG AROUND AT ALL IN SUCH A SITUATION IS MOST UNWISE!

*R584 0 -3
YOU ARE ONE OUT IN TIME SEQUENCE...

*R75 0 0 1
 WASHINGTON (D.C.) IS THE CAPITAL OF THE USA
```

Frame #570 (above) simply prints the text line below the control line; frame #584 substracts 3 from the current score before printing the text; and frame #75 adds 1 to the current value in the running 'sum' register, after writing out the text line. (In frame numbers 584 and 75 a zero 'display' parameter is added to prevent ambiguity).

In general, *R(eturn) frames can only be effectively used in association with conditionally branching *Q(uestion) or *M(arking) frames. A sequence of frames such as the following:

```
*T55 0 0 0 56
NOW GO TO FRAME 56
*R56
THIS IS FRAME 56
```

would obviously comprise a loop, in which the two text messages would be printed alternately, and no exit would be possible, since if a frame has no exit address (e.g. *R56) control remains with the frame which called it (*T55).

## The F(lag) frame

To control branching in accordance with the response to an earlier question, it may be convenient to set a flag to some specified value, and later to make a conditional branch depending on the value of the flag. The parameters of a *F(lag) frame control line are similar to those of the standard *T frame, except that the 3rd parameter now specifies the value to be taken by the flag. The 'FLAG' is an integer initialized as 1, with a maximum value of 11. When the Driver encounters a frame such as:

```
*F 8 0 0 2 9
```

and reads the 3rd parameter ('2'), it sets the FLAG to that value.

The value of FLAG may also be set dynamically, depending on the score, if a zero value for the 3rd parameter is given. For example, the control line

```
*F 8 0 0 0 9
```

would set the value of FLAG to an integer between 1 and 11 in accordance with the following rough and ready calculations: If the current score is:

100 (maximum), the value of FLAG becomes 1
90 (to the nearest ten), FLAG becomes 2
80 (to the nearest ten), FLAG becomes 3 . . . etc.,

until, if the score is zero – it is not allowed to fall below zero – the flag becomes 11. That is to say, FLAG takes up a value of (110-SCORE)/10.

It is also possible to change or set the value of FLAG within a special-purpose sub-program called from the master Driver.

As with every type of frame except *S(ubroutine) and *A(nswer), any associated text is printed when the frame is read by the Driver, at the same time as the FLAG is set.

## The I(f) frame

This frame controls transfer to an address which depends on the value that FLAG has at the time the frame is read. The *I-frame control line therefore should supply an appropriate number of exit addresses. There can be less than 11 of these if it is certain that the value of FLAG can never reach 11. For example the following *I(f) frame (from the illustrative exercise in Chapter 3) has only two addresses (1060 and 1070):

```
*I1050 0 0 -1 1060 1070
```

If, when this frame is called, FLAG = 1 (the user had stated his sex was male when answering *Q(uestion) frame # 7 – see p. 25 – and no change had been made in the default value of 1), control would be transferred to frame #1060. If FLAG = 2 (sex female, flag set to 2 by frame #8, as described above), control would pass to frame #1070. Insufficient addresses in a *I-frame will stop the program with an appropriate error message, or (in 'authoring' mode), return control to 'COMMAND:' (see p. 104).

## The E(nd) frame

This has a frame number, and (optionally) a 'display' parameter e.g.:

```
*E2001
THANK YOU
```

When this frame is encountered, any associated text is first printed, then the program is stopped. The example above is the last frame of the illustrative text file of Chapter 3, though it need not have been the last frame. Any number of *E(nd) frames can be used in a text file.

## The Q(uestion) frame

This frame is used for most general purposes, to prompt the user for some response and to branch conditionally on his response. It has the same general form as the standard *T(ext) frame, e.g.

```
Q7 0 0 0 'M',10   'F' 8 'WOM'8
WHAT IS YOUR SEX? - TYPE M OR F AND PRESS 'RETURN' KEY AGAIN
```

i.e. a frame number ('7'), a 'display' parameter (the 1st zero), a 'score' parameter (the 2nd zero), a 3rd parameter (the 3rd zero) and alternative addresses (frame # 10, if the answer begins (or is) 'M', and frame # 8 (if the answer is or begins 'F' or 'WOM'). In any *Q frame there must be at least one exit address, unless control is to be transferred by a *G(lobal) keyword (see p. 58), and normally there would be at least two exit addresses, though any number of addresses is allowed.

The response to a *Q frame can be of any type:

(1) Numeric (integer or 'floating point' – i.e. a decimal number).

(2) Numeric range (i.e. between a lower and upper limit).

(3) A character or succession of characters (of any length), i.e. usually a word, or the first part of a word.

Round brackets, e.g. (2), (−3.5, −.01) or ( ) are used if a numeric answer is expected. (2) would only be satisfied if the user typed '2', '02', '2.0' or some equivalent; (−3.5, −.01) would be satisfied by any number between −3.5 and −.01 inclusive, and () would be satisfied by any number at all including negative and zero numbers. Examples from the illustrative text exercise in Chapter 3 are:

```
*Q170 3400 0  0 (1)180 (2)185
WOULD YOU LIKE TO KNOW YOUR SCORE?  TYPE 1 FOR YES, 2 FOR NO

*Q1775 2300 2 0 (-3,5,-.01)1780 ''1785
WHAT WAS YOUR VALUE FOR FACTOR 3?
```

Single inverted commas are used if a character of any kind is expected. Indeed, *Q frame #170 (above) could be written:

```
*Q170 3400 0 0 '1'180 '2'185
```

However, since the characters in a *Q(uestion) frame answer are read from left to right, entries of '01' or '02' would be rejected (because the 1st characters of both are zero), but would be accepted by:

```
*Q170 3400 0  0 (1)180 (2)185
```

Blanks may be included in a *Q frame answer. If, for example, the only correct answer to a question was 'RHEUMATIC FEVER' this whole character string could be specified, e.g.:

```
*Q3000 0 0 0 'RHEUMATIC FEVER'3001 ''3002
```

Note that in this case two adjacent single inverted commas ('') will accept any input whatever. For example, in the following frame

```
*Q15 2000 0 0 'Y'30 '',20
 ARE YOU READY TO PROCEED?
```

any answer, other than 'Y' (or any answer not beginning with 'Y') will cause transfer of control to frame #20.

It is possible to extend the use of the *Q(uestion) frame by the use of dictionaries, and this will be described in the next chapter (p. 59). However, there is no limit to the size of a *Q frame, which can be extended by any number of continuation lines, with '+' in column 1 of the first and any subsequent lines, e.g.:

```
*Q201 0 0 0 'Y'205 'AFFIRMATIVE'205 'I WOULD'205 'SCORE',205
+ 'N'305
```

If the user's input cannot be matched by the main control line, the next line is examined, and if it is a continuation line, its characters or words are checked by the Driver.

It is also possible to use a *Q-frame to transfer control according to the running score or running total, making use of the numeric or numeric range facility. Examples from the illustrative exercise of Chapter 3 are frames *Q107 and *Q1000. Since the values of both the running 'score' and the running 'sum' or 'total' can be changed within specially-written subprograms, Q-frames can be used to transfer control conditionally on some manoeuvre performed within the subprogram. The facility will be further described in Chapter 8.

Inspection of the above examples, and of the '*Q' frames in the illustrative text exercises of Chapter 3, shows that commas and spaces are optional. For example, 'Y'205 'Y',205 and 'Y' 205 are all legal ways of writing the control line.

## The M(arking) frame

It is possible to use *Q(uestion) frames throughout for all questioning purposes, but this means that each question has to be posed singly and answered singly. This is particularly tedious and inconvenient for exercises such as multiple choice questions. The M(arking) frame allows from 1 to 9 questions to be posed in a single block, and their answer or answers to be given also as a single block.

The simplest marking frame invites a YES/NO answer to a single question, e.g.:

```
*M 1601 3400 0 12 1700, 1699 0
/USE 15
```

The 3rd parameter ('12') signifies that the question expects 1 answer, with 2 alternatives. The 4th parameter ('1700') is the final exit address. 'N' or 'NO' is always translated as zero, and 'Y' or 'YES' as one. There are two possible responses here. If the answer is 'N', 'NO', (or '0') control passes to frame #1699. If the answer is 'Y', 'YES' (or '') the answer is 'correct', or expected (last address = 0), no message is printed, and control now passes to the main exit address (frame #1700). The sequence of frames

```
*M 1601 3400 0 12 1700, 1699 0
/USE 15

*T1700 2000 0 -1 1710
I SHALL NOW PLOT A SIMPLE GRAPH OF Y AGAINST X...   Y=5X
```

has exactly the same effect (when 'Y' is typed) as one using the following *Q-frame:

```
*Q1601 3400 0 0 'Y'1700 'N'1699
/USE 15
*T1700 2000 0 -1 1710
 I SHALL NOW PLOT A SIMPLE GRAPH OF Y AGAINST X...   Y=5X
```

In a *M(arking) frame any response except an integer between 0 and 4, or any letter other than 'Y', 'N' or 'E' is translated as '2'. The effect is illustrated in the multiple choice question in the text exercise of Chapter 3:

```
*M70 2500 0 62 100, 0 75,0 76,77 0,0 78, 0 79,
+0 80
```

```
 WHICH OF THE FOLLOWING STATEMENTS ARE TRUE?
1.NEW YORK IS THE CAPITAL OF THE USA
2.MICHELANGELO PAINTED THE 'MONA LISA'
3.97 IS A PRIME NUMBER
4.ELECTRONS ARE POSITIVELY CHARGED
5.THE OPERA 'MARRIAGE OF FIGARO' WAS WRITTEN BY ROSSINI
6.SOCRATES WAS THE DISCIPLE OF PLATO
 TYPE YOUR ANSWERS ACROSS A LINE, E.G.YYNN?Y - THEN PRESS RETURN KEY
```

In the answer shown opposite this part of the illustrative text (on p. 26) – "YYNNXY" – the 'X' is treated as an indeterminate answer ('2') and the appropriate error message given. The first two addresses of *M-frame 70 ('0 75') mean: "On answer 'N' or '0' to the 1st question take no action, and proceed to the next answer; on answer 'Y' or '1', print the corrective response given by frame #75 before proceeding."

Exit to frame #100 is not normally made until all the answers have been processed, providing that the numbered addresses are all of *R(eturn) frames. The pairs of instructions for each question appear in sequence. The first pair in the example above is '0 75', the second pair is '0 76', the third '77 0', and so on until '0 80'. (This last pair of instructions appears on a continuation line).

The *M(arking) frame does not demand a correct ('0') address for each or any question. If, for example, '74 75' was substituted for '0 75' the Driver would print the text of frame #74 on the answer 'N' and that of frame #75 on the answer 'Y'. In the case of any ambiguous answer, the text of the frame with the higher number (in this case '75') would be displayed. If one answer is 'correct' – i.e. the address is zero – e.g. '0 75' in the above example – an indeterminate answer will print the text of frame #75.

In the above example, the third parameter ('62') again gives information to the Driver. The first digit (in this case '6' gives the number of questions posed by the text. The second (in this case '2') signifies the number of possible grades of reply. In this case there are only two – either 'N' (or '0' – i.e. zero), or 'Y' (or '1'). The first digit has a maximum value of 9, i.e. a M(arking) frame cannot process the answers to more than nine questions at once.

### *Graded responses in a M(arking) frame*

The second digit of the 3rd parameter can be given any value between 2 and 5. This allows the possibility of asking questions to which the answer is not necessarily 'YES' or 'NO' but might be, for example

| 0 | 1 | 2 |
|---|---|---|
| NO | YES | DON'T KNOW |

| 0 | 1 | 2 | 3 |
|---|---|---|---|
| NO | YES | DON'T KNOW | EXPLAIN |

| 0 | 1 | 2 | 3 | 4 |
|---|---|---|---|---|
| NEVER | OCCASIONALLY | SOMETIMES | QUITE OFTEN | ALL THE TIME |
| MUST NOT DO | MIGHT DO | COULD DO | SHOULD DO | MUST DO |
| NONE AT ALL | VERY SLIGHT | MODERATE | FAIRLY BAD | VERY BAD |

It should be noted that any input character except 'N', 'Y' and 'E' codes as '2'. The first example above does not need numerical input at all (though responses of '0', '1' or '2' would have the same effect as 'N', 'Y', and '?'). The response 'E' ('Explain') is treated as '3', thus allowing character entry even for the 4-point scale 0–1–2–3 (e.g. *N*o–*Y*es–*D*on't know–*E*xplain). For a 5-point scale numerical entries are essential.

There are very many examples of questions which can be rated on a 3, 4 or 5-point scale. The illustrative text exercise of Chapter 3 has an example of a 4-point scale (frame #20). An example of a 'grading' question is the following:

```
*M552 2500 2 35 580,  0 555 555 555 555, 560 560 -1 0 -1,
+ 570 570 570 570 0
 IF YOU WERE DRIVING ALONG A DESERTED COUNTRY HIGHWAY AND
 YOU SAW A CAR SLEWED OFF THE ROAD, WITH A FRONT WING BUCKLED AGAINST A
 TREE, HOW WOULD YOU GRADE THE FOLLOWING COURSES OF ACTION?
1. STOP THE MOTOR;
2. GET OUT AND LOOK TO SEE IF ANYONE WAS INJURED;
3. IF NO-ONE IS IN SIGHT, IMMEDIATELY GET BACK AND DRIVE ON
  -    GRADE EACH QUESTION ON THE SCALE 0-1-2-3-4,   EG. 042
```

In this example, **3** questions are being asked, and a graded response on a **5**-point scale (0–1–2–3–4) requested, so that the 3rd parameter is '35'. The exit address is '580'. The first question is analysed by the sequence of frame numbers '0 555 555 555 555'. This means that the only completely correct answer is the first number in the 5-point scale 0–1–2–3–4, i.e. zero. The answers '1', '2', '3' or '4' are regarded as incorrect, and will result in the output of the text of frame #555. Question 2 is controlled by the sequence of numbers '560 560 −1 0 −1'. In this case, the only completely correct response is '3' (the 4th position in the series 0–1–2–3–4). As before, answers '0' or '1' are treated as incorrect, with output of the text of frame #560. The answer of '4' to this question (as in the example on p. 32) gives an intermediate response in which the Driver prints the message:

```
Q.2. ACCEPTABLE - THOUGH MY GRADE WOULD BE SLIGHTLY LOWER
```

A response of '2' would have given a similar style of response, suggesting the ideal response or grade would be slightly higher. In other words, '−1' (as a *M(arking) frame address) codes for an acceptable but not quite ideal answer.

Unless modifications are made to the Driver, the largest possible value of the 3rd parameter of a *M(arking) frame is '95', i.e. 9 questions in a block, with 5 grades possible for each question.

The modes of operation of different types of *M-frame are illustrated by the text exercise in Chapter 3. It is perhaps worth noticing (e.g. see the dialogue on p. 30) that after three incorrect responses either to a *Q or to a *M frame the question is repeated. This is to guard against the text disappearing off the screen of a visual display unit used in 'roll' mode. However, if structured screen display is in use (see Chapter 8) the Driver holds the question stationary on the screen, while incorrect responses are successively overwritten, and corrective messages displayed. In this case the question is not automatically repeated.

The *M(arking) frame has the capacity for automatic scoring, which will be fully described in Chapter 7.

The commas shown in the *M-frame examples of Chapter 3 make the grouping of conditional addresses easier to see at a glance, but their use is entirely optional, as in *Q-frames.

## SUMMARY

The main types of 'executable' frame are described, i.e. those frames which are numbered and which form part of the predetermined or conditional transfers of control. These frames comprise:

(1) The *T(ext) frame, which is mainly to display text.
(2) The *R(eturn) frame, to do the same without transferring control.
(3) The *F(lag) frame, to set the value of a flag.
(4) The *I(f) frame, to branch according to the value of a flag.
(5) The *E(nd) frame, to stop the Driver.
(6) The *Q(uestion) frame, to get numerical or character answers, in order to control conditional branching.
(7) The *M(arking) frame, to handle groups of questions together (as in multiple choice questionnaires) and to allow up to 5 grades of answer, in addition to simple 'YES/NO' responses.

The text of any frame can be used in place of, or to supplement, the text of any other frame, thus avoiding any need to duplicate text.

# 6
# Un-numbered, non-executable and special purpose frames

In the last chapter we described the structure and function of those frames which form the substance of a branching exercise or dialogue. In this chapter we shall describe the other frames and control lines which also begin with an asterisk (*) in column 1, but which are not part of the text proper (*C(omment), *B(egin), *G(lobal) and *D(ictionary)).

## The *C(omment) line

We mentioned briefly in Chapter 3 that for easier intelligibility, MACAID allows the text file to have an unlimited number of 'comment lines', i.e. lines which are neither control lines nor part of the text material, but which serve to remind the author, or someone else editing or changing the text, about the purpose of each section of the program. Providing the line begins with an asterisk in column 1 (i.e. in the 1st character position on the 72-character line of the text file), and providing it has the capital letter 'C' in column 2 (i.e. in the 2nd character position), the Driver will ignore it completely. The line will not be treated as a control line, nor will it be treated as part of a text frame (since the printing or display of text is terminated as soon as an asterisk is encountered at the beginning of a line).

The use of COMMENT lines is illustrated extensively in the model interrogative program in Chapter 3. It is worth noting that the only ill consequence of incorporating many comment lines is that the file storage space has to be proportionately increased. The size of the directory, and thus the time taken for the Driver to locate any particular numbered frame, depends only on the number of control frames, and not at all on the length of the text file.

## The *B(egin) line

Mention of this essential part of a MACAID text file has already been made in the last chapter. Although the *B-frame contains two numbers (the first is the number of the frame which the Driver is instructed to operate on at the start of a run, and the second is the line address of the text file directory) the author has only to supply the first one, the number of the starting frame. If, therefore (as in the illustrative text exercise of Chapter 3) the author wishes the Driver to start at Frame #1, he just makes the first line of the file

```
*B 1
```

and the Driver does the rest. When it is called up in 'AUTHOR' mode (see p. 100) with the 'authoring' password, and the question 'NEW DIRECTORY?' is answered in the affirmative, the Driver reads the whole file, locates the end-of-text line (beginning '**'), automatically constructs the directory and places it immediately after the '**' line. The address of the directory (i.e. the number of the text file line at which it is stored) is automatically entered on the *B(egin) line as the 2nd number. In the illustrative text exercise, for example, after the directory has been made, the *B-line is changed from

```
*B 1
```

to

```
*B    1  396
```

A *B(egin) line *must* be the first line of a text file. Any other line will be interpreted by the Driver to mean that the file is blank or defective. The operator will then be offered a choice of stopping, of creating a new file, with blank but numbered frames, or of performing a rescue operation by inserting a new *B(egin) line and a new frame for it to access (p. 89). A*B line occurring anywhere else in the file will result in an appropriate error message, and in ordinary use, stops the Driver altogether. In 'AUTHOR' mode (p. 100) control returns to the operator with 'COMMAND:'.

## The *G(lobal) line

The global facility is optional, except that the Driver always has one built-in 'global' command, i.e. a command which can be entered anywhere and at any time during a text dialogue. This is 'AUTHOR', which is described fully on p. 89, and which allows a wide range of editing commands to be given. The effect of this entry is shown below (see frame #7 of the illustrative text exercise in Chapter 3):

```
WHAT IS YOUR SEX? - TYPE M OR F AND PRESS 'RETURN' KEY AGAIN
? AUTHOR
COMMAND:
```

However, up to 5 further GLOBAL instructions can be entered on the *G-line, which, if present, *must form the 2nd line of the text file.* In the illustrative text exercise of Chapter 3, the *G-line is as follows:

```
*G 'SCORE',300 'STOP'2001
```

Any sequence of up to 5 characters, including numbers, symbols and blanks can be used as a keyword in a Global line, providing it does not exceed 5 characters in length. For example, '999', '£' and 'RUN M' would all be legal and permissible Global keywords. The frame address which follows each keyword (contained between single inverted commas) is the transfer address. If at any time during the dialogue the user of the illustrative exercise typed 'STOP', for example, control would pass at once to frame #2001. However, if he typed 'SCORE' control would pass only temporarily to frame #300, because the latter is a *R(eturn) frame (see p. 49). After the text had been displayed, therefore, and the 2nd and 3rd parameters (if present) acted upon, control would return to the calling frame. In the text exercise of Chapter 3 (p. 30) the user typed 'SCORE', instead of the expected answer. This transferred control temporarily to frame #300, with the result that the current value of the score was printed.

The only absolute limitation on *G(lobal) operations is that they are (in the FORTRAN version of the Driver contained in this book) limited to five 5-character keywords or character combinations. In principle it would be possible, by enlarging the storage arrays, to increase this number and size as much as a user wished. However, the practical disadvantages are considerable. The search for GLOBAL keywords other than 'AUTHOR' (which is always, as mentioned, a global keyword) takes a small but not completely insignificant amount of computer time. A search for 5 keywords takes roughly 5 times as long as the search for one.

## The *D(ictionary) frame

This frame, though it may have a reference number, is not part of the sequence of control lines and frames. It is used only to augment the function of *Q(uestion) frames, to make possible 3 extensions of use:

(1) To allow more than one keyword or character sequence to be recognized.
(2) To allow other words to be interspersed between or before designated keywords, without preventing recognition of the keywords themselves.
(3) To allow the same group of keywords to be searched for in response to more than one *Q-frame question.

Up to 14 separate dictionaries are permitted in the version of the MACAID Driver described here (since allowance is at present made for 14 5-digit numbers, representing the line addresses of the 14 dictionaries, to be indexed in the directory across a single 72-character line of the text file). There are 3 main rules concerning dictionaires, which are:

(1) They must be placed after the 2nd line of the text file (i.e. not in the positions of the *B(egin) or *G(lobal) lines), and before the text terminator line (**).
(2) They must be sequentially numbered, in digits (starting at #1), according to their position in the file.
(3) Words or character strings treated as keywords must not contain blanks.

Dictionaries may be of any length by extending them with continuation lines. The individual keywords may also be of any length. The illustrative text exercise of Chapter 3 has two dictionaries. The first follows frame *Q190 (p. 31);

```
*D 1      'JERS',1 'PEN' 2 'OHIO'3 'IND'4 'ILL'4 'VIRG'5 'KENT'5
+ 'MARY'5 'HAWA'6
```

and the second follows frame *Q581 (p. 33):

```
*D 2 'CHAMBER'1 'CHURCHILL'2417 'BALDWIN'3
```

The line addresses of these 2 dictionary frames (183 and 281) are automatically entered as the last line of the directory when this is created by the Driver (see p. 89). Note that dictionary 1 comes before dictionary 2 in the file, and that each of the keywords or character sequences in each dictionary is given a reference number, which is an integer (of up to 4 digits).

The *Q-frames described in the last chapter had mostly a 3rd parameter of zero, e.g.:

```
*Q15 2000 0 0 'Y'30 '',20
 ARE YOU READY TO PROCEED?
```

This means "no dictionary to be consulted". In the case of frame #581, however

```
*Q581 2300 0 2 <1>590 <2417>584 <3>584 'H'582 ''583
WHO WAS THE BRITISH PRIME MINISTER AT THE OUTBREAK OF THE 1939-45
WAR - THE ONE WHO ACTUALLY DECLARED WAR WITH GERMANY?
```

the 3rd parameter is '2', which means "search dictionary #2 for match of keyword(s) before processing the *Q-frame control line". Thus if, in the illustrative exercise (p. 32) the user enters 'CHURCHILL', the Driver finds a match in dictionary 2 (above) and records the integer '2417'. Since no other words were entered, control passes to the rest of the *Q581 control line, and a match is found between conical brackets for the integer '2417', so that control passes to frame #584, which prints the message

```
YOU ARE ONE OUT IN TIME SEQUENCE...
```

In ordinary use a *Q-frame examines only the first non-blank character and those that immediately follow it. For example, although the line:

```
*Q581 2300 0 0 'CHURCHILL'584
```

would transfer control to frame #584 if the user entered
CHURCHILL
If he had entered
IT WAS CHURCHILL
no match would be found for 'I', 'IT', 'IT W' or 'IT WAS CHURCHILL'. However, if 'CHURCHILL' is put in a dictionary (as it is in dictionary #2, used by frame #581), the user could have typed

I THINK IT WAS CHURCHILL
and the Driver would have picked out 'CHURCHILL' from the other words.

The Driver examines each 'word' (i.e. a sequence of characters separated by blanks from other character sequences) in turn, and checks it against the whole dictionary, including all the continuation lines, if present. In the example above 'I' is first checked, then 'THINK', then 'IT', then 'WAS' before 'CHURCHILL' is recognized.

The *D(ictionary) frame may be used to identify up to 6 keywords, providing they occur in the correct sequence. For example, in the dialogue involving frame #190 in the illustrative text exercise (see p. 30), the Driver examined the finally correct answer
NEW JERSEY, THEN PENNSY, THEN OHIO
checked 'NEW' and found no match; checked 'JERS', found a match, and recorded '1' for the first keyword; checked 'THEN' and found no match; checked 'PEN', found a match, and recorded '2' for the 2nd keyword; checked the 2nd 'THEN' and ignored it; and finally checked 'OHIO', found a match, and recorded '3' for the 3rd keyword. Then when the control line was read, the sequence <1+2+3> transferred control to frame #191, giving the message

```
ABSOLUTELY RIGHT!
```

On the other hand, the sequence

```
NEW JERSEY, THEN OHIO THEN PENNSYLVANIA
```

would have produced <1+3+2> and would have given the message in frame #192:

```
RIGHT STATES - WRONG ORDER!
```

and a partially correct answer such as

```
FIRST PENNSY, THEN OHIO
```

would have produced <2+3> which would have given the reply

```
YOU HAVE FORGOTTEN NEW JERSEY - AN EASY MISTAKE TO MAKE
```

In practice, 6 keywords and 10 words in all are enough for virtually all purposes, but the Driver is constructed in such a way that these limits could be readily extended by slight changes to the *Q-frame Driver segment.

Note that in the event of no dictionary match being found, the standard *Q-frame notation can be mixed up with dictionary search results (e.g. see the third line of frame #190, p. 29). Since the control line is read from left to right, a line such as

```
*Q190 2300 0 1 <1+2+3>191 'HIN'199 <1+3+2>192
```

would have first checked the correct sequence of keywords, before checking whether 'HINTS' had been asked for. This sequential interpretation of different types of input allows great flexibility in the conditional branching logic of questions and answers.

Dictionaries can be placed anywhere in a file (after line 3) and need not follow the relevant *Q-frames, though if they do it normally makes the conditional branching easier to follow.

## SUMMARY

Special-purpose, unnumbered and non-executable frames are described, including:

(1) The *C(omment) line, which simply comments on the text.
(2) The *B(egin) line, which instructs the Driver which frame to access at the start of a run.
(3) The *G(lobal) line, which supplies a limited number of character strings which are tested for every time input is entered.
(4) The *D(ictionary) frame, which is used in conjunction with one or more *Q(uestion) frames, to allow a limited number and sequence of keywords to be recognized, even if interspersed within other words or phrases.

# 7
# Types of visual display; use of the 'display' parameter

The Teletype printing terminal made the 'roll' mode of displaying text familiar. Each line is typed across the paper, the paper moves up one line, and then the next line is typed, just as in a manually operated typewriter. When visual display units (using cathode-ray tubes) were introduced, it was natural to adopt the same mode of presentation, and it is standard practice that lines of characters are displayed at the foot of the screen, and that each line-feed instruction moves the text up the screen. A slightly more sophisticated form of display allows the screen to be periodically cleared of old text, and for new text to be written from the top downwards (as one might write on paper) rather than from the bottom (as on a typewriter). This allows the text already printed to remain stationary on the screen, at least until the screen is filled up, after which further material causes the display to 'roll up', line by line.

The standard full-size visual display unit provides for 72 (or 80) characters to be displayed across a single line, and for 24 lines to be displayed simultaneously, making a matrix of 72×24 cursor positions. Many visual display units now allow the cursor (i.e. the position at which the next character will be printed) to be moved to any of the 72×24 screen character positions, and for the screen to be selectively cleared of residual text (usually below and to the right of the cursor position). It seems to us certain that this type of facility will become standard on all visual display units within the next few years. Therefore we felt that MACAID should provide adequate facilities for clearing the screen of a display unit, and for appropriately positioning the cursor. Obviously if the display unit is a hard-copy printer, or a visual display unit without cursor control, this facility is superfluous, and therefore it is necessary for the Driver to identify the type of terminal in use, before starting any interrogative dialogue.

This is done by an initial question, e.g.:

```
TYPE  1  FOR THE HEWLETT-PACKARD TERMINALS,
TYPE  2  FOR ALL OTHER VISUAL DISPLAY UNITS,
OTHERWISE JUST PRESS THE *RETURN* KEY
?_
```

The Driver then sets an internal flag determining the effect of terminal-specific display codes which are acted on every time before the computer displays text on the screen. (Obviously the question above is just an example showing how different available terminals might be identified. If only one type of terminal is in use in a time-sharing computer system the question can be deleted).

In addition to control of the screen cursor by the master text file it might be necessary also to control external devices such as a random-access slide projector or video-disc. Although the standard FORTRAN version of the master driver listed in this book (Appendix I) does not exemplify this facility, it could be readily added to the 'display' subroutine.

### The 1st ('display') parameter

Since it is obviously necessary to control the cursor of a visual display unit before text is displayed, the MACAID control line (p. 45) provides for display instructions to be given by the 1st 'parameter' e.g.:

| *T | 23 | 1000 | 0 | 0 | 24 |
|---|---|---|---|---|---|
| 'Type' letter | Frame number | 1st ('display') parameter | 2nd ('score') parameter | 3rd ('add') parameter | Exit address |

The three control parameters, and the exit address, are read from left to right. The first integer after the frame number is the 'display parameter'. This is normally either zero or '1000' (if no special display instructions are to be given), or, alternatively, some other 4-digit number, e.g. '3400'.

When the Driver reads the 'display parameter' it checks whether this is greater than zero, and the type of terminal in use. If (1) the terminal allows cursor control and (2) a positive display parameter has been found, the 4-digit integer is then read and interpreted by the Driver. The 4 digits are separately read, and used as follows:

Digit 1: controls screen clearing and cursor setting prior to the display of the text of a frame.

Digit 2: controls the position on the screen at which questions are posed by *Question and *Marking frames, and at which corrective and other messages are displayed.

Digits 3 and 4: (in the Driver described in this book) are spare and are provided for other types of display control, such as the control of the position of the cursor *across* rather than *down* the screen, and the control of external devices such as slide projectors, audio-tapes, video-discs, graphics terminals or animated models.

Obviously, to avoid ambiguity in reading these 4 digits it is necessary for four digits always to be specified (except when the display parameter is zero). The frame renumbering facility (chapter 11) automatically removes leading zeros, e.g. '0012' becomes '12'. We have therefore arranged for the Driver to treat '1' as equivalent to '0'. Thus a display parameter of '1111' conveys no display instructions to the Driver, and it is equivalent to '1000', '0000' or '0'. Only digits 2–9 are effective.

The choice of display will obviously depend on the terminal or terminals available. Assuming a screen of 72–80 columns width, containing 24 lines, we have found the following coding convenient:

Digit values: 0 or 1 = no action
2 = clear whole screen, set cursor top left;
3 = set cursor at line 6, clear screen below;
4 = ,, ,, ,, ,, 8, ,, ,, ,,
5 = ,, ,, ,, ,, 10, ,, ,, ,,
6 = ,, ,, ,, ,, 12, ,, ,, ,,
7 = ,, ,, ,, ,, 14, ,, ,, ,,
8 = ,, ,, ,, ,, 16, ,, ,, ,,
9 = ,, ,, ,, ,, 18, ,, ,, ,,

i.e. the cursor will be positioned at line 2N and the screen cleared below this point, when 'N' is the value of a display digit greater than 2. Other users may find other types of display more satisfactory, and it is a simple matter to change the display instruction section of the Driver.

## Examples of types of structured screen display

The illustrative text exercise of Chapter 3 contains several examples of cursor-controlling frames. The 2nd frame

```
*T2 2000 0 -1 3
```

has no associated text, and has the sole function of clearing the screen so that subroutine #4 (which asks for the current date and date of birth, and works out age) can start by displaying its first question at top left on an empty screen.

Later, there is the following sequence

```
*Q15 2000 0 0 'Y'30 '',20
 ARE YOU READY TO PROCEED?

*M20 3400 0 14 30, 0 25 26 27
 IS THIS BECAUSE YOU ARE UNCERTAIN OF YOUR ABILITY? (ANSWER
'YES', 'NO', 'DON'T KNOW', OR 'EXPLAIN')
```

The display parameter ('2000') in frame #15 clears the screen, so that "ARE YOU READY TO PROCEED?" is printed across the top of the screen. The system will then await an entry from the user, and if this is anything other than 'Y' frame 20 will be processed. This frame has a display parameter of '3400'. As the first digit is '3', the cursor moves down to line 6, still leaving the preceding question in place across the top of the screen, so that "IS THIS BECAUSE . . . EXPLAIN" appears on lines 6 and 7 of the screen. The 2nd digit of the *M frame display parameter is '4' (3400) which means "locate the questions and corrective replies from line 8 onwards" (see key code above).

A more complicated *M-frame is:

```
*M70 2500 0 62 100, 0 75,0 76,77 0,0 78, 0 79,
+0 80
```

```
 WHICH OF THE FOLLOWING STATEMENTS ARE TRUE?
1.NEW YORK IS THE CAPITAL OF THE USA
2.MICHELANGELO PAINTED THE 'MONA LISA'
3.97 IS A PRIME NUMBER
4.ELECTRONS ARE POSITIVELY CHARGED
5.THE OPERA 'MARRIAGE OF FIGARO' WAS WRITTEN BY ROSSINI
6.SOCRATES WAS THE DISCIPLE OF PLATO
 TYPE YOUR ANSWERS ACROSS A LINE, E.G.YYNN?Y - THEN PRESS RETURN KEY
```

The display parameter of this frame is '2500'. The initial '2' clears the screen and prints the text across the top 8 lines of the screen (there are 8 lines of text). The cursor is thereafter controlled by the 2nd digit ('5') which moves the cursor to line 10. The invitation "TYPE RESPONSES FOR EACH QUESTION ALONG A LINE" is then displayed. After the user has entered his answers (see example on p. 26) the cursor is returned to line 10, the screen cleared below, and the check display printed in the same place, e.g.:

```
 FOR QUESTIONS -> 1 2 3 4 5 6
IS THIS RIGHT? -> Y Y N N ? Y ?
```

In the event of the user entering 'N(O)' at this point, the screen would again be cleared from line 10, and an invitation given to enter a revised answer. Once accepted, the appropriate corrective message for each question in turn would be displayed, with the question number appearing two lines lower (on line 12), and the response two lines lower still (on line 14), as each question is successively analysed.

Within a *Q(uestion) or *M(arking) frame all screen clearing and cursor movements are controlled by the first two digits of the display parameter. The 2nd digit will normally be larger than the first, because a display parameter of '3200', for example, could hardly allow the user time to read the text displayed before it was wiped off by the 2nd digit ('2') which clears the entire screen!

The general effect of this type of cursor control is to make the system easier and pleasanter to use, since it is simple to arrange that the text remains stationary on the screen at all times, and does not 'roll up' in a manner which inexperienced visual display unit users often find irritating and difficult to read. Also, it is confusing if the question posed has disappeared from view by the time the corrective answers are displayed.

## Other types of display control

In the Driver described in this book no use is made of the last 2 digits of the 4-digit display parameter, but obviously these 'spare' digits could readily be made to control more sophisticated screen clearing and cursor positioning, and also to control external devices. In the FORTRAN version of the driver, such controls would operate from subroutine MCDISP (see Appendix I). Available options can be increased by using characters+digits.

## Removal of the 'display' parameter

Obviously a user with no facilities or no need for cursor control may be tempted to remove the short section of the master Driver which interprets the 'display' parameter, and also to remove the superfluous display parameters throughout all the text files in use. We would advise against doing this, because:

(1) His own text files would not be immediately transferrable to someone else's system.
(2) He would be unable to use MACAID text programs prepared elsewhere, without modifying all the frames to remove the display parameters throughout.

It is very little more trouble to make a practice of inserting an extra 'zero'. For example

```
*T180 0 7 1 185
```

instead of

```
*T180 7 1 185
```

The delay in execution time in reading an extra digit is small, and the preparation for display control will allow this to be added easily if the visual display units in use are later upgraded, without any need to change extensively all the files on the system.

## SUMMARY

MACAID provides for every control line a 'display parameter' which can be used to clear (or partly clear) the screen, and to position the cursor of a visual display unit, according to instructions contained in the text file. This facility allows structured screen display in which, for example, a question may remain stationary at the top of the screen while answers and corrective or other messages may be displayed below. Provision has been made for space control digits to be used for other purposes such as the control of external devices.

# 8
# Running scores and running totals

In the three preceding chapters reference has been made several times to the 2nd or 'score' and the 3rd or 'add' parameters of control lines in the text file. In this chapter we shall describe the ways in which these parameters may be used.

## The 2nd or 'score' parameter

In a frame of the following form (taken from the illustrative exercise in Chapter 3)

```
*R584 0 -3
YOU ARE ONE OUT IN TIME SEQUENCE...
```

'584' is the frame number, '0' is the 1st or 'display' parameter (whose use was described in the last chapter), and '−3' is the 2nd or 'score' parameter. Whenever the Driver encounters a *negative* integer as its 2nd parameter in any control line of the text file, the value specified is subtracted from the running score, providing that the scorer is switched on. When the Driver is started, the score is initialized at 100 and the scorer is switched off. A score parameter of zero means 'do nothing to the score'. For example

```
*A1 0 0 0 2
```

has no effect on the score, since the 2nd parameter is 0. Positive integers between 3 and 7 are used to control the scorer, by instructing the Driver, as follows:

'3' means 'switch off the scorer – make no change in the score';
'4' means 'switch on the scorer – make no change in the score';
'5' means 'reset the score to 100 – but don't display anything';
'6' means 'reset the score to 100, and switch on the scorer';
'7' (or any positive integer greater than 7) means 'print the current score, in the form
YOUR SCORE IS . . .'

A score parameter of '1' or '2' has a special use concerned with recording answers on an output file, and will be described in Chapter 9.

The five score instruction codes allow most kinds of manipulation which a designer is likely to need. For example, in the illustrative exercise in Chapter 3, the designer wanted to ask a multiple question (*M552) without allowing the answer to change the score, so before this question was posed he switched off the scorer by

```
*T540 2000 3 0  552
```

and after the question had been posed and answered he switched it on again with:

```
*T580 0 4 0 581
```

Before the technical questions started, in the early part of the exercise, the scorer was switched on and set to 100 by the control line

```
*T60 1000 6 0  70
```

and the final score was printed when the Driver read the line

```
*T180 0 7 1 185
```

As mentioned before, the 'score' starts at 100, and cannot be more than 100; also, it is not allowed to fall below zero. Unless it is reset to 100, as just described, the score can be decremented but never incremented.

To find out at any moment what the score is and whether the scorer is switched on or not, it is only necessary to enter 'COMMAND:' mode and ask for 'TRACE' (p. 90). Figure 11.3 (p. 91) shows an example of the display of the state of the score and of the score switch, in TRACE mode. Note that the figure (0) in brackets after the score signifies the score switch is off, and (1) signifies that it is on.

## *Automatic scoring in M(arking) frames*

In all other types of frame, the score can only be changed by an amount set by the score parameter, as already explained. However, in certain situations, especially multiple-choice questions, the program designer may want a standard type of scoring throughout a test. If the scorer is switched on when the Driver encounters a Marking frame, a wholly correct answer leaves the score unchanged, a wholly wrong answer reduces it by 2, and an indeterminate answer to a multiple-choice question reduces it by 1. For questions involving multiple grades there is a similar system (i.e. correct = no change, incorrect = −2) and an answer judged 'ACCEPTABLE THOUGH MY GRADE WOULD BE SLIGHTLY HIGHER/LOWER' reduces the score by 1. All this automatic scoring is additional to any other changes to the score brought about by the score parameters of individual frames.

No other automatic scoring is performed by the Driver, but an auxiliary subroutine could be written to process the score in any other way a designer might wish (see Chapter 10).

### *Conditional branching using the score*

MACAID provides two means of branching conditional on the score:

(1) By setting the FLAG (p. 50) using a *F(lag) frame; and subsequently branching with an *I(f) frame (p. 51).
(2) By using the *Q(uestion) frame in a special way.

The first is obvious. A frame sequence such as

```
*F40 0 0 0 45
*I45 0 0 0 46 47 48 49 50 51 52 53 54 55 56
```

would first set the value of FLAG to an integer between 1 and 11, depending on the score (according to the formula FLAG = (110−SCORE)/10), after which the *I(f) frame would transfer control to one of the 11 frame addresses according to the value of FLAG. As explained in chapter 5, this method is simple but somewhat rough and ready.

To get more discrimination for special-purpose branching it is necessary to use a *Q(uestion) frame whose 3rd parameter is '−1'. In the following frame (from the illustrative test exercise of Chapter 3)

```
*Q1000 0 0 -1 (0,78)1010 (75,90),1020 ()1030
```

the 3rd parameter (−1) instructs the Driver "take as input the current value of 'score' and branch accordingly". Thus if the score, when the Driver encountered this frame, was between 0 and 75, inclusive, control would be transferred to frame #1010; between 76 and 90, also inclusive, the frame address 1020 would be used; and for 91–100, frame #1030. (This control instruction could also have been written (90, 100) 1030 since the score is not allowed to rise above 100, nor fall below zero – but ()1030 is equally explicit, shorter, and marginally quicker in execution).

## The 3rd (or 'add') parameter – keeping a running total

In certain frames the 3rd parameter is reserved for special purposes and has nothing to do with keeping a running total. Such special frames include:

*Q(uestion) frames – 3rd parameter determines use (or not) of a dictionary, or branching conditional on the running score;

*M(arking) frames – 3rd parameter instructs the driver how many questions and answers to analyse, and in how many grades;

*F(lag) frames – 3rd parameter sets the value of the flag.

However, the 3rd parameter in *T(ext), *R(eturn) and *I(f) frames has no special, dedicated use, and is available for keeping a running total, or 'sum'. When the Driver is first started up, the sum is set to 0.0 and the adder is switched off. After the adder has been switched on, any positive number (whether integer or floating point) as the 3rd or 'add' parameter in a *T(ext), *R(eturn) or *I(f) control line will cause the Driver to add that amount to the running sum or total in the adder. To take an example from the text exercise in Chapter 3:

```
*R77 0 0 1
YOU CAN'T DIVIDE 97 EXACTLY BY ANY SMALLER NUMBER, THEREFORE IT IS PRIME
```

The 1st ('display') and the 2nd ('score') parameters are zero, but the 3rd ('add') parameter is '1', so the cumulative sum is increased by 1.0. The 'add' parameter is the only one in which any notice is taken of decimal points. If, for example, the 'sum' was already 7.63 and frame 77 had been

```
R77 0 0 1.16
```

then after printing the text of the frame the Driver would alter the running sum from 7.63 to 8.79.

Whereas in the case of the score, only subtractions are permitted, in the case of the 'add' parameter, only additions are allowed. The 'sum' can never have a value smaller than zero, but it has no upper limit.

Negative values for the 'add' parameter in *T, *R and *I frames are used to control switching on and off, and the resetting of the adder, in a way similar to the comparable positive values for the 'score' parameter control instructions:

'−3' means 'switch off the adder – make no change in the sum';
'−4' means 'switch on the adder – make no change in the sum';
'−5' means 'reset the sum to zero, but don't display anything';
'−6' means 'reset the sum to zero, and switch on the scorer';
'−7' (or any more negative number) means 'print the current sum, in the form 'PRESENT TOTAL IS . . .' (to 1 decimal place).

These five instructions to the adder allow the same flexibility as the comparable instructions given to the scorer. For example, in the illustrative exercise of chapter 3 the adder is switched on (to record the total number of wrong answers in the succeeding question) by:

```
*T13 0 0 -6 15
```

Each wrong answer to the question of *M70 adds 1 to the running sum, e.g.

```
*R77 0 0 1
```

and when the analysis is complete control passes to

```
*T100 2000 0 -7 105
```

in which '−7' instructs the Driver to print the current total (of wrong answers). Subsequently the adder is used for another purpose – to keep a tally on the number of times the user requests the score – and the 'sum' is reset to zero by

```
*T160 2000 0 -6 170
```

At the end, the sum is not displayed at the terminal, but printed on the output (answer) file by

```
*A1501 0 0 -2 1600
```

*A(nswer) frame instructions, however, will not be further discussed here, but are fully described in the next chapter.

As in the case of the scorer and the score, the current state of the adder switch (on or off) and of the 'sum' can be followed by the use of the 'TRACE' command (see Figure 11.3, p. 91). Zero, in brackets after TOTAL (e.g. 'TOTAL (0.) = . . .') means that the adder is turned off, and '1.' means that it is turned on.

Values of −1 and −2 for the 'add' parameter have special uses, just as values of +1 and +2 have for the 'score' parameter. If the 'add' parameter is −1 or −2 in a *T or *I frame this instructs the Driver "continue to the next frame with no pause or prompt". For example, in the sequence

```
*T30 2000 0 -1 60
 RIGHT - LET'S GO
*T60 1000 6 0  70
 NOW FOR SOME GENERAL KNOWLEDGE QUESTIONS. I SHALL PUT THESE IN THE FORM
 OF A MULTIPLE-CHOICE QUESTION, TO WHICH YOU SHOULD ANSWER 'YES' OR 'NO'
```

the second text line would follow the first without interruption (see p. 26). If, on the other hand, the 'add' parameter has a value of zero in a *T or *I frame, the Driver issues a prompt, 'PRESS *RETURN*'. For example, in the sequence

```
*T191 0 0 0 200
 ABSOLUTELY RIGHT!
*T200 2000 0 -1 201
 WHEN I AM MARKING DIFFICULT GEOGRAPHY TESTS, I MARK YOU ACCORDING
 TO YOUR DEGREE OF IGNORANCE. WOULD YOU LIKE TO KNOW YOUR SCORE NOW?
```

after the first text line is printed, a prompt is requested (p. 30 shows an example of an actual run of this text file sequence).

### *Conditional branching using the sum, or value, in the adder*

We have described above (p. 70) how a Q(uestion) frame may be made to process the value in 'score' by making the 3rd parameter '−1'. If the 3rd parameter of a *Q frame is '−2', the Driver will treat the sum in the adder as the answer, and branch conditionally as the *Q-control line instructs it. The Chapter 3 illustrative text exercise gives an example:

```
*Q107 0 0 -2 (0,.99)110 (.99,2)120 (2,5)130 (),140
```

When the Driver reads this line and the running 'sum' is, say, 1.0, control is transferred to frame #120. A value of, say, 6.5 could only be satisfied by '()' and control would therefore pass to frame #140.

### Types of use for running scores and running totals

The use of a score is obvious. The running total or 'sum' (incrementable by the 3rd parameter) can be used, as in the illustrative text exercise of Chapter 3, to keep a check on some quantity (e.g. the number of wrong answers – as described on p. 28). Subsequently in the same exercise the add parameter is used to keep a check on the number of requests for 'score'. In the setting of a clinical exercise the adder could be used to keep a check on, say, the passage of time, or the cumulative cost of investigations.

The reader will appreciate that the MACAID Driver provides three different types of local storage, determined by a user's answers:

(1) setting of the flag (integer range 1 to 11)
(2) the cumulative score, diminishing to zero from a starting value of 100 (integer range 100 to 0)
(3) the cumulative sum, increasing from a starting value of 0.0 (floating point – no upper limit)

A few control lines can easily change one type of information storage to another. The setting of the flag in accordance with the score has already been described. It is also simple to change the score (or the sum in the adder) in accordance with the flag by arranging that an *I(f) frame addresses other frames which make adjustments to the score or to the running 'sum' in the adder.

### Changes to the flag, the score and the sum in subroutines

The variables corresponding to these indices can readily be passed to and from specially written subprograms, in which any manipulations can be carried out. For example, the value of FLAG might be changed according to a user's answers in a subroutine, so that on return to the text program, an *I(f) frame could be used to branch conditionally.

### SUMMARY

In addition to maintaining one type of memory of previous user input in the form of a flag (described in Chapter 5), the MACAID Driver also maintains two other different types. One is a 'running score', initialized at 100, and diminished by integer subtractions according to instructions in the text file. The other is a 'running total' or 'sum', initialized at 0.0, and incrementable by floating point additions. Instruction codes allow printing of the value of 'score' and 'sum' on demand; and it is also possible to arrange branching conditional on the current values of 'score' and 'sum' by the special use of the previously described Q(uestion) frame.

It is a simple matter to interconvert the three different types of memory, to change them within special-purpose subroutines, and to use them flexibly for virtually every type of conditional branching.

# 9
# Recording users' answers — the Answer file and the A(nswer) frame; recording free text

Many programs for computer-assisted learning stand alone, and no record is made (or needed) of a user's activities. However, if such a record is made, or can be made, the designer can insert traces to find the way in which different people use the program, or to record the average and individual performances of users in an assessment exercise. Furthermore, it also becomes possible to transform a user's entries into a précis or even a virtual narrative which summarizes and collates them in a predetermined logical manner.

MACAID makes provision for recording all, or any selected entries by a user on an Answer file which has the form of a simple output file written sequentially as the dialogue proceeds. Various forms of output recording can be programmed in the text file, and many can be specified by the A(nswer) frame (see below).

## The Answer file

The current version of the Driver specifies that the Answer file is built up with successive 72-character lines, though this could easily be changed. The first 7 columns allow the recording of frame types, frame numbers and 'global' commands, thus allowing a designer to trace a complicated branching sequence. Any comments or headings supplied to the output file by the text file are printed from column 8 onwards, and any user entries in response to free text, simple questions or grading exercises, and the display of scores and totals appear at column 10. Figure 9.1 shows a typical example of the completed Answer file which was built up in the course of the illustrative text exercise in Chapter 3. This shows some 'trace' codes (Q6, T27, M552, Q1775) which record that a user encountered these frames. Any GLOBAL commands entered are also printed in the margin column. Text subheadings (e.g. "NAME, SEX, AGE and ADDRESS") are indented, and accepted user entries (e.g. "DICKINSON, C. J.") and free text entries

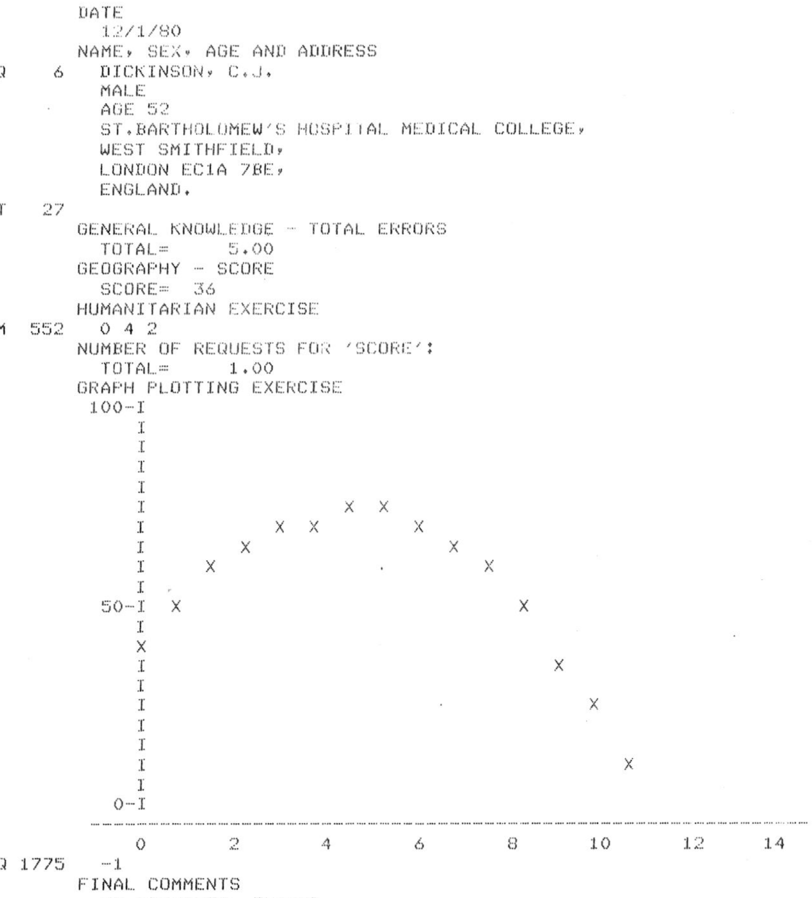

```
         DATE
           12/1/80
         NAME, SEX, AGE AND ADDRESS
Q    6     DICKINSON, C.J.
           MALE
           AGE 52
           ST.BARTHOLOMEW'S HOSPITAL MEDICAL COLLEGE,
           WEST SMITHFIELD,
           LONDON EC1A 7BE,
           ENGLAND.
T   27
         GENERAL KNOWLEDGE - TOTAL ERRORS
           TOTAL=        5.00
         GEOGRAPHY - SCORE
           SCORE=  36
         HUMANITARIAN EXERCISE
M  552     0 4 2
         NUMBER OF REQUESTS FOR 'SCORE':
           TOTAL=        1.00
         GRAPH PLOTTING EXERCISE
          100-I
              I
              I
              I
              I
              I                    X  X
              I              X  X        X
              I           X                 X
              I        X                       X
              I
           50-I  X                                X
              I
              X
              I                                      X
              I
              I                                         X
              I
              I
              I                                            X
              I
            0-I
         ------------------------------------------------------------
              0       2       4       6       8      10      12      14
Q 1775     -1
         FINAL COMMENTS
           NO COMMENTS, THANKS
```

**Figure 9.1** Example of an output or Answer file, created during the running of the illustrative program of Chapter 3. Note entries of trace codes in the margin column, headers derived from the text, indented user entries, totals and scores, and a graph stored from subroutine #5 (Appendix III)

are indented further, as are records of the score and of the 'sum'. At the end of the Answer file is the record of a graph made by the user (with the assistance of the graph-plotting subroutine listed in Appendix III) and stored at the user's command (p. 36).

## *Recording frame numbers and user entries on the Answer file*

In the last chapter we described the use of the 2nd, or 'score' parameter of a control line. Negative integers are subtracted from the running score, and positive integers greater than 2 are used to switch the scorer on and off, and to reset or print the score. However, if the value of the 2nd parameter is '1', as in the control line

```
*T27 0 1 0 15
 I WANTED JUST TO CHECK THAT YOU WERE REALLY READY TO GO BEFORE
 WE STARTED - I HOPE WE ARE NOW!
```

then the Answer file will record that the Driver encountered this frame (see Figure 9.1) and hence (in the illustrative text of Chapter 3) that in response to the M(arking) frame question 20 the user asked the program to 'E(xplain)'.

If the 'score' parameter is 2, then not only will the frame type and number be written in the margin of the Answer file, but also the answer itself. In the frame

```
*M552 2500 2 35 580,   0 555 555 555 555, 560 560 -1 0 -1,
+ 570 570 570 570 0
```

the 2nd or 'score' parameter ('2') directs the Driver to store on the output file

```
M  552    0 4 2
```

(see Figure 9.1), when the answers '0', '4' and '2' are given to the 3 questions posed in M(arking) frame 552.

Similarly, a 'SCORE' parameter of 2 in a Q(uestion) frame is also an instruction to write an accepted entry on the Answer file, e.g.:

```
*Q6 0 2 0 ''7
PLEASE TYPE YOUR NAME, THEN AGAIN PRESS THE 'RETURN' KEY
```

instructs the Driver, after printing the text, to enter the frame type and number on the Answer file, followed by the user's entry. (As described in Chapter 5, '' in a *Q-frame means that any answer is acceptable, and will transfer control to frame 7 as soon as the "RETURN" key is pressed.) In the Chapter 3 example, the Answer file (Figure 9.1) reads:

```
Q    6    DICKINSON, C.J.
```

### Recording free text on the Answer file

As described above, free text can be entered into a *Q-frame question, but once the entry or 'carriage return' key is pressed, the *Q-frame has been fully interpreted, and control passes to the exit address. To allow the unlimited entry of free text, MACAID provides that if the 'score' parameter in a *T(ext) frame control line is 2, unlimited amounts of free text can be entered on successive lines and transferred to the Answer file. The reading is only terminated if the entry or 'return' key is pressed after a null entry. The following is an example from the illustrative text exercise of Chapter 3:

```
*T12 2000 2 0 13
NOW PLEASE GIVE ME YOUR ADDRESS - PRESS RETURN KEY AT THE END OF
EACH LINE, AND TWICE AT THE END
```

The user's entry, on 5 lines, is shown in the dialogue on p. 24, and the resultant Answer file in Figure 9.1. The user's final comments were recorded by a similar *T(ext) frame:

```
*T2000 2000 2 0 2001
THAT IS THE END.  THANK YOU FOR YOUR COOPERATION.
IF YOU HAVE ANY COMMENTS, PLEASE TYPE THEM IN NOW, AND PRESS
 *RETURN* KEY TWICE
```

## Use of the A(nswer) frame

An A(nswer) frame has a frame number, a 1st or 'display' parameter, a 2nd ('score') parameter, a 3rd ('add') parameter, and an exit address, e.g.:

```
*A1 0 0 0 2
DATE
```

As the text of an *A-frame is not printed or displayed at the user's terminal, but rather entered on to the Answer file, the 1st or 'display' parameter controls what is entered on the answer file. '0' (or any number less than zero) causes any associated text of the *A(nswer) frame to be printed on the Answer file. An integer 'N' greater than zero gives the instruction 'prepare to read from the text file, starting N line(s) after the last directory line'. Thus the *A(nswer) frame:

```
*A11 2 0 1 12
```

copies from line 2, after the directory, on to the Answer file (this line contains the age in years previously worked out by subroutine #4, described in the next chapter).

The 2nd or 'score' parameter of the *A-frame is used for scoring purposes exactly as described for other frames (p. 68).

The 3rd or 'add' parameter ('N'), if greater than zero, instructs the Driver to copy on to the Answer file N lines, beginning at the address specified by the 1st ('display') parameter. Thus the frame

```
*A11 2 0 1 12
```

instructs the Driver as follows: 'go to the 2nd line after the end of the directory, and copy out one line at this address on to the Answer file'.

If the 3rd or 'add' parameter is '−1', then the current score will be copied on to the Answer file, in the form

```
SCORE= 93
```

and if the 3rd parameter is '−2' (or any more negative number), the 'sum' will be printed, in the form

```
TOTAL=      4.00
```

In both cases, this entry will be indented from the margin.

The use of the spare end lines of the text file itself for intermediate storage of text or numerical values is convenient, and more economical than setting up extra storage arrays in the Driver but it has the (obvious) limitation that only one user can be accessing the text file at any one time – otherwise material written there by one user may be overwritten by another before there has been time to copy it out again. If this is *not* a possibility, however, this facility has many advantages.

### Direct printing on the output file by a subroutine

It is obviously easy to arrange that a purpose-built computational subroutine can write directly to the answer file, and the illustrative text exercise of Chapter 3 shows an example.

When the frame

```
*S1760 0 0 5 1775
1
```

is accessed, the user is invited to 'store' his graph, for later inspection, with the result illustrated in Figure 9.1. (The 'STORE' instruction in subroutine # 5 is listed in subroutine SUB5, Appendix III, p. 171; Statements 250–300.)

## SUMMARY

MACAID provides for an output or 'answer' file for recording any or all of the following:

1. A list of frames or selected frames accessed;
2. A user's accepted entries in response to text questions;
3. A user's entry of free text;
4. Predetermined headings and other text material;
5. Running scores and 'sum' totals;
6. Text or numerical values previously written on the spare lines at the end of the text file;
7. Direct output from a subroutine.

Categories 1, 2 and 3 are achieved by codes which use the 2nd or 'score' parameter; categories 4, 5 and 6 use the special *A(nswer) frame; and 7 is arranged within the subroutine concerned. The format of a complete 'answer' file is shown in Figure 9.1.

# 10
# Simulation packages and other subprograms – linkage with interrogative text; the *S(ubroutine) frame

As we mentioned in the first chapter, our activities in computer-assisted learning since 1970 have mainly comprised writing programs simulating various aspects of normal and disordered human physiology. These programs allow a user to study simultaneously a number of related aspects of human bodily function (e.g. respiration and blood gas transport) by means of a digital computer model which, if perturbed, behaves quantitatively as well as qualitatively in a realistic manner.

To avoid wasteful duplication of effort we wrote all these simulation programs in standard FORTRAN IV, and we have been gratified by their wide distribution to medical schools throughout the world, by their proven portability and generally good reception (e.g. Tidball, 1978) and by their increasing utilization within instructional courses as well as for clinical and research use.

When we began in 1972 the earliest versions of the MACAID Driver and text-file system described in this book, we also wrote the Driver in standard FORTRAN IV. As in the case of the models, we had in mind eventually producing an equally portable comprehensive interpretive system. The task, as previously mentioned, has taken 8 years to complete, because MACAID has been repeatedly revised, extended, condensed and in other ways improved during this time.

These two activities (i.e. physiological simulation and text-handling design) continued in parallel for some years, but independently of one another. We gradually realized that it might be both possible and advantageous to combine the models with explanatory or interrogative text. As described fully in the published version of the respiratory model 'MacPuf' (Dickinson, 1977) it is possible to condense a large set of instructions to the model into a string of numbers separated by 'slashes' (/), whose meaning is 'suppress the dialogue and take as next user input the number that follows'. For example, in the respiratory model 'MACPUF' a user who is familiar with the interactive dialogue can type:

1/1/100/3/1/3000/2

which tells the model 'connect a rebreathing bag to the mouth, fill the bag with 3000 cc of 100% oxygen, rebreathe from the bag for a standard 3-minute run period, display $PO_2$ and $PCO_2$, and print all relevant values at the end of the period'.

It soon became obvious to us that a string of numbers of this type could make up a line of the MACAID text file, thus allowing a text file to give unlimited sets of different instructions to a computer simulation model or subprogram.

## The S(ubroutine) frame

The S(ubroutine) frame completes the list of frame types available with the basic MACAID Driver (though others could readily be added). As in other frames the control line has 3 parameters, and an exit address, e.g.:

```
*S1710 0 0 5 1720
0/1/2/5/2/4
```

The first zero (in the control line) is the 'display' parameter which, if positive, can give display or storage instructions to the Driver. The 2nd ('score') parameter is available for all the purposes described in Chapter 8. The 3rd parameter (= 5) is the code number of the subroutine which is called up by this frame.

'0/1/2/5/2/4' is the string of instructions passed to subroutine #5, and #1720 is the final exit address.

By way of illustration and example, the model text exercise in Chapter 3 utilizes two compiled subprograms, which are given the code numbers 4 and 5. The standard FORTRAN version of the Driver is given in Appendix I, and in subroutine MCSUBR the subprograms are given the names 'SUB4' and 'SUB5'. The subroutines are given in full in Appendix III. SUB4 is a short subroutine which asks for the current date and the user's date of birth, works out his age, and stores the result for later recall and printing on the Answer file. SUB5 is a subroutine which plots a digitized graph of the equation

$$y = (1)+(2)x+(3)x^{(4)}$$

where (1), (2), (3) and (4) are constants which can be changed at will by a user. This subroutine allows a user to change any of or all the 4 parameters of the equation, and then automatically to plot the graph when ready. Inspection of the dialogue on pages 34 and 36 shows how the text program first plots a graph of $y = 5x$ by way of illustration, using the code mentioned. In the text line

```
*T27 0 1 0 15
*S1710 0 0 5 1720
0/1/2/5/2/4
```

'0' says 'call the subprogram, but don't print anything';

'1' says 'a factor is to be changed';
'2' says 'factor 2 (in the equation above) is to be changed';
'5' says 'make this equal to 5';
'2' says 'plot and display the resultant graph at the terminal';
'4' says 'exit from the subprogram'.

Inspection of the dialogue and its result on p. 36 should make the sequence of operations clear.

In the example, the user is challenged to change the 4 parameters to produce a graph which cuts the $y$ axis at 40, goes up, then down again to cut the $x$ axis around 12. The user eventually gives the instruction

1/1 2 3 4/40/12/−1/2/2

The first part says 'change (1) then make
Factor 1 = 40
Factor 2 = 12
Factor 3 = −1
Factor 4 = 2',
and the last instruction is a second '2', which means 'plot and display the graph'.

When the user is satisfied, he can type '3' which is an instruction to 'store' the graph – i.e. copy it on to the Answer file (see dialogue on p. 36). The instruction '4' (to 'stop') then exits from the model back into the text. The question 'what was your value for factor 3?' is then asked, and the answer checked for correctness and recorded on the Answer file by the frame

```
*Q1775 2300 2 0 (-3.5,-.01)1780 ''1785
WHAT WAS YOUR VALUE FOR FACTOR 3?
```

Subroutine 5, once called, operates independently of the text file, and, indeed, of the Driver. However, subroutine #4 is called with the 'display' parameter = 1:

```
*S3 1 0 4 4
```

The subprogram is written to utilize this number, and to implement the instruction 'print result starting at line 1 on the text file, immediately after the directory'. This has the result that the current date and the user's computed age are entered on 2 successive blank unused lines of the text file. For example, after the illustrative exercise of Chapter 3 has been run through, the end lines of the file appear as in Figure 10.1.

```
1010   3011020   3051030   3071050   3131060   3141070   3161500   3191501   322
1600   3261601   3351699   3371700   3401710   3471720   3501730   3521740   357
1750   3671760   3731775   3761780   3781785   3801790   3832000   3882001   393
  183   281     0     0     0     0     0     0     0     0     0     0     0     0
          12/1/80
          AGE 52
```

**Figure 10.1** Example of a user's entry and a computational result entered on to the end of a text file (by subroutine #4, Appendix III, running the illustrative text exercise of Chapter 3). The first 4 lines are the last lines of the directory. '12/1/80' is the user's entry, 'AGE 52' is the computer result worked out by SUBROUTINE SUB4

The A(nswer) frame control line allows material from this location to be printed on the output file. The line

```
*A4 1 0 1 5
```

means 'go to the first line of the text file, immediately after the directory, and prepare to print what is there on the output file' (1st parameter = 1) and also instructs 'print 1 line from this location' (3rd parameter also = 1).

Later in the dialogue, when the sex has been recorded on the Answer file, the age is printed by the control line

```
*A11 2 0 1 12
```

which instructs the Driver 'go to the 2nd line of the end-of-file space' (1st parameter = 2) and then 'print 1 line from this location' (3rd parameter = 1).

## Intermediate storage

Obviously this type of 'intermediate' storage of text or numerical values depends firstly on having the necessary 2 spare lines, and secondly on having the text file for one user's exclusive use. If the text file is accessible to and used by many users at the same time, extensive intermediate storage would demand that a subprogram carried a running or intermediate store space which was shared with the Master Driver itself. The method of storage used by subroutine SUB4 is, however, simple and economical to use, if it is permissible.

## Other uses of subprograms

The subprograms SUB4 and SUB5 are simply examples of the unlimited number and variety of computational exercises which MACAID can handle. The only limit to the number, size and complexity of subprograms is given by the size of storage space available in the computer system in use, or by the convenience and ease of overlaying programs. Since the Driver is written in FORTRAN IV, and adaptable very simply to FORTRAN 77 standard, it is extremely simple to write any necessary FORTRAN subroutines to handle any computational problem. Conditional branching under control of the Driver is also possible by changing the values of FLAG (p. 50), SCORE (p. 68) or SUM (p. 70) (all of which are in a labelled COMMON block) within a subroutine.

A few years ago the provision of a large and comprehensive Driver in itself might have appeared to be an unwarranted and expensive luxury, and a combined text/subprogram Driver even more extravagant. We believe that educational and interrogative users will increasingly capitalize on the cheaper and physically smaller, but computationally more powerful microprocessors, and will also make extensive use of solid-state and fast access disc storage devices. Within a few more years, even the relatively sophisticated and comprehensive Driver we have designed will doubtless be extended. Hitherto no portable system has provided the almost complete design freedom available with MACAID. Linked text and computational programs are in their infancy. However, to provide an illustration of a realistic teaching exercise, capitalizing heavily on a computational subprogram which is itself a large and well-tried physiological model of human respiration ('MacPuf'; Dickinson, 1977), we have written a complete text file to teach some principles of basic and applied human respiratory physiology. This is available from the authors at nominal cost (Appendix VI, p. 178).

## SUMMARY

MACAID allows the text file, through the special *S(ubroutine) frame, to call up any compatible standard FORTRAN subroutine and to use this flexibly within the context of a teaching exercise. Examples are given of the ways in which this can record and make use of a user's answers. The future of this linked text/subprogram system seems very promising.

# Part 3
# The MACAID Driver

# 11
# 'Authoring' commands and the text file editor; the renumbering and checking facility; practical aspects of writing and editing MACAID texts

The means by which a text file may be changed is known as an *editor.* Any computer of the current (1980) 'mini' size will undoubtedly have available a comprehensive text editor, by means of which a file of text may be created *ab initio,* lines may be changed, whole lines inserted and deleted, and global editing manoeuvres performed. Equally useful editors are becoming available on microprocessor systems. One might therefore question the need for a possibly redundant text editor within the MACAID system.

There are two reasons for providing one. Firstly, a text editor makes the whole system independent and, providing that the master Driver can be compiled and loaded, and can directly access sequentially numbered lines of a text file, no other facility need be provided at all. Secondly, and much more important, is that once a text exercise or interrogative routine is about half-developed, and in partial working order, it is best tested on the bench by the designer interacting with it, to see that it behaves in the correct way. It is difficult, even for an experienced text author, to write a complicated branching program free from errors. Such errors will be not only in mundane things like punctuation and spelling, but also in the instructions for the transfer of control between individual frames and different parts of the program. It is almost essential to be able to correct mistakes while running the program.

## Starting with a blank file

Suppose that an author knows he wants to create an interrogative text of about 400 lines, which he has already written down on sheets of paper. All he needs to do is to provide the master Driver with a rather larger blank direct-access file of standard 'card-image' type, i.e. a series of, say, 440 72-column blank lines on a file held on a disc or other more rapid memory device. When the Driver is started up, after giving the 'authoring' password (see below), it reads the first line of the file, and finds no information there, i.e. the *B(egin) frame is not present. The computer then responds:

```
*** DIRECTORY OR FILE INADEQUATE - PLEASE REPORT
*B(EGIN) FRAME MISSING - CREATE NEW FILE?
?_
```

On the reply 'YES', the question is then posed:

```
HOW MANY FRAMES?
?_
```

If the author wants about 100 frames, he replies '100'. The program then asks:

```
*B     10    404
*G
*T   10 1000 0 0    20
...
...
...
*T   20 1000 0 0    30
...
...
...
*T   30 1000 0 0    40
...
...
...
*T   40 1000 0 0    50
...

...
*T 990 1000 0 0 1000
...
...
...
*T1000 1000 0 0 1010
...
...
...
**
 101     0
   0     2  10     3  20     7  30    11  40    15  50    19  60    23  70    27
  80    31  90    35 100    39 110    43 120    47 130    51 140    55 150    59
 160    63 170    67 180    71 190    75 200    79 210    83 220    87 230    91
 240    95 250    99 260   103 270   107 280   111 290   115 300   119 310   123
 320   127 330   131 340   135 350   139 360   143 370   147 380   151 390   155
 400   159 410   163 420   167 430   171 440   175 450   179 460   183 470   187
 480   191 490   195 500   199 510   203 520   207 530   211 540   215 550   219
 560   223 570   227 580   231 590   235 600   239 610   243 620   247 630   251
 640   255 650   259 660   263 670   267 680   271 690   275 700   279 710   283
 720   287 730   291 740   295 750   299 760   303 770   307 780   311 790   315
 800   319 810   323 820   327 830   331 840   335 850   339 860   343 870   347
 880   351 890   355 900   359 910   363 920   367 930   371 940   375 950   379
 960   383 970   387 980   391 990   3951000   399
     0     0     0     0     0     0     0     0     0     0     0     0     0     0
```

**Figure 11.1** Blank file (ready for entering text) created on demand by the Driver, following the instructions described in the text. Note sequential frames, and automatically created frame directory. The *G(LOBAL) line counts as frame #0, so there are 101 frames in all, numbered in 10's. The second number of each pair of directory numbers is the line number address of the frame

```
HOW MANY LINES PER FRAME?
?
```

On the answer '3' the driver will create a functional, though largely blank file which looks like Figure 11.1 opposite.

If, now, in response to 'COMMAND:', the user responds 'GO', the 3 lines of frame #10 will be displayed at the terminal, and the program will request a pause (3rd parameter of each *T-frame = 0).

## Editing a file

Any file which has the 4 essential components (described in Chapter 4), i.e. a *B(egin) line, at least one numbered executable frame, a text terminator ('**') and a directory, can be edited by the MACAID Driver. A text file lacking a directory cannot be edited until the 'authoring' mode question:

```
NEW DIRECTORY?
?_
```

is answered in the affirmative. The Driver will thereupon construct a directory by reading through the text file, building up an address table, and storing it at the end of the file. A newly created file (see above) will automatically be given its directory (e.g. Figure 11.1). If the *B line is missing, and a new file is *not* requested, the Driver will automatically insert a new *B-line, with first frame number = 1, and (on line 2) a simple *T-line

```
*T1    0    0    0    2
```

If the text terminator (**) is missing, it will be automatically inserted, as far down the file as possible. Both manoeuvres might be necessary before a corrupted file could be edited.

Whenever a new directory has been made, or whenever the universal 'authoring' key word 'AUTHOR' (or just 'AUTHO') is typed during the running of any program, the Driver prompts with

```
COMMAND:
```

which allows a number of 'authoring' commands to be given.

## 'Authoring' commands

Apart from using the Editor facilities (p. 92) to change text, it is an advantage to be able to move control about within the program at will, overriding the automatic and conditional branching logic. This can be done by the 'GO' command. Other authoring commands are 'TRACE', 'UNTRACE', 'STOP' and 'RESTART', in addition to 'EDIT', which brings the text editor into action. All these are available any time if the global keyword 'AUTHOR' is typed in, and the 'RETURN' key pressed. This can be done as soon as user input is awaited at any stage in running a text exercise.

### *I. 'GO'.*

This command has the form GO ⟨N⟩, in which the integer 'N' is the number of one of the frames. For example, if in the course of running the illustrative text exercise (Chapter 3) 'AUTHOR' is typed, it is possible to use the 'GO' command to skip about within the text. For example (starting at *Q7):

```
WHAT IS YOUR SEX? - TYPE M OR F AND PRESS 'RETURN' KEY AGAIN
? AUTHOR
COMMAND: GO1700
I SHALL NOW PLOT A SIMPLE GRAPH OF Y AGAINST X...   Y=5X
```

The command 'GO 1700' skips over the whole dialogue/text sequence from frame 8 to frame 1699 inclusive. If no frame is specified, the command 'GO' returns control to the previous frame. In the example of Figure 11.2 'GO' transfers control back to the calling frame after an 'EDIT' manoeuvre.

```
 WHAT IS YOUR SEX? - TYPE M OR F AND PRESS 'RETURN' KEY AGAIN
?AUTHOR
COMMAND: EDIT
/M7,1
  WHAT IS YOUR SEX? - TYPE M OR F AND PRESS 'RETURN' KEY AGAIN
-                                        RESCAPE
  WHAT IS YOUR SEX? - TYPE M OR F AND PRESS 'ESCAPE' KEY AGAIN
-
/END
COMMAND: GO
 WHAT IS YOUR SEX? - TYPE M OR F AND PRESS 'ESCAPE' KEY AGAIN
?M
NOW PLEASE GIVE ME YOUR ADDRESS - PRESS RETURN KEY AT THE END OF
EACH LINE, AND TWICE AT THE END
?_
```

**Figure 11.2** Example of the return of control to the text file, after an editing manoeuvre (described later in the chapter) by the command 'GO'

When starting any exercise or interrogative program, 'GO' (no frame specified) transfers control to the first frame, designated as such by the *B(egin) frame.

### *II. 'TR(ACE)'*

When editing, or tracing a logical fault in conditional or other branching, it is an advantage to know which frame is being acted upon. After the command 'TRACE' (or just 'TR') the Driver prints for every frame a note of the number of the current and of the previous frame, the value of 'FLAG', the current score and the 'sum' and also indicates whether the scorer and adder are on or off. The sequence of Figure 11.3 illustrates the effect of the 'TRACE' command applied during the running of the Chapter 3 illustrative exercise.

It is easy to keep track of (1) the value of 'FLAG' (in this case it was set at 2 after 'F' had been entered in a previous question about sex), (2) the switching on of the scorer by frame #60 ('SCORE(0) = ' changes to 'SCORE(1) =)', and (3) the branching logic.

```
 ARE YOU READY TO PROCEED?
?_AUTHOR
COMMAND:_TRACE
COMMAND:_GO
*LAST=    -1   CURR=    15   FLAG= 2   SCORE(0)=100   TOTAL(0.)=         0.0
 ARE YOU READY TO PROCEED?
?_YES
*LAST=    15   CURR=    30   FLAG= 2   SCORE(0)=100   TOTAL(0.)=         0.0
 RIGHT - LET'S GO
*LAST=    30   CURR=    60   FLAG= 2   SCORE(0)=100   TOTAL(0.)=         0.0
 NOW FOR SOME GENERAL KNOWLEDGE QUESTIONS. I SHALL PUT THESE IN THE FORM
 OF A MULTIPLE-CHOICE QUESTION, TO WHICH YOU SHOULD ANSWER 'YES' OR 'NO'
PRESS *RETURN*
?_
*LAST=    60   CURR=    70   FLAG= 2   SCORE(1)=100   TOTAL(0.)=         0.0
 WHICH OF THE FOLLOWING STATEMENTS ARE TRUE?
1.NEW YORK IS THE CAPITAL OF THE USA
2.MICHELANGELO PAINTED THE 'MONA LISA'
 ...
```

**Figure 11.3** Illustrative dialogue showing the effect of switching on the TR(ACE) facility during a test run

## *III. 'UN(TRACE)'*

This command simply switches off the 'TRACE' facility (Figure 11.4).

```
*LAST=    12   CURR=    13   FLAG= 2   SCORE(1)=100   TOTAL(0.)=         0.0
 THANK YOU.
*LAST=    13   CURR=    15   FLAG= 2   SCORE(1)=100   TOTAL(1.)=         0.0
 ARE YOU READY TO PROCEED?
?_AUTHO
COMMAND:_UNTRACE
COMMAND:_GO
 ARE YOU READY TO PROCEED?
?_YES
 RIGHT - LET'S GO
 NOW FOR SOME GENERAL KNOWLEDGE QUESTIONS. I SHALL PUT THESE IN THE FORM
 OF A MULTIPLE-CHOICE QUESTION, TO WHICH YOU SHOULD ANSWER 'YES' OR 'NO'
PRESS *RETURN*
?_
```

**Figure 11.4** Illustration of the effect of switching off the TRACE facility by the UN(TRACE) command

## *IV.. 'ST(OP)'*

This stops the program altogether, e.g. frame #7 of the illustrative exercise;

```
 WHAT IS YOUR SEX? - TYPE M OR F AND PRESS 'RETURN' KEY AGAIN
?_AUTHOR
COMMAND:_STOP
PROGRAM STOP
:_
```

## *V. 'RE(START)'*

This has the same effect as 'R' or 'RESTART' typed in during EDIT manoeuvres (Figure 11.8, p. 100) and sets the Driver back to starting conditions, in 'authoring' mode (p. 94).

The first option ('RENUMBER AND CHECK TEXT FILE?') is described on p. 100. If it is not used (i.e. the answer is 'NO'), the simple command 'Y' in response to the question 'NEW DIRECTORY?' instructs the Driver to read the whole text file and construct a directory automatically, similar in form to that at the end of the illustrative text exercise in Chapter 3 (see p. 37).

### *VI. 'EDIT'*

When 'COMMAND:' appears the most usual entry at this point is 'EDIT' (or just 'ED'). The prompt then changes from 'COMMAND:' to a slash (/). At this point a number of editing commands may be entered. These have the general form X⟨N⟩, ⟨K⟩ where 'X' is a single letter identifying the operation, which may be 'T(YPE)', 'L(IST)', 'E(ND)', 'M(ODIFY)', 'O(VERWRITE)', 'A(DD)', 'D(ELETE)', 'C(ONDENSE)', 'S(PACED LIST)' and 'R(ESTART)'.

If an integer N is specified, it must refer to a valid frame number, otherwise an error message will be issued. If N is not given, the operation will start at the 2nd line of the text file (if editing is just beginning), or at the line immediately following the line where the last editing manoeuvre finished. K is a second, also optional, parameter defining the number of lines down the file (if positive) or up the file (if negative) that the desired operation should be performed, with reference to frame #N. The following examples should make these operations clear.

## 'Editing' commands

### *I. 'TYPE'*

The simplest editing command is 'TYPE' (or just 'T'), which instructs the Driver to display or print the control line or lines of the frame specified, and any text associated with it. Any preceding comment lines are omitted. The Editor goes on printing successive lines until one beginning with a column 1 asterisk is encountered, after which a further EDIT command is invited.

To give some realistic examples of the 'TYPE' instruction, refer to the first page of the illustrative text exercise in Chapter 3 (p. 25) to interpret the editing manoeuvres illustrated by the following editing dialogue:

```
 WHAT IS YOUR SEX? - TYPE M OR F AND PRESS 'RETURN' KEY AGAIN
? AUTHO
COMMAND: ED
/ T5
```

(Note that only the first 5 characters of 'AUTHOR' need be typed.) This prints the control line and text of frame #5, as follows:

```
*A5 0 0 0 6
NAME, SEX, AGE AND ADDRESS
```

If the editing command had been

the Editor would respond by displaying only the single line

```
 NAME, SEX, AGE AND ADDRESS
/_
```

In the case of the command:

```
/_T5,-1
```

it would print the preceding comment line

```
 *C INSERT ANOTHER HEADING ONTO THE ANSWER FILE
/_
```

Although the *B and *G lines have no reference frame number, they can be accessed by going backwards the necessary number of lines from the first numbered frame, e.g.:

```
/_T1,-6
 *B     1   396
/_
```

and

```
/_T1,-5
 *G 'SCORE',300 'STOP'2001
 TEST EXERCISE INCORPORATING VIRTUALLY ALL FEATURES OF 'MACAID'
 (NORMALLY COMMENT LINES REQUIRE A *C TO IDENTIFY THEM, BUT IF THEY
  IMMEDIATELY FOLLOW THE *G FRAME, THIS IS NOT NEEDED)
```

To reiterate, the T(ype) command displays the line specified and goes on displaying further lines sequentially until a line beginning with an asterisk is encountered.

## *II. 'LIST'*

This command also prints lines on the command 'LIST' (or just 'L'), but its operation is independent of a *-control line. Thus on the instruction

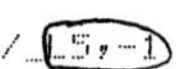

```
/_L5,-1
```

The Editor first displays the line identified:

```
*C INSERT ANOTHER HEADING ONTO THE ANSWER FILE
```

then asks

```
HOW MANY LINES?
?_
```

If the reply is '7', the dialogue proceeds as follows:

```
/ L5,-1
 *C INSERT ANOTHER HEADING ONTO THE ANSWER FILE
HOW MANY LINES?
? 7
*C INSERT ANOTHER HEADING ONTO THE ANSWER FILE
*A5 0 0 0 6
NAME, SEX, AGE AND ADDRESS
*C NEXT QUESTION CAN BE SATISFIED BY ANY ANSWER ('').
*C SCORE PARAMETER (=2) IS AN INSTRUCTION TO RECORD THE ANSWER GIVEN
*C ON THE OUTPUT FILE
*Q6 0 2 0 ''7
/_
```

If an attempt is made to use the 'TYPE', 'LIST' or any other commands to access a non-existent frame or an address outside the text file, the Editor will give an error message, e.g. for the illustrative text exercise of Chapter 3:

```
/_T21
NON-EXISTANT FRAME NUMBER
*INVALID*
/_L1,-7
LINE(S) OUTSIDE LIMITS OF FILE
*INVALID*
/_L2001
 *E2001
HOW MANY LINES?
?_500
LINE(S) OUTSIDE LIMITS OF FILE
*INVALID*
/_
```

### *III. 'END'*

The EDIT mode can be terminated by typing 'E' or 'END', in response to the computer instruction '/'. The Driver responds as follows:

```
/_E
COMMAND:_
```

and the user can then enter other 'authoring' commands or return to running the text again, e.g.:

```
/ T7
 *Q7 0 0 0 'M',10   'F' 8 'WOM'8
  WHAT IS YOUR SEX? - TYPE M OR F AND PRESS 'RETURN' KEY AGAIN
/_E
COMMAND: TE
COMMAND: GO7
*LAST=    7  CURR=    7  FLAG= 1  SCORE(0)=100  TOTAL(0.)=     0.0
 WHAT IS YOUR SEX? - TYPE M OR F AND PRESS 'RETURN' KEY AGAIN
?_
```

## Other editing commands, involving writing on the text file or using the lineprinter

The TYPE and LIST commands do not involve writing on to the text file – they only read from it. These commands can be given any time a user response is requested by entering the global keyword 'AUTHO(R)', and then asking to 'ED(IT)' as described above. The other editing commands now to be described can actually change the text file permanently, and their use (like that of the lineprinter for SPACED LIST (p. 100)) is prohibited unless, when starting the Driver, in response to:

```
TO START, TYPE   GO   , THEN PRESS *RETURN* KEY
?_
```

the user enters the chosen 'authoring password' (see Figure 11.5) (in the FORTRAN version of the Driver in Appendix I this is defined in the DATA statement of the master program as a 5-letter word – 'PASSW' – but the user could of course make this somewhat more original!). Thereafter, the full range of editorial operations is allowed.

```
TO START, TYPE   GO  , THEN PRESS *RETURN* KEY
?_PASSW
TYPE  1   FOR THE HEWLETT-PACKARD TERMINALS,
TYPE  2   FOR ALL OTHER VISUAL DISPLAY UNITS,
OTHERWISE JUST PRESS THE *RETURN* KEY
?_
RENUMBER AND CHECK TEXT FILE?
?_
NEW DIRECTORY?
?_
```

**Figure 11.5** Entry of special 'authoring' password, instead of 'GO', thus releasing special options not otherwise available

## *IV. 'MODIFY'*

To the command 'MODIFY' (or just 'M') the Editor displays the line specified, e.g.:

```
/_M7
 *Q7 0 0 0 'M',10    'F' 8 'WOM'8
```

and then invites modifications in it. The possible operations of MODIFY are R(eplace), I(nsert), D(elete) and # (blank a character). The operation starts at that point in the line that R, I, D or # are typed. To replace some or all of the line, type 'R' beneath the first character to be replaced, followed by the new character(s), e.g.:

```
/_M7
 *Q7 0 0 0 'M',10    'F' 8 'WOM'8
                             R9 'N'11
 *Q7 0 0 0 'M',10    'F' 8 'WOM'9 'N'11
```

To insert characters, type 'I' followed by the desired character string, at the point at which an insertion is wanted, e.g.:

```
/_M7
 *Q7 0 0 0 'M',10    'F' 8 'WOM'9 'N'11
          I'WHY',12
 *Q7 0 0 0 'WHY',12'M',10    'F' 8 'WOM'9 'N'11
```

The Insert command will insert and the Replace command will replace leading and embedded blanks, but neither command can deal with trailing blanks, since they cannot be distinguished from a null entry. A 'hash' (#) is therefore used to symbolize a blank for *Insertions*, though for the Replace manoeuvre, the hash will be treated as a character, e.g.:

```
/_M7
 *Q7 0 0 0 'WHY',12'M',10    'F' 8 'WOM79 'N'11
                   I##
 *Q7 0 0 0 'WHY',12  'M',10    'F' 8 'WOM'9 'N'11

/_M7
 *Q 0 0 0  'WHY',12  'M',10    'F' 8 'WOM'9 'N'11
                     R#
 *Q7 0 0 0 'WHY',12  '#',10    'F' 8 'WOM'9 'N'11

/_
```

To delete characters or blanks, and thus to close up a line, type D for each character to be removed, e.g.:

```
/ M7
 *Q7 0 0 0 'WHY',12  '#',10   'F' 8 'WOM'9 'N'11
          DDDDDDDDDDD
 *Q7 0 0 0 '#',10   'F' 8 'WOM'9 'N'11
                              DDDDD
 *Q7 0 0 0 '#',10   'F' 8 'WOM'9
```

To blank characters, without closing up the line, type # for each character to be blanked, e.g.:

```
/ M7
 *Q7 0 0 0 'WHY',12  '#',10   'F' 8 'WOM'9 'N'11
          ###########
 *Q7 0 0 0             '#',10   'F' 8 'WOM'9 'N'11
/
```

*Combined Deletion and Insertion under MODIFY* – In general 'MODIFY' allows only a single manoeuvre to be performed at one time, but the exception is combined deletion and insertion. If 'D' is typed in for each character to be deleted, it is then possible to type 'I' (for 'Insert') followed by the characters to be inserted, as in the examples above. In the following example the operator typed in an instruction to delete 6 characters and to insert 9 characters and 2 blanks (the latter coded as 'hashes').

```
/ M7
 *Q7 0 0 0 'M',10  'F'8  'WOM'8
          DDDDDDI'MALE',10##
 *Q7 0 0 0 'MALE',10   'F'8   'WOM'8

/ T7
 *Q7 0 0 0 'MALE',10   'F'8   'WOM'8
  WHAT IS YOUR SEX? - TYPW M OR F AND PRESS 'RETURN' KEY AGAIN
/
```

The only limitation on this facility is that if it is used to delete and insert large numbers of characters at the end of a line, some may be lost, since in the current version of the Driver the size of the input buffer available is limited to 72 characters.

All the above commands operate on a *copy* of the line, held by the Driver. If no command is given, and the 'return' key pressed, the edited line is copied back into the text file, overwriting the original line. However, if the author decides not to change the line, the M(odify) operation can be terminated any time by typing a double slash (//), which leaves the original text unchanged, e.g.:

```
/ M7
 *Q7 0 0 0 'WHY',12  '#',10   'F' 8 'WOM'9 'N'11
          DDDDDDDDDDD
 *Q7 0 0 0 '#',10   'F' 8 'WOM'9 'N'11
                              DDDDD
 *Q7 0 0 0 '#',10   'F' 8 'WOM'9
 //
/ M7
 *Q7 0 0 0 'WHY',12  '#',10   'F' 8 'WOM'9 'N'11
```

### V. 'OVERWRITE'

As in the M(odify) command described above, the Overwrite command first types the line specified, on the command 'O', e.g.:

```
/_O7
*Q7 0 0 0              '#',10   'F' 8 'WOM'9 'N'11
```

Any characters or embedded blanks can then be simply overwritten, and the new edited line will be entered as soon as the 'return' key is pressed without making an entry. As in M(odify), it is necessary to type hashes (#) to blank characters, unless the blank is embraced by text. An O(verwrite) manoeuvre can be terminated, like a M(odify) one, by typing a double slash. A null entry, however, does not return the Driver to EDIT mode, but proceeds to the next line in the file, after overwriting the previous one. Typing a double slash (//) is therefore the *only exit* from O(verwrite) mode. A few examples will make the O(verwrite) command clear:

```
/_Q7
*Q7 0 0 0              '#',10   'F' 8 'WOM'9 'N'11
        'M',10  'F'8   'WOM'8
*Q7 0 0 0 'M',10  'F'8   'WOM'8F' 8 'WOM'9 'N'11
                       ################
*Q7 0 0 0 'M',10  'F'8   'WOM'8

 WHAT IS YOUR SEX? - TYPE M OR F AND PRESS 'RETURN' KEY AGAIN
                                          ESCAPE
 WHAT IS YOUR SEX? - TYPE M OR F AND PRESS 'ESCAPE' KEY AGAIN

*C IF ANSWER INDICATES FEMALE SEX, SET FLAG TO 2, FOR USE LATER
//
/_T7
*Q7 0 0 0 'M',10  'F'8   'WOM'8
 WHAT IS YOUR SEX? - TYPE M OR F AND PRESS 'ESCAPE' KEY AGAIN
/_
```

In general, the M(odify) command is more convenient for editing an already completed file, since only a few lines will need to be changed. The O(verwrite) command is provided chiefly to enable large blocks of text, or, indeed, a whole file, to be typed in at one sitting, each line being edited or retyped if necessary before being entered into the file.

### VI. 'ADD'

The command ADD⟨N⟩, ⟨K⟩ or simply A⟨N⟩, ⟨K⟩ first displays the specified line, then asks HOW MANY LINES?, e.g.:

```
/_A1775,1
 WHAT WAS YOUR VALUE FOR FACTOR 3?
HOW MANY LINES?
?_
```

On the reply (for example) '2' the Editor adds 2 new dummy lines immediately before the line specified, and then issues the message

```
 2 LINE(S) ADDED
/_
```

The lines added are not completely blank. Columns 1, 2 and 3 contain full stops, and columns 4–72 are all blank. Figure 11.6 gives an example of the text before and after the addition of 2 lines before frame #1775(+1).

The A(DD) command, like the D(ELETE) and C(ONDENSE) commands described below, are very slow in operation, especially if used at the start of a large file, since every line has to be read and copied back into a new location.

```
*C NUMERIC RANGE QUESTION
*Q1775 2300 2 0 (-3.5,-.01)1780 ''1785
WHAT WAS YOUR VALUE FOR FACTOR 3?
*T1780 0 0 0 1790
A GOOD ESTIMATE - CONGRATULATIONS!
*T 1785 0 0 0 1790
IT HAS TO BE NEGATIVE, AND NOT TOO BIG - AROUND -2 IS CORRECT
/_A1775,1
 WHAT WAS YOUR VALUE FOR FACTOR 3?
HOW MANY LINES?
?_2
  2 LINE(S) ADDED
/_
*C NUMERIC RANGE QUESTION
*Q1775 2300 2 0 (-3.5,-.01)1780 ''1785
...
...
WHAT WAS YOUR VALUE FOR FACTOR 3?
*T1780 0 0 0 1790
A GOOD ESTIMATE - CONGRATULATIONS!
*T 1785 0 0 0 1790
IT HAS TO BE NEGATIVE, AND NOT TOO BIG - AROUND -2 IS CORRECT
/_
```

**Figure 11.6** Example of adding 2 lines before a specified line of the text file (1 line after control line #1775). The resultant expanded text is shown below

## *VII. 'DELETE'*

This is the same type of operation as 'ADD' except that the line displayed is normally deleted, plus N-1 further lines (where 'N' is the number specified) – i.e. 'N' lines in all. The commands DELETE ⟨N⟩, ⟨K⟩ or D⟨N⟩, ⟨K⟩ display the specified line before asking for deletion instructions. For example, the lines added in the example of Figure 11.6 could be deleted as follows:

```
/_D1775,1
 ...
HOW MANY LINES?
?_2
  2 LINE(S) DELETED
/_
```

## *VIII. 'CONDENSE'*

A new, blank file can be supplied with sequentially numbered frames and blank lines starting with '. . .' (as described on p. 87) by an initial request to create a file. In addition, the 'ADD' command (see above) allows expanding an existing file any number of extra lines, again beginning '. . .'. Using the M(odify) or O(verwrite) editor commands described above (p. 95), any of these lines can be changed to new control lines and new text lines. However, when the exercise is complete there may be redundant or surplus dummy lines, which will be displayed or printed if they form part of a text section. All such lines can be removed by the C(ONDENSE) command, which operates on the file from the line specified to the end of the file. Figure 11.7 gives an example of a text file listing (from the Chapter 3 illustrative exercise), before and after the operation of the C(ONDENSE) command.

If 'ADD', 'DELETE' or 'CONDENSE' have been used, the operator will automatically be presented with options for renumbering the file, and also for making a new directory (see Figure 11.7). It is necessary to respond 'Y' to

```
*T 1785 0 0 0 1790
IT HAS TO BE NEGATIVE, AND NOT TOO BIG - AROUND -2 IS CORRECT
...
...
*C ANSWER FILE HEADING
*A1790 0 0 0 2000
FINAL COMMENTS
*C FINAL COMMENTS - FREE TEXT ENTRY PROMPTED BY 2ND PARAMETER = 2.
*C NOTE THAT "*RETURN*" IN THE LAST TEXT LINE HAS TO BE INDENTED
*C BY 1 SPACE TO PREVENT THE TEXT LINE BEING TREATED AS A CONTROL LINE
*T2000 2000 2 0 2001
THAT IS THE END.  THANK YOU FOR YOUR COOPERATION.
IF YOU HAVE ANY COMMENTS, PLEASE TYPE THEM IN NOW, AND PRESS
 *RETURN* KEY TWICE
*C FINAL FRAME
*E2001
...
...
...
THANK YOU
**
/_C1785
 *T 1785 0 0 0 1790
  5 LINE(S) DELETED
/_L1785
 *T 1785 0 0 0 1790
HOW MANY LINES?
?_16
*T 1785 0 0 0 1790
IT HAS TO BE NEGATIVE, AND NOT TOO BIG - AROUND -2 IS CORRECT
*C ANSWER FILE HEADING
*A1790 0 0 0 2000
FINAL COMMENTS
*C FINAL COMMENTS - FREE TEXT ENTRY PROMPTED BY 2ND PARAMETER = 2.
*C NOTE THAT "*RETURN*" IN THE LAST TEXT LINE HAS TO BE INDENTED
*C BY 1 SPACE TO PREVENT THE TEXT LINE BEING TREATED AS A CONTROL LINE
*T2000 2000 2 0 2001
THAT IS THE END.  THANK YOU FOR YOUR COOPERATION.
IF YOU HAVE ANY COMMENTS, PLEASE TYPE THEM IN NOW, AND PRESS
 *RETURN* KEY TWICE
*C FINAL FRAME
*E2001
THANK YOU
**
/_E
*** WARNING - NEW DIRECTORY IS NOW ESSENTIAL ***
RENUMBER AND CHECK TEXT FILE?
?_N
NEW DIRECTORY?
?_Y
  96 CONTROL FRAMES.       395= LAST TEXT LINE NUMBER
COMMAND:_
```

**Figure 11.7** Example of the use of the C(ONDENSE) command. Note removal of the 5 'dummy' lines beginning '. . .' and that an attempt to end editing gave a warning message and put the Driver in RESTART mode, so that a new directory could be created before proceeding further

the request for a new directory, otherwise the old one will persist, and the Driver will not work properly when either running the text, or editing the file. Indeed, it is very likely that an execution error will occur, since the Driver may be compelled to read an incorrectly-formatted incomplete directory.

### *IX. 'SPACED LIST'*

If the 'authoring' password has been given (p. 94) and the user gives the instruction SPACED LIST (or just S), a special kind of listing of the whole file is printed.

If a lineprinter is available, the Driver asks:

```
LINEPRINTER LISTING?
?_
```

and then either on the terminal or the lineprinter (as requested) a specially spaced text listing is printed, starting at line 1, terminating at the last line of the text material, and incorporating a space between each successive frame, to aid intelligibility. (The listing of the illustrative text exercise of Chapter 3 was made in this way.)

### *X. 'R(ESTART)'*

Typing 'R' in Editing mode (providing the 'authoring' password was given at the onset of the exercise – see p. 94) – has exactly the same effect as typing 'RE(START)' in response to

```
*COMMAND*
```

(see Figure 11.8). It allows checking and renumbering of the file as well as making a new directory.

```
 WHAT IS YOUR SEX? - TYPE M OR F AND PRESS 'RETURN' KEY AGAIN
?_AUTHO
COMMAND:_RESTART
RENUMBER AND CHECK TEXT FILE?
?_NO
NEW DIRECTORY?
?_YES
  96 CONTROL FRAMES.        395= LAST TEXT LINE NUMBER
COMMAND:_
```

**Figure 11.8** 'Authoring' command RE(START) and its effect, giving the options of renumbering and checking the file (see later, this chapter) and of remaking the directory. Note that the abbreviation 'AUTHO' is a sufficient global keyword. The command 'R' or 'RESTART' can also be given any time in EDIT mode

## Checking, renumbering and tidying a text file

Whenever the Driver is started up in 'authoring' mode (by giving the author's password – see p. 94), or when the global command 'AUTHO(R)' is entered during a text exercise run in 'authoring' mode, and the command 'RE(START)' is typed, the Driver responds:

```
RENUMBER AND CHECK TEXT FILE?
?_
```

If the 'return' key is now pressed, or any entry other than 'Y' entered, the Driver will continue with the invitation:

```
NEW DIRECTORY?
?_
```

whose use and significance has been already discussed above. However, the answer 'Y' (or 'YES') to:

```
RENUMBER AND CHECK TEXT FILE?
?_
```

produces the confirmatory query:

```
HAVE YOU A COPY IN CASE OF ACCIDENTS?
?
```

If the answer to this question is 'NO', the Driver will take no further action, because a computer failure during a renumbering procedure may degrade the text in such a way that extensive re-editing may be needed before it can be used again. If possible, therefore, a copy should be kept. When the answer 'Y' (or 'YES') is given, the checking and renumbering routine will start.

The checking and renumbering facility is rather slow when operating on a large file, because it reads the whole file twice, in sequence from top to bottom, then copies out the renumbered file, replacing the original. The complete sequence of operations is as follows:

(1) Each numbered control line is read, starting at the first numbered frame, and continuing until the end-of-text line '**' is encountered (or until the Driver discovers that the allotted file length is insufficient, in which case it inserts this essential text terminator as far down the file as possible).

(2) Error messages are issued for any out-of-numerical-sequence frames or duplicate-numbered frames.

(3) A table of all numbered frames is printed, in 10-column format, giving a complete list of all the original numbered frames.

(4) The original list of frame numbers is stored in sequential array in the Driver.

(5) Each control line of each original frame is read a second time, starting from the first line.

(6) A new frame number is supplied by the Driver to each numbered frame in sequence of tens – i.e. the first control frame becomes 10, the second 20, the third 30, and so on – regardless of what the original frame numbers were.

(7) All frame exit addresses, or conditional addresses in *Q(uestion) or *M(arking) frames are renumbered to conform to the renumbered frames.

(8) The type letter is checked against a list of 'legal' type letters, and error messages report the presence of blank or illegal frame types.

(9) Unmatched parentheses, unmatched single inverted commas or unmatched conical brackets are detected, an appropriate error message issued, and the offending conditional branching deleted.
(10) All unnecessary extra blanks are removed from the control and continuation lines and from dictionaries, and leading zeros from control line parameters and addresses are also removed.
(11) All text (i.e. non-control) lines are transcribed without change into the renumbered file.
(12) All floating point numbers (except those in the 'add' parameters) are truncated to integers, and numbers of more than 4 digits are truncated (from the right) to 4-digit numbers.
(13) Any residual space at the end of each control, dictionary or continuation line is filled up with asterisks.
(14) A warning message is issued for each frame which is not accessed anywhere in the text file.
(15) A warning message is issued for any exit or conditional branching address which attempts to access a non-existent frame.
(16) A non-descript number (in fact, the total number of control frames) is assigned to any non-existent address.
(17) A new directory is constructed.

### *An example of the checking and renumbering facility in action*

Figure 11.9 is a modified version of the start of the illustrative exercise of Chapter 3 in which certain changes have been made. The 3 frames from the

```
*B    1  396
*G 'SCORE',300 'STOP'2001
TEST EXERCISE INCORPORATING VIRTUALLY ALL FEATURES OF 'MACAID'
(NORMALLY COMMENT LINES REQUIRE A *C TO IDENTIFY THEM, BUT IF THEY
 IMMEDIATELY FOLLOW THE *G FRAME, THIS IS NOT NEEDED)
*C ANSWER FILE HEADING
*K1790 0 0 0 2000
FINAL COMMENTS
*C FINAL COMMENTS - FREE TEXT ENTRY PROMPTED BY 2ND PARAMETER = 2.
*C NOTE THAT "*RETURN*" IN THE LAST TEXT LINE HAS TO BE INDENTED
*C BY 1 SPACE TO PREVENT THE TEXT LINE BEING TREATED AS A CONTROL LINE
*T2000 2000 2 0 2001
THAT IS THE END.  THANK YOU FOR YOUR COOPERATION.
IF YOU HAVE ANY COMMENTS, PLEASE TYPE THEM IN NOW, AND PRESS
 *RETURN* KEY TWICE
*C FINAL FRAME
*E3001
THANK YOU
*C NEXT *A FRAME WRITES HEADING ONTO ANSWER FILE
*A1 0 0 0 2
DATE
*C NEXT *T FRAME HAS NO TEXT.  ITS ONLY FUNCTION HERE IS TO CLEAR SCREEN
*C AND SET CURSOR TO TOP LEFT OF SCREEN (IF AN APPROPRIATELY
*C CONTROLLABLE VISUAL DISPLAY UNIT IS AVAILABLE) -
*C DISPLAY PARAMETER TO CODE THIS INSTRUCTION = 2000.  3RD ('ADD')
*C PARAMETER (=-1) IS AN INSTRUCTION TO PROCEED WITHOUT PROMPTING
*T2 2000 0 -1 3
```

**Figure 11.9** Rearranged text file of the illustrative text exercise of Chapter 3 in which 3 frames from the end of the file have been transposed to the beginning of it, and deliberate (ringed) errors introduced (an invalid type letter for frame #1790, a mis-numbered frame – *E3001 instead of *E2001)

end of the file (1790, 2000, 2001) have been placed at the front of the file, thus making the original line numbering non-sequential; and other (ringed) deliberate errors have been introduced. The consequential operations of the checking and renumbering facility are illustrated in Figure 11.10, and need

```
RENUMBER AND CHECK TEXT FILE?
?_Y
HAVE YOU GOT A COPY IN CASE OF ACCIDENTS?
?_Y
OLD FRAME # 1790 ILLEGAL, OR TYPE LETTER NOT IN COLUMN 2
OLD FRAME    1 WAS DUPLICATE OR OUT OF SEQUENCE & WILL BE RECODED
OLD CONTROL FRAMES WERE..
 1790  2000  3001     1     2     3     4     5     6     7
    8     9    10    11    12    13    15    20    25    26
   27    30    60    70    75    76    77    78    79    80
  100   104   105   106   107   110   120   130   140   160
  170   180   185   190   191   192   193   194   195   196
  197   198   199   200   201   205   300   305   510   520
  530   540   552   555   560   570   580   581   582   583
  584   590   600  1000  1010  1020  1030  1050  1060  1070
 1500  1501  1600  1601  1699  1700  1710  1720  1730  1740
 1750  1760  1775  1780  1785
NEW FRAME    0 ATTEMPTS ACCESS OF NON-EXISTENT OLD FRAME 2001
NEW FRAME   20 ATTEMPTS ACCESS OF NON-EXISTENT OLD FRAME 2001
   50 TEXT LINES PROCESSED
  100 TEXT LINES PROCESSED
  150 TEXT LINES PROCESSED
  200 TEXT LINES PROCESSED
  250 TEXT LINES PROCESSED
  300 TEXT LINES PROCESSED
  350 TEXT LINES PROCESSED
FRAME #    30 (OLD FRAME 3001) NOT ACCESSED ANYWHERE
ADD MORE FRAMES?
?_NO
NEW DIRECTORY WILL BE MADE
  96 CONTROL FRAMES.        395= LAST TEXT LINE NUMBER
COMMAND:_GO
```

**Figure 11.10** Print of the Driver's activities when checking and renumbering the text file illustrated in Figure 11.9. Note warnings of illegal type letter, out-of-sequence frames, attempted access of non-existent frame #2001 by the *Global line (= frame 0) and by the new frame #20 (old frame #2000), and non-accession of old frame #3001. Note also invitation to add further blank or dummy frames

no elaborate description, since examples of various types of error and their consequences are illustrated. Figure 11.11 shows the first part of the checked and renumbered file. Note that both the *B(egin) and *G(lobal) line addresses have been changed appropriately, and that any punctuation commas have been left intact. Note also that extra sequentially-numbered blank frames can be inserted before the end of the operation.

As previously described, the rows of asterisks help to make the divisions between successive frames easier to read, and also speed up the Driver's response time by terminating the reading of each control or continuation line as soon as an asterisk is encountered.

### *Uses of the checking and renumbering facility*

Obviously a large number of sequential operations on the text file are carried out each time the renumbering facility is used. Since the text file will commonly be stored on a disc, two 'in' and one 'out' transfers will be needed

```
*B   40  396
*G 'SCORE',570 'STOP', 96  ****************************************************
TEST EXERCISE INCORPORATING VIRTUALLY ALL FEATURES OF 'MACAID'
(NORMALLY COMMENT LINES REQUIRE A *C TO IDENTIFY THEM, BUT IF THEY
 IMMEDIATELY FOLLOW THE *G FRAME, THIS IS NOT NEEDED)
*C ANSWER FILE HEADING
*K 10 0 0 0 20  ******************************************************
FINAL COMMENTS
*C FINAL COMMENTS - FREE TEXT ENTRY PROMPTED BY 2ND PARAMETER = 2.
*C NOTE THAT "*RETURN*" IN THE LAST TEXT LINE HAS TO BE INDENTED
*C BY 1 SPACE TO PREVENT THE TEXT LINE BEING TREATED AS A CONTROL LINE
*T 20 2000 2 0 96  ***************************************************
THAT IS THE END.  THANK YOU FOR YOUR COOPERATION.
IF YOU HAVE ANY COMMENTS, PLEASE TYPE THEM IN NOW, AND PRESS
 *RETURN* KEY TWICE
*C FINAL FRAME
*E 30 0  *************************************************************
THANK YOU
*C NEXT *A FRAME WRITES HEADING ONTO ANSWER FILE
*A 40 0 0 0 50  ******************************************************
DATE
*C NEXT *T FRAME HAS NO TEXT.  ITS ONLY FUNCTION HERE IS TO CLEAR SCREEN
*C AND SET CURSOR TO TOP LEFT OF SCREEN (IF AN APPROPRIATELY
*C CONTROLLABLE VISUAL DISPLAY UNIT IS AVAILABLE) -
*C DISPLAY PARAMETER TO CODE THIS INSTRUCTION = 2000.  3RD ('ADD')
*C PARAMETER (=-1) IS AN INSTRUCTION TO PROCEED WITHOUT PROMPTING
*T 50 2000 0 -1 60  **************************************************
```

**Figure 11.11** The same text file as in Figure 11.9 after the renumbering and checking operation shown in Figure 11.10. Note that the *B(egin) line now accesses new frame #40, and the global line and all other transfer addresses have been appropriately changed. However, the old address '2001' was non-existent, and has been redesignated by a nondescript number (96, = number of control frames) in the *G(lobal) line), and in new frame #20 (ringed). Note also that redundant space in all control lines is filled up with asterisks. The illegal type letter of new frame #10 ('K') persists, and will produce an error message when it is accessed during a run, as also will any non-existent transfer address

for each line of the file, and this is likely to make the renumbering procedure slow. We would therefore recommend that its use should be restricted to the stage at which a complete exercise has been fully developed and the designer is ready to make a comprehensive check on the entire program before releasing it. Most of the grosser errors will be thrown up by the renumbering facility. Minor and more subtle errors will produce messages such as

```
*** NOT ENOUGH ADDRESSES FOR *M  70 FRAME - PLEASE REPORT
COMMAND:_
```

or

```
*** DICTIONARY # 2 CALLED FROM *Q 581 NOT FOUND - PLEASE REPORT
COMMAND:_
```

during the actual running of the program, even though such errors will not be detected by the checking and renumbering facility. We would recommend that the first few check runs of the program should be made in 'authoring' mode (p. 94) in which, if errors of this type are detected, the Driver prompts at once with 'COMMAND:', as shown above, so that the text editor (described in the last chapter) can be used to correct the offending line, without causing the Driver to stop. This facility allows the Driver to act in effect as an *interpreter* (e.g. like a BASIC or MUMPS interpreter). In ordinary usage, nowever, when the 'authoring' password has not been given, the program will stop altogether when any fatal error of this kind occurs, so that needless confusion will be avoided. The error message will, however, be printed, so that a user whose program has gone adrift may be able to tell the author what has happened.

## Practical aspects of writing and editing MACAID interrogative or teaching programs

Enormous amounts of time can be wasted trying to compose MACAID or any other computer-aided instructional material 'on-line', by typing the text material directly into a computer file. Except for very short exercises, or for trivial and utterly simple texts, it is much more satisfactory and saves a great deal of time in the end to write the text out first on sheets of paper. For MACAID (just as for COURSEWRITER and most other systems) it is best to use separate sheets of paper for each frame. These can then be moved around freely until the final order of text frames is decided upon. Since there is no effective delay in finding any frame of the text, the program does not have to be sequential in its logical progression, but it is much easier and quicker subsequently to edit the file if the frame sequence runs with the dialogue.

We would recommend first numbering sheets of paper in 10's, i.e. 10, 20, 30, 40, etc. and deciding in advance that certain frames will be 'nodes', i.e. the origins or central branching points of main sections of the text. However, the numbering order is not unduly important, since a single run through the RENUMBER and CHECK facility (described in the next chapter) will sequentially renumber any text file in 10's. It is of course necessary to avoid giving duplicate numbers for frames. We would therefore advise numbering all the sheets of paper for the text file before writing down any material. There are considerable advantages in preprinting a stack of forms like that illustrated in Figure 11.12, which shows how the designer might have designed frame #552 of the illustrative exercise of Chapter 3 (p. 33).

There are two ways of then creating the text file. The quickest is probably to use the extensive editing facilities available on most computers to type the whole text into a new file and make corrections to it there before loading it as a direct-access file. The main body of the file should be preceded by BEGIN and GLOBAL lines, e.g.:

```
*B 10
*G
```

Only one number needs to be supplied to the *B(egin) line (that of the first frame number to be accessed – in this case '10') and the *G line is prepared for but left blank. At the end of the file place a double-asterisk line

```
**
```

to mark the end of the text, and allot some blank extra lines for the directory. These should be at least 5% (better 10%) as many as the total lines of the text file – more if the file is to be later enlarged. For a 400-line text file, it would be adequate for most purposes to provide about 440 lines in all. Then

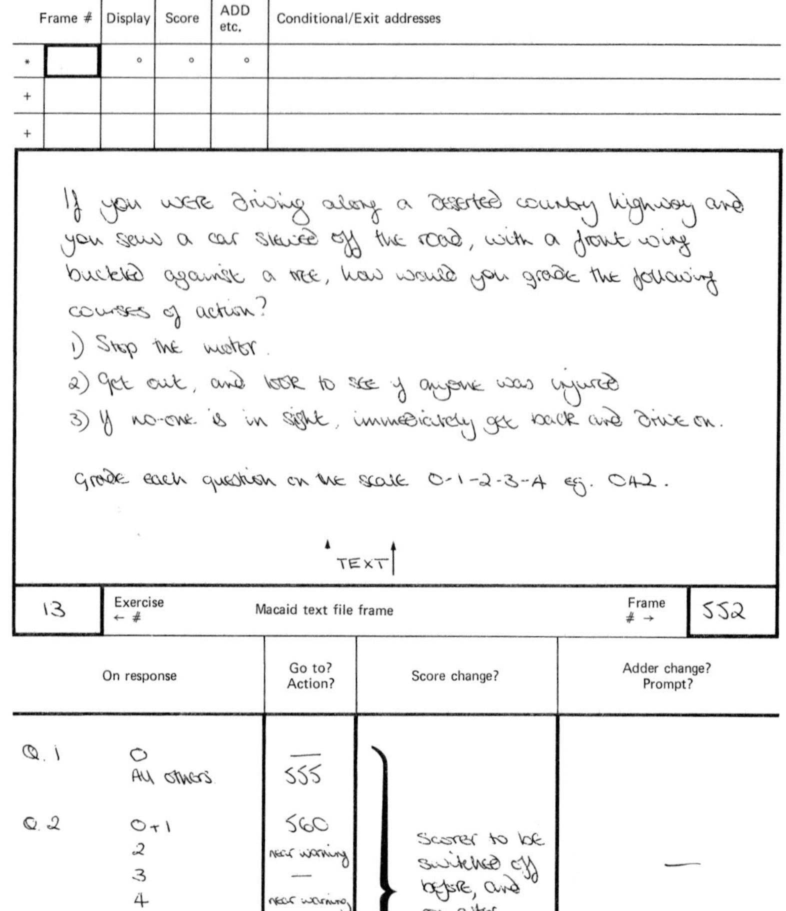

| | Frame # | Display | Score | ADD etc. | Conditional/Exit addresses |
|---|---|---|---|---|---|
| * | | ○ | ○ | ○ | |
| + | | | | | |
| + | | | | | |

If you were driving along a deserted country highway and you saw a car slewed off the road, with a front wing buckled against a tree, how would you grade the following courses of action?

1) Stop the motor.

2) Get out, and look to see if anyone was injured

3) If no-one is in sight, immediately get back and drive on.

Grade each question on the scale 0-1-2-3-4 eg. 042.

TEXT

| 13 | Exercise ← # | Macaid text file frame | Frame # → | 552 |
|---|---|---|---|---|

| | On response | Go to? Action? | Score change? | Adder change? Prompt? |
|---|---|---|---|---|
| Q. 1 | 0 | — | Scorer to be switched off before, and on after. | — |
| | All others | 555 | | |
| Q. 2 | 0+1 | 560 | | |
| | 2 | near warning | | |
| | 3 | — | | |
| | 4 | near warning | | |
| Q. 3 | 0,1,2,3 | 570 | | |
| | 4 | — | | |
| | Then exit to | 580 | | |

Exit To # 580

**Figure 11.12** Example of a pre-printed form to simplify the creation of new text exercises, before they are entered formally on to a MACAID text file. The designer would add the appropriate control lines at the top when the exercise was complete

in the Driver set NNST to the first line number (usually = 1) and NNEND to the last line number (440 in the example mentioned). When starting the Driver up with appropriate passwords (p. 94) the Driver reads the file and on command automatically creates and stores a directory of frame addresses at the end (after the double-asterisk line) (p. 37). The file can then be run and further edited on-line, in 'authoring' mode, as just described.

Alternatively a text exercise already written on sheets of paper can be entered directly on to a suitably prepared blank file. In the example above, once NNST and NNEND have been set to 1 and 440 respectively, the Driver is started up. If the question

```
CREATE NEW FILE?
?_
```

(p. 88) is answered in the affirmative, the Driver will create a blank file complete with *B, *G and ** (terminator) lines together with a directory. It is then possible to ask for 1 frame of 400 lines. The O(VERWRITE) edit facility can be used to enter, and if necessary, correct each line of the text file. Each entry or correction to it is displayed repeatedly until a blank line is entered. Alternatively a dummy numbered text like Figure 11.1 can be created and then edited.

The apparent complexity of a MACAID text file at first sight resides in the numbers associated with each control line. When setting out a text it is simplest to begin by making the 1st, 2nd and 3rd parameters all zero. Thus successive control lines might be:

```
*T10 0 0 0 20
*T20 0 0 0 30
*T30 0 0 0 40
*T40 0 0 0 50
"""
```

and so on, with text following each frame control line. The Driver will on appropriate command create a new (blank) file of this type, though all the 'display' parameters will be set to 1000 rather than zero, e.g.

```
*T    10 1000 0 0    20
```

If such a text file is run on line, each frame of associated text will be displayed in sequence, after pressing the 'return' key for each prompt.

Next, insert conditioned branching points by editing each appropriate 'T' line, changing the frame type from 'T' to, for example, 'Q' to construct *Q(uestion) frame nodes.

When the file is complete and gross errors have been removed, it is then helpful to ask for 'RE(START)' and to 'RENUMBER AND CHECK' the text file (as described in the next chapter). When this is complete, and the main errors rectified, it is a simple matter to obtain a spaced lineprinter listing by the 'edit' command 'S(PACED LIST)'. Such a listing is almost essential for efficient editing.

Before starting to run a new program, type the 'authoring' command 'TR(ACE)'. If then some error is seen, the number of the faulty frame will have been printed, and corrections to it can be entered before continuing further.

In the case of text programs with very complicated branching sequences it is possible that a later user may uncover some circular or incorrect behaviour. Unless the special 'authoring' password (p. 94) was given, the Driver would normally stop with an informative error message. In 'authoring' mode on-line direct editing of the file can be performed any time the program comes to a halt through some error in the text file.

### *Multiple single files or one single large file?*

This choice may be dictated by the machine hardware. For microprocessors, each user would have a precompiled Driver, and each program of text might be given a fixed-length direct-access file, e.g. of 1000 lines. This allows writing on the end of the text file for intermediate storage (p. 77). In larger systems with many time-sharing terminals we have found it satisfactory to maintain a large text file of, say, 20,000 lines, and to preface this file with a master directory which can supply the Driver with first (NNST) and last (NNEND) line numbers. One way of doing this is illustrated by Appendix IV (the large file directory) and by Appendix V (a supervisory program to set NNST and NNEND before calling the main Driver as a subroutine – 'MACRUN').

## SUMMARY

The provision of a comprehensive text file editor makes the Driver self-sufficient and independent of an external editor. The MACAID Driver has an editor which can rapidly edit or list specified lines, or prepare a special list of the whole file, and which can rather slowly add or delete whole lines. All editing manoeuvres can be performed *during running of a text program* and then running the program can be resumed at any point. It is also possible to renumber and check comprehensively entire programs.

Various practical suggestions are made to enable text files to be prepared and run with least difficulty.

# 12
# A brief description of the Master Driver

In this chapter we shall describe in outline the functions of each of the main segments of the Driver before listing the equivalent FORTRAN subroutines. Our objective is to simplify the task of writing a version of the Driver in some other language, and also to make it easier for those using the FORTRAN version to modify it for special purposes.

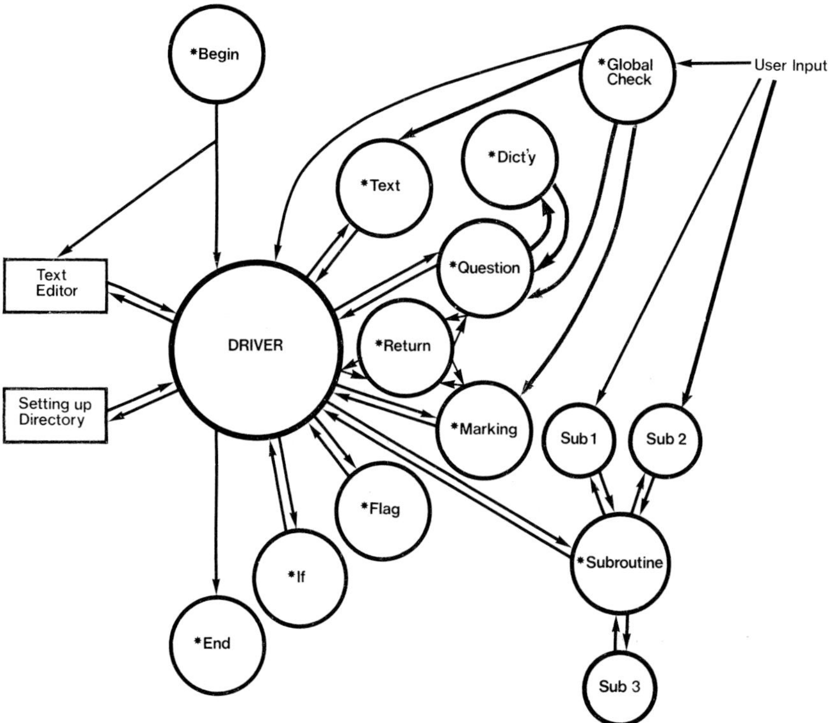


**Figure 12.1** Schematic layout of the master Driver showing the interrelationships of various program segments (see text)

The segments of the Driver can be arranged in a functional hierarchy:

I. Essential components.
II. Components needed for processing particular types of frame.
III. Components needed only for 'authoring', and editing the text file.

Figure 12.1 illustrates the interrelationships of the various components.

## I. Essential components

These comprise a *START* section, a *MACAID* main control section, and sections to *INITIALIZE*, to obtain *INPUT*, to *LOCATE* a frame address, to read a free format *NUMBER*, to display or *PRINT* a text line, and to *READ* a specified text file line.

1. *START* gives the opportunity of entering a special 'author' password, and checks the terminal type in use before calling up the MACAID main section.

2. *MACAID* is the main section. All subsequent operations of the Driver are channelled through this section. Repeated operations incorporate most or all of the following sequence:

(a) Locate frame address and read control line.
(b) Identify frame type.
(c) Read and act on 1st (display and cursor control) instructions.
(d) Read and act on 2nd ('score') parameter instructions.
(e) Print the text of the frame.
(f) Call special purpose processing routines.
(g) Record a user's answers.
(h) Read and act on 3rd ('add') parameter instruction.
(i) Read exit address.

3. The *INITIALIZE* section reads in the directory of frame addresses (stored at the end of the text file) and also reads and stores any 'global' keywords specified and their exit addresses.

4. *INPUT* from a user is checked against previously stored 'global' keywords, and numerical input separately identified.

5. The *LOCATE* section finds the line address of a specified frame by binary search, using the previously stored directory of frame addresses.

6. *NUMBER* is a routine to read along a line of characters from a specified pointer position and to extract therefrom the next number present.

7. The *PRINT* routine displays or prints at the terminal a specified line of text, and goes on printing sequential lines of text until the next control frame is reached.

8. *READ* is a section to read into the Driver a single line from the text file.

## II. Components needed to interpret special frames or types of display

The essential components listed above comprise the minimum structure possible for the Driver. With these components the Driver can print a predetermined sequence of text frames, and also obtain the entry of free text at any predetermined points on an Answer file. To allow conditional branching it is necessary to use either the *Q(uestion) frame (p. 51) or the *M(arking) frame (p. 53). If the text contains only *Q frames, routine *QFRAME* alone will be needed, if it contains *M frames, routine *MFRAME* will be needed, and if it contains both types of frame, both sections will be needed. If *R(eturn) frames are to be used, routine *RETURN* will be needed to print from them. In addition, if any *S(ubroutine) frames are specified, and computative subroutines used, then the *SUBROUTINE* section will also be needed. If screen cursor control (by instructions in the text file) is needed, this is obtained by use of a *DISPLAY* section.

1. Section *QFRAME* obtains a user's response to a question posed in the text, and compares it with possible alternative answers envisaged in the text file, and asks for further input if no matching entry is given. It is also possible to use one or more dictionaries to allow given sequences of keywords to be identified, ignoring other intervening words or characters. This section of the Driver can also be used to check numbers, or numerical ranges, and can also be used to bring about branching conditional on the numerical values of the running score or running total.

2. Section *MFRAME* processes frames which pose from 1 to 9 separate questions, each having binary or numerical types of answer, with 2 to 5 alternatives (see p. 53). this section of the Driver first reads in the addresses of frames whose text is printed or to which control is passed when a specific answer is given to each question. It then requests input from the user. The answers are converted into numbers in a 0–4 integer scale (if necessary), checked for completeness, then compared against the table of addresses. Corrective and other messages are printed from *R(eturn) frames by the RETURN routine (see below).

3. The *RETURN* section has the sole function of printing the text of *R(eturn) frames, under the control of *Q and *M frames, without returning control to the main Driver.

4. The *SUBROUTINE* section of the Driver identifies the code number of the subroutine specified, and calls it up.

5. The *DISPLAY* section is only needed if cursor control is in operation. It is then called into action prior to any display instruction by the MACAID Driver, or by sections QFRAME or MFRAME. By its use the 4-digit 'display' parameter is decoded, the cursor positioned and the screen cleared in appropriate parts.

### III. 'Authoring' and editing components

The previously described components only *read from* the text file and cannot change it. To prepare a text file in the first place, and to edit it on-line (i.e. while actually running the program) certain other components are needed. The most essential is the *DIRECTORY* section, which automatically creates a new directory of frame addresses. The *EDIT* section allows text editing, the *RENUMBER* section allows renumbering and checking of a text file, and the *NEWFILE* section allows the creation of a blank (but editable) text file.

1. The *DIRECTORY* section reads the whole file, stores the line address of each control frame or dictionary, and writes (or overwrites) at the end of the text file a directory of addresses (which can be read subsequently by the INITIALIZE section already described on p. 110).

2. The *EDIT* section implements various 'authoring' commands such as 'TRACE', 'RESTART' and 'GO' (to a specified frame number). It also allows various editing manoeuvres including changing text or control lines, and inserting or deleting lines in the text file.

3. *RENUMBER* is an optional section of the Driver which performs the non-essential but highly convenient functions of renumbering all numbered frames in sequential 10's, and comprehensively checks the whole text file for errors such as attempts to access non-existent frames, wrong or inconsistent frame types, mismatched parentheses and non-accessed frames.

The RENUMBER facility of the Driver can be used to make a file work again after massive transpositions or insertions of frames out of sequence. Such changes in the text file would otherwise prevent it being used.

4. The *NEWFILE* section allows the creation of, or overwriting the existing text file by, a new file with sequential control lines and intervening blank or dummy text lines (which can then be edited). This facility is not needed if direct-access text files can be readily edited on the computer itself, but is otherwise an important part of the Driver, allowing text exercises to be written on-line.

## THE FORTRAN VERSION OF THE MASTER DRIVER

The components of the Driver comprise, in the FORTRAN version, the following, which are given in the order in which they are printed in Appendix I. A magnetic tape or card deck of this whole program, plus the illustrative test program of Chapter 3 and the subroutines of Appendix III is available from the authors (see Appendix VI).

### 1. Essential components

| *Description* | *FORTRAN routine or subroutine name (all begin 'MAC')* | *Number of statements (excluding COMMON)* |
|---|---|---|
| START | MACRUN | 31 |
| MACAID | MACAID | 170 |
| INITIALIZE | MACINL | 73 |
| INPUT | MACINP | 23 |
| LOCATE | MACLOC | 15 |
| NUMBER | MACNUM | 39 |
| PRINT | MACPRN | 16 |
| | MACPRT | 35 |
| READ | MACRND | 10 |
| | Total | 412 |

## 2. Special purpose components

| Description | FORTRAN sub-routine name (all begin 'MC') | Number of statements (excluding COMMON) |
|---|---|---|
| QFRAME | MCQFR1 | 75 |
| | MCQFR2 | 68 |
| | MCQFR3* | 69 |
| MFRAME | MCMFRM | 137 |
| RETURN | MCRETN | 28 |
| SUBROUTINE | MCSUBR | 26 |
| DISPLAY | MCDISP | 40 |
| | Total | 443 |

* This subroutine is only needed if dictionaries are to be used with *Q-frames.

## 3. 'Authoring' and editing facilities

| Description | FORTRAN subroutine name (not beginning 'MAC' or 'MC') | Number of statements (excluding COMMON) |
|---|---|---|
| DIRECTORY | AUTHR1 | 95 |
| EDIT | AUTHR2 | 228 |
| RENUMBER | RENUM1 | 205 |
| | RENUM2 | 28 |
| NEWFILE | NEWFIL | 41 |
| | Total | 597 |
| | GRAND TOTAL | 1452 |

The functions of each part shown are described by comment lines in the source program (Appendix I) and by comments describing each subroutine.

## SUMMARY

The essential components of the Master Driver comprise:

## 1. Essential components, including the following sections:

START
MACAID (Main)
INITIALIZE (setting up)
INPUT
LOCATE
NUMBER
PRINT
READ
} (performing frequently needed operations)

**2. Special frame interpreters and display controllers:**

| | |
|---|---|
| QFRAME | (for *Q-frames) |
| MFRAME | (for *M-frames) |
| RETURN | (for *R-frames) |
| SUBROUTINES | (for *S-frames) |
| DISPLAY | (for cursor controls on visual display units) |

**3. 'Authoring' and editing facilities**

DIRECTORY (to create a directory)
EDIT (to control and edit on-line)
RENUMBER (to renumber and check a text file)
NEWFILE (to create a new, blank text file).

The corresponding FORTRAN subroutines are listed. All are available on magnetic tape from the authors (see Appendix VI).

# References

Abrahamson, S., Denson, J. S. and Wolf, R. M. (1969). Effectiveness of a simulator in training anesthesiology residents. *J. Med. Educ.*, **44**, 515–19

Aida, K., Minamikawa, T., Takai, Y., Fujimasa, I., Takasugi, S. and Miwa, T. (1977). A simulation model CAI system for diagnosis and treatment in cardiology. In Shires/Wolf (eds.) Proceedings *MEDINFO 77.* Pp. 841–845. (Amsterdam: North Holland)

Bloch, R., Sweeney, G., Ahmed, K., Dickinson, C. J. and Ingram, D. (1980). 'MacDope': A simulation of drug disposition in the human body. Applications in clinical pharmacokinetics. *Brit. J. clin. Pharmacol.* (in Press)

Deland, E. C. (1978). (ed.) *Information Technology in Health Science Education,* (New York: Plenum Press)

Deland, E. C., Winters, W. W., Dell, R. B. and Zuckerman, A. (1972). FLUIDMOD: A versatile CAI system for medical students. *In: Proceedings of the USA-Japan Computer Conference, Tokyo, October 1972.* (Am. Fed. Inf. Soc.)

Dickinson, C. J. (1977). *A Computer Model of Human Respiration.* (Lancaster: MTP Press)

Dickinson, C. J., Allen, L., Ingram, D. and Sinclair, J. (1980). A computer model of respiration and gas exchange in the premature infant. (submitted for publication)

Dickinson, C. J., Sackett, D. L. and Goldsmith, C. H. (1973). MacMan: A digital computer model for teaching some basic principles of haemodynamics. *J. Clin. Comput.*, **2**, 42–50

Dickinson, C. J. and Shephard, E. P. (1972). A digital computer model of the systemic circulation and kidneys, for studying renal and circulatory interactions involving electrolytes and body fluid compartments (MACPEE). *J. Physiol. (London)*, **216**, 11–12P

Forman, M. H., Pengov, R. E. and Burson, J. L. (1979). A network for sharing health care learning resources with Ohio health care facilities and educational institutions. In E. C. Deland (ed.) *Information Technology in Health Science Education* (New York: Plenum Press)

Gottlieb, G. L., Beers, R. F., Bernecker, C. and Samter, M. (1972). An approach to automation of medical interviews. *Comput. Biomed. Res.*, **5**, 99–107

Guyton, A. C., Coleman, T. G. and Grainger, H. J. (1972). Circulation: overall regulation. *Ann. Rev. Physiol.*, **34**, 13

Harless, W. G., Drennon, G. G., Marxer, J. J., Root, J. A. and Miller, E. E. (1971). CASE: A computer-aided simulation of the clinical encounter. *J. Med. Educ.*, **46**, 443–448

Harless, W. G., Drennon, G. G., Marxer, J. J., Root, J. A., Wilson, L. L. and Miller, G. E. (1973). GENESYS – A generating system for the CASE natural language model. *Comput. Biol. Med.*, **3**, 247–268.

Helppi, R. K., Macinnis, P. J., Sherwood, J. D. and Wolf, H. K. (1977). User frustration with poor program Design. *Comput. Biomed. Res.*, **10**, 319–321

Lucas, R. W., Mullin, P. J., Crean, G. P., Card, W. I. and Knill-Jones, R. P. (1977). The acceptability of computers for the interrogation of patients. *In: Proceedings MEDCOMP 1977.* Pp. 861–878. On-line Computers Ltd. (Uxbridge, England)

Murray, T. S. (1977). Developing methods of evaluation appropriate to the undergraduate teaching of general practice of Glasgow University. Ph.D. thesis, University of Glasgow

Rushby, N. J. (1979). *Introduction to Educational Computing.* (London: Croom Helm)

Seidel, R. J. and Rubin, M. (1975). (eds.) *Computing and Communications: Implications for Education.* (New York: Academic Press)

Senior, J. R. (1976). *Towards the Measurement of Competence in Medicine.* (Philadelphia: National Board of Medical Examiners)

Summerville, S., Evans, C. R., Pobgee, P. J. and Bevan, N. S. (1979) MICKIE – Experiences in taking histories from patients using a micro-processor. *In* B. Barber, F. Grémy, K. Uberla and G. Wagner (eds.) *Proceedings Medical Informatics Berlin*, pp. 713–722. (Berlin: Springer-Verlag)

Svedlow, D. B., Barnett, G. O., Grossman, J. H. and Souder, D. E. (1972). A simple programming system ('Driver') for the creation and execution of an automated medical history. *Comput. Biomed. Res.*, **5**, 90–98

Tidball, C. S. (1978). A digital computer simulation of cardiovascular and renal physiology. *Physiol. Teacher*, 37–42

USA Congress office of Technology Assessment (1979). *Computer Technology in Medical Education and Assessment.* (Washington, D.C.: U.S. Congress (OTA–BR–H–1))

Warner, H. R., Woolley, F. R. and Kane, R. L. (1974). Computer-assisted instruction for teaching clinical decision making. *Comput. Biomed. Res.*, **7**, 564–574

Weber, J. C. and Wagamen, W. D. (1972). ATS: A new system for computer-mediated tutorials in medical education. *J. Med. Educ.*, **47**, 637–644

# Appendices

# Appendix I

## THE COMPLETE FORTRAN PROGRAM OF THE MASTER DRIVER.

```
C    M A C A I D (MCMASTER COMPUTER-ASSISTED INSTRUCTIONAL DRIVER)
C                    MCMASTER         AHMED      INGRAM    & DICKINSON
C      VERSION 80.27 -  1 FEBRUARY 1980
C
C    A GENERALIZED FORTRAN DRIVER FOR COMPUTER AIDED INSTRUCTION
C    OR INTERROGATION (CAI)
C    AUTHORS : DR.K.AHMED
C              COMPUTER SERVICES UNIT, HEALTH SCIENCES CENTRE,
C              MCMASTER UNIVERSITY, HAMILTON, ONT., CANADA, LBS 4J9
C            : DR.D.INGRAM AND DR.C.J.DICKINSON
C              DEPT. OF MEDICINE, ST. BARTHOLOMEW'S HOSPITAL MEDICAL
C              COLLEGE, WEST SMITHFIELD, LONDON, EC1A 7BE, ENGLAND.
C
C* N.B. ALL LOCAL ARRANGEMENTS WHICH OTHER USERS MIGHT NEED TO
C*       CHANGE ARE PRECEDED BY A COMMENT CARD BEGINNING WITH 'C*'.
C*       THE NUMBER OF STARS REFERS TO THE TYPE OF CHANGE,
C*       AS FOLLOWS:
C
C**** FOUR STARS COMMENT CARD INDICATES SOME LOCAL ARRANGEMENT
C      FOR CURSOR POSITIONING ON THE DISPLAY SCREEN, OR
C      INSTRUCTIONS FOR OPERATING AN EXTERNAL DEVICE (E.G.
C      A SLIDE PROJECTOR)
C
C*** THREE STARS INDICATES SOME GENERAL LOCAL ARRANGEMENT -
C     E.G. 'RETURN', 'ESCAPE' KEY TO BE PRESSED, SIZE OF STORE
C     ARRAYS, FILE LENGTH, LOGICAL UNIT DEVICES, ETC.
C
C** ALL ANSWER FILE 'WRITE (KA' STATEMENTS ARE PRECEDED BY A 2-STAR
C    COMMENT CARD BEGINNING WITH 'C** ', SO THAT USERS WISHING TO
C    CHANGE OUTPUT FILE ARRANGEMENTS CAN EASILY LOCATE THESE LINES.
C    IN PARTICULAR, SOME COMPUTERS MAY NOT NEED A 'CARRIAGE CONTROL'
C    CHARACTER IN THE FIRST POSITION OF A FORMAT STATEMENT
C
C* FOR FORTRAN COMPILERS ALLOWING CHARACTER DESIGNATION,
C  CHARACTER STRINGS ARE SHOWN AS ALTERNATIVES TO SOME INTEGER
C  VARIABLES PRECEDED BY A 1-STAR COMMENT CARD BEGINNING WITH 'C* '.
C  IF CHARACTER TYPE STATEMENTS ARE USED, THE INTEGERS
C  REDESIGNATED SHOULD BE REMOVED FROM THE INTEGER TYPE STATEMENTS
C
C=======================================================================C
C    NOTE ON MACHINE-DEPENDENT FEATURES:                                C
C    APART FROM THE FILE ATTACH OR DEFINE INSTRUCTIONS (WHICH FOLLOW)   C
C    THERE IS ONLY ONE FEATURE OF FORTRAN USED IN MACAID THAT MUST BE   C
C    AVAILABLE FOR USE. THIS IS THE DIRECT-ACCESS (OR RANDOM-ACCESS)    C
C    READ/WRITE ON A FIXED-LENGTH DISC FILE (IN THIS VERSION 72-COLUMN) C
C                                                                       C
C    A DIRECT-ACCESS READ OR WRITE ON FILE 'KF' AT ADDRESS 'N' IS:      C
C          READ (KF'N,100) X,Y,Z        WRITE (KF'N,100) .. ETC.        C
C    100   FORMAT (.......) ,  ETC.                                     C
```

MAIN PROGRAM
CONTINUED

```
C                                                                          C
C   THIS, OR EQUIVALENT PROCEDURE, IS AN ESSENTIAL FEATURE OF MACAID,      C
C   AND IS EXTENSIVELY USED THROUGHOUT THE PROGRAM                         C
C                                                                          C
C   THE ANSWER FILE 'KA' IS ONLY NEEDED IF SELECTED FRAME NUMBERS AND      C
C   ANSWERS TO QUESTIONS ARE TO BE KEPT FOR LATER ANALYSIS -               C
C   OTHERWISE THE FILE SHOULD BE DUMMY, OR THE 'WRITE' STATEMENTS          C
C   REMOVED                                                                C
C                                                                          C
C==========================================================================C
C   LOGICAL FILE UNITS USED IN THIS PROGRAM ARE:                           C
C   KF = TEXTFILE (CARD IMAGES DISC FILE, ALLOWING RANDOM ACCESS)          C
C   KA = ANSWER FILE TO COLLECT ANSWERS, WHEN REQUIRED (NOT PRINTED)       C
C   INI = INPUT FILE (TERMINAL)                                            C
C   KT = OUTPUT FILE (TERMINAL)                                            C
C   KL = OUTPUT FILE (LINEPRINTER OR TERMINAL)                             C
C         (THIS DEVICE IS NOT USED IN THE MASTER DRIVER, BUT 'KL' IS       C
C          EXTENSIVELY USED WITHIN SIMULATION MODELS, WHICH MAY BE         C
C          ATTACHED, TO RUN OFF LONG RUNS ON A LINEPRINTER)                C
C   (KN) - NOT A BLANK COMMON VARIABLE LINE THE OTHERS ABOVE, BUT IS       C
C          USED (OPTIONALLY) IN ONE PLACE ONLY (S/R AUTHR2) TO MAKE A      C
C          COMPLETE SPACED LISTING OF THE TEXT FILE.  'KN' SHOULD BE       C
C          SET IN THIS SUBROUTINE TO 7, OR TO THE LOGICAL UNIT NUMBER      C
C          OF THE LINEPRINTER                                              C
C==========================================================================C
C*** LOCAL ARRANGEMENT FOR FILE ATTACH MAY BE NEEDED HERE
C     ATTACH FILE 3 (DIRECT ACCESS)
C     ATTACH FILE 4 (OUTPUT)
C*
C     CHARACTER AUTHR(5),PASSW(5),BUF(72),KWDS,BLANK
C     CHARACTER ATTACH*50
      INTEGER AUTHR(5),PASSW(5),BUF(72),BLANK
      INTEGER FLAG,SCORE
C STANDARD BLANK COMMON BLOCK, AS USED IN ALL MCMASTER SIMULATION MODELS
C KT,KL,INI ARE OUTPUT AND INPUT DEVICES (SEE BELOW).
C NW1 TO NEOF ARE USED TO OPERATE FREE-FORMAT INPUT USING
C AN INPUT SUBROUTINE (NXTWD), WHICH IS STANDARD IN MCMASTER MODELS
C NPRT IS USED IN THE MODELS AS A PRINT SUPPRESSION INDEX
      COMMON KT,KL,INI,NW1,NW2,JKL,NPRT,LDISP,KA,ITRIG(73),NEOF
      COMMON /FLS/ KF,LADRS,NPP,NNST,NNEND,MODE,FLAG,ION,SCORE,AION,SUM
C*** LOCAL ARRANGEMENTS
C ARRAY KEY(2,250) CONTROLS MAXIMUM NUMBER OF CONTROL *-FRAMES WHICH
C CAN BE HANDLED BY THE DIRECTORY OR DURING RENUMBERING (I.E. 250)
      COMMON /TABLE/ NTOT,NKA,NFR,KYMAX,KEY(2,250),NDFR(14)
      COMMON /GLB/ NG,NGFR,KWDS(6,5),KNUM(6)
C*** LOCAL ARRANGEMENTS TO DEFINE AUTHOR AND PASSWORD CODES (5-LETTER)
C* IN FORTRAN 77, THE DATA STATEMENTS AND 'RECOGNITION' DO LOOPS
C  COULD BE MUCH SIMPLIFIED
      DATA AUTHR/'A','U','T','H','O'/
      DATA PASSW/'P','A','S','S','W'/
C*** LOCAL ARRANGEMENTS FOR DIRECT ACCESS FILE DEFINITION/ATTACHMENTS
C    AND ATTACHMENT OF AN ANSWER FILE
      DEFINE FILE 3(440,72,E,NPP)
C    OPEN NECESSARY FILES
C     ATTACH[50:1]=:15C
C     ATTACH[1:49]='FILE FTN03=TEXT,OLD;SHR'
C     CALL COMMAND(ATTACH,I,J)
C     ATTACH[1:49]='FILE FTN04=CHAP,OLD'
C     CALL COMMAND(ATTACH,I,J)
C     ATTACH[1:49]='FILE FTN07;DEV=LP;CCTL'
C     CALL COMMAND(ATTACH,I,J)
C INITIATE MACAID
C
C*** LOCAL ARRANGEMENTS FOR LOGICAL UNIT NUMBERS
C SET LOGICAL UNITS (INI=INPUT, KT AND KL=OUTPUTS (KT=CONSOLE,
C KL=LINEPRINTER IF AVAILABLE), KF=TEXT FILE - DIRECT ACCESS,
C KA=ANSWER FILE FOR RECORDING SELECTED REPLIES TO QUESTIONS)
      INI=5
      KT=6
```

MAIN PROGRAM
CONTINUED

```
      KL=6
      KF=3
      KA=4
C*** KYMAX IS THE LIMIT TO NUMBER OF CONTROL FRAMES BEGINNING WITH '*-'
C AND SHOULD BE THE SAME AS THE 2ND DIMENSION OF ARRAY 'KEY' IN
C LABELLED COMMON /TABLE/
      KYMAX=250
C
C INSTRUCT DRIVER TO LOOK FOR *B FRAME IN FIRST RECORD OF FILE
C
C*** LOCAL ARRANGEMENTS - IF A LARGE FILE OF TEXT IS TO BE USED
C WITH SUCCESSIVE EXERCISES, EXTRA CODE WILL BE NEEDED TO SELECT THE
C NUMBER OF THE EXERCISE, AND TO SET NNST TO THE CORRECT POSITION
C IN THE FILE TO START EACH PARTICULAR TEXT EXERCISE.  IT IS HIGHLY
C DESIRABLE IF POSSIBLE TO SET NNEND TO THE LINE NUMBER OF THE LAST
C RECORD IN THE FILE, TO GIVE WARNING OF EXTENDING THE FILE BEYOND
C ITS END.  ALTERNATIVELY, NNEND OF ONE SECTION CAN = NNST OF THE NEXT,
C OR NNEND COULD BE DEFINED AS COMING A FEW LINES AFTER THE END OF THE
C DIRECTORY, IN WHICH CASE IT COULD BE SET IN SUBROUTINE MACINL
C
      NNST=1
      NNEND=440
C SET UP 'AUTHO(R)' (OR OTHER MASTER WORD) AS A GLOBAL KEYWORD
      NG=1
      DO 10 I = 1,5
   10 KWDS(1,I)=AUTHR(I)
      KNUM(1)=0
      WRITE (KT,20)
C*** LOCAL ARRANGEMENTS FOR INPUT OF REPLIES (E.G. RETURN, ESCAPE, ETC.)
   20 FORMAT (1X,'TO START, TYPE   GO   , THEN PRESS *RETURN* KEY')
C IF 'PASSW' ENTERED AT THIS POINT, MODE=1; OTHERWISE MODE=2
      MODE=2
      CALL MACINP (BUF,X,NFLG)
      DO 30 I = 1,5
      IF (BUF(I).NE.PASSW(I)) GO TO 40
   30 CONTINUE
      MODE=1
   40 NTERM=0
C**** LOCAL ARRANGEMENTS - IF CURSOR CONTROLS OR EXTERNAL
C     CONTROLS ARE WANTED, NEXT 5 STATEMENTS WILL BE NEEDED TO
C     IDENTIFY TYPE OF TERMINAL IN USE  - OTHERWISE DELETE ALL
      WRITE (KT,50)
   50 FORMAT (1X,'TYPE  1  FOR THE HEWLETT-PACKARD TERMINALS,',/,
     X 1X,'TYPE  2  FOR ALL OTHER VISUAL DISPLAY UNITS,',/,
     X 1X,'OTHERWISE JUST PRESS THE *RETURN* KEY')
      CALL MACINP (BUF,X,NFLG)
      IF (IFIX(X).EQ.1) NTERM=1
C     IF (IFIX(X).EQ.2) NTERM=2
      CALL MACAID (NTERM)
      STOP
      END
```

SUBROUTINE MACAID

```
      SUBROUTINE MACAID (NTERM)
C
C THIS IS THE ACTUAL DRIVER
C*
C     CHARACTER TYPE,BLANK,STAR,BUF(72),TPLST(10),KWDS
      INTEGER TYPE,BLANK,STAR,BUF(72),TPLST(10)
      INTEGER FLAG,SCORE,TRACE
      COMMON KT,KL,INI,NW1,NW2,JKL,NPRT,LDISP,KA,ITRIG(73),NEOF
      COMMON /FLS/ KF,LADRS,NPP,NNST,NNEND,MODE,FLAG,ION,SCORE,AION,SUM
      COMMON /TABLE/ NTOT,NKA,NFR,KYMAX,KEY(2,250),NDFR(14)
      COMMON /GLB/ NG,NGFR,KWDS(6,5),KNUM(6)
      EQUIVALENCE (BUF(2),TYPE)
      DATA TPLST/'S','A','F','I','T','R','E','M','Q','Z'/
      DATA STAR,BLANK/'*',' '/
C
C======================= INITIALIZATION ================================
C SCORE STARTS AT 100. SCORE SWITCH IS ION (1=ON, 0=OFF)
   10 SCORE=100
      ION=0
C SUM STARTS AT 0.  SUM SWITCH IS AION (1=ON, 0=OFF)
      SUM =0.
      AION=0.
C TRACE IS A FLAG TO ENABLE TRACING PATH THROUGH FRAMES (1=ON, 0=OFF)
      TRACE=0
C START COUNTER FOR NUMBERS OF CONTROL FRAMES IN THE TEXT FILE
      NTOT=0
C NKA IS A SWITCH TO RECORD ANSWERS ON ANSWER FILE (1=ON, 0=OFF)
      NKA=0
C READ IN DIRECTORY AND FIND STARTING FRAME # NSTRT
      CALL MACINL (NSTRT)
C NFR=NEXT FRAME NUMBER, LASTF=LAST FRAME NUMBER
C FLAG CAN BE 1 TO 11 - SET = 1(DEFAULT VALUE)
   20 NFR=NSTRT
      LASTF=NFR
      FLAG=1
C SET COUNTER FOR NUMBER OF 'GLOBAL' KEYWORD FRAME NUMBERS
      NGFR=0
C IF IN 'AUTHOR MODE' GO TO S/R AUTHR2 BEFORE STARTING
      IF (MODE-1) 780,780,70
C===============CHECKS AND ERRORS SECTION===============================
C SAVE PREVIOUS FRAME NUMBER IN CASE NO ADEQUATE ADDRESS SUPPLIED
   30 LASTF=NFR
      NFR=IFIX(FR)
      IF (NFR) 40,60,70
C GLOBAL KEYWORD WAS ENTERED, BRANCH TO FRAME NGFR (SEE SUBR. MACINP)
   40 IF (NGFR) 780,780,50
   50 NFR=NGFR
      GO TO 70
C ZERO FRAME - USE PREVIOUS FRAME
   60 NFR=LASTF
C TURN OFF OUTPUT FILE ANSWERS INDEX
   70 NKA=0
C WRITE TRACING INFORMATION IF SWITCH IS ON (TRACE=1)
      IF (TRACE-1) 100,80,100
C================== PROCESS CURRENT FRAME NUMBER NFR ===================
   80 WRITE (KT,90) LASTF,NFR,FLAG,ION,SCORE,AION,SUM
   90 FORMAT (1X,'*LAST=',I5,2X,'CURR=',I5,2X,'FLAG=',I2,2X,'SCORE(',I1,
     X ')=',I3,2X,'TOTAL(',F2.0,')=',F8.1)
C LOCATE ADDRESS OF THE CURRENT FRAME ON TEXTFILE
  100 CALL MACLOC (IADRS)
      IF (IADRS) 110,110,130
  110 WRITE (KT,120) NFR,LASTF
  120 FORMAT (1X,'*** FRAME #',I5,'(CALLED FROM #',I5,') NOT FOUND - PLE
     XASE REPORT')
      IF (MODE.EQ.1) GO TO 780
      STOP
C READ CONTROL LINE OF THE FRAME FROM TEXTFILE
C NPP IS POINTER TO THE LINE NUMBER OF THE TEXTFILE
  130 NPP=IADRS
```

SUBROUTINE MACAID
CONTINUED

```
C READ CONTROL LINE NPP INTO ARRAY 'BUF'
      CALL MACRND (BUF,IERR)
C CHECK FRAME TYPE
      DO 140 N = 1,10
      IF (TYPE.EQ.TPLST(N)) GO TO 160
  140 CONTINUE
      WRITE (KT,150) TYPE,NFR
  150 FORMAT (1X,'*** FRAME *',A1,I5,' ILLEGAL - PLEASE REPORT')
      IF (MODE.EQ.1) GO TO 780
      STOP
C============ PROCESS DISPLAY CODE AND SCORE FOR THIS FRAME ============
C  SKIP OVER FRAME NO. AND LEAVE POINTER (IP) AT THE FIRST NON-BLANK
C  CHARACTER AFTER THE FRAME NUMBER
  160 IP=3
      CALL MACNUM (BUF,IP,X,NFLG,R)
C RECORD DISPLAY INSTRUCTION INTEGER
      CALL MACNUM (BUF,IP,X,NFLG,R)
      LDISP=IFIX(X)
C**** LOCAL ARRANGEMENTS - IF THE POSSIBILITY EXISTS, AND IS WANTED,
C OF STRUCTURED SCREEN DISPLAY, THE 1ST PARAMETER (LDISP) CAN BE USED AT
C THIS POINT TO POSITION THE CURSOR OR FOR EXTERNAL CONTROLS, EG.
C OF A SLIDE PROJECTOR.  ALL THESE ARE BEST DONE BY S/R MCDISP.
C IF THIS IS NOT POSSIBLE OR WANTED, NEXT LINE COULD BE DELETED
C AND SUBROUTINE MCDISP COULD BE REMOVED.  NTERM GIVES TYPE OF TERMINAL
C IN USE.  2ND ARGUMENT (=1) MEANS: 'ACT ON THE 1ST DIGIT OF LDISP'
      IF (NTERM.GT.0) CALL MCDISP (NTERM,1)
C READ SCORE INTEGER
      CALL MACNUM (BUF,IP,SCR,NFLG,R)
C IF SCR INDEX IS 2., SWITCH ON OUTPUT FILE RECORDER (NKA=1)
      IF (SCR-2.) 180,170,180
  170 NKA=1
      GO TO 280
C IF SCR INDEX = 1., RECORD FRAME NUMBER ON OUTPUT FILE
  180 IF (SCR-1.) 210,190,210
C** WRITE ON OUTPUT FILE
  190 WRITE (KA,200) BUF(2),NFR
  200 FORMAT (1X,A1,I5)
      GO TO 280
C UPDATE SCORE
  210 IXX=IFIX(SCR)
      IF (IXX) 270,280,220
  220 IF (IXX.GT.7) IXX=7
C SEE COMMENTS IN T-FRAME HANDLING LATER FOR THE NEXT BRANCH
      GO TO (280,280,260,240,250,230,280), IXX
  230 SCORE=100
  240 ION=1
      GO TO 280
  250 SCORE=100
      GO TO 280
  260 ION=0
      GO TO 280
C IF SCR WAS NEGATIVE, ADD IT TO TOTAL SCORE
  270 SCORE=SCORE+SCR*ION
C PREVENT SCORE EVER GOING NEGATIVE
  280 IF (SCORE) 290,300,300
  290 SCORE=0
C PRINT SCORE, IF 'SCORE' PARAMETER = 7
  300 IF (IXX.EQ.7) WRITE (KT,310) SCORE
  310 FORMAT (1X,'YOUR SCORE IS ',I3,/)
C SAVE LINE POINTER IN CASE NPP GETS CHANGED LATER
      NPPX=NPP
C======== PRINT TEXT FROM THIS FRAME (EXCEPT S & A-FRAMES) =============
      IF (N-2) 330,330,320
  320 I=NFR
      CALL MACPRN (IADRS)
C RESTORE ORIGINAL FRAME NUMBER IN CASE '/USE' HAS ALTERED IT
      NFR=I
C READ 'ADD' PARAMETER, EXCEPT FOR *E, *M AND *Q FRAMES
  330 IF (N.LT.7) CALL MACNUM (BUF,IP,ADD,NFLG,R)
```

```
SUBROUTINE MACAID
CONTINUED

C
C  BRANCH TO THE APPROPRIATE SECTION TO EXECUTE THE FRAME.
      GO TO (570,430,580,610,340,670,650,420,410,660), N
C       TYPES: S , A , F , I , T , R , E , M , Q , Z  RESPECTIVELY
C=====================================================================
C  FRAME TYPE: T(EXT)
C  *T  NFR  LDISP  SCR  ADD  FR
C     NFR - REFERENCE NUMBER OF THE FRAME
C     LDISP - USER DEFINED 4-DIGIT INTEGER TO CONTROL DISPLAY
C           TYPE AND POSITION.  UNLESS NTERM>0 THIS HAS NO ACTION
C     SCR - IF NEGATIVE:  INTEGER TO BE ADDED TO 'SCORE'
C           IF ZERO        0= NO CHANGE OF SCORE, NO RECORDING OF OUTPUT
C           IF POSITIVE (+)1= WRITE FRAME NUMBER ON OUTPUT FILE
C                          2= WRITE FRAME NUMBER ON OUTPUT FILE, AND
C                             ALSO COLLECT FREE TEXT, TERMINATING AS
C                             SOON AS A BLANK LINE IS ENTERED
C                          3= TURN OFF SCORER, LEAVE SCORE UNCHANGED
C                          4= TURN ON SCORER, LEAVE SCORE UNCHANGED
C                          5= RESET SCORE TO 100 WITHOUT PRINTING
C                          6= SET SCORE TO 100, AND TURN ON SCORER
C                          7 (OR >7)= PRINT SCORE
C     ADD - IF POSITIVE:  AMOUNT TO BE ADDED TO 'SUM'
C           IF ZERO        0= PROMPT NEEDED BEFORE GOING TO NEXT FRAME
C           IF NEGATIVE   -1 (OR ANY NUMBER OTHER THAN ZERO) =  NO PROMPT
C                             NEEDED BEFORE GOING TO NEXT FRAME
C                         -3= TURN OFF ADDER, LEAVE SUM UNCHANGED
C                         -4= TURN ON ADDER, LEAVE SUM UNCHANGED
C                         -5= RESET SUM TO ZERO, WITHOUT PRINTING
C                         -6= RESET SUM TO ZERO, AND TURN ON ADDER
C                         -7 (OR <-7)= PRINT SUM
C     FR = NEXT FRAME TO BE EXECUTED
C
  340 CALL MACNUM (BUF,IP,FR,NFLG,R)
C CONTROL INSTRUCTIONS FROM SCR (FREE INPUT=2) AND FROM ADD:
C PAUSE IF ADD=0,  OR SIMPLY JUMP TO THE NEXT FRAME IF ADD=NEGATIVE
      IF (SCR-2.) 350,380,350
  350 IF (ADD) 670,360,670
  360 WRITE (KT,370)
C*** LOCAL ARRANGEMENTS FOR PROMPT ('RETURN', 'ESCAPE' ETC.)
  370 FORMAT (1X,'PRESS *RETURN*')
      CALL MACINP (BUF,X,NFLG)
      IF (NFLG) 670,670,40
C ACCEPT ANY NO. OF LINES - BRANCH TO THE NEXT FRAME ON A BLANK LINE
  380 CALL MACINP (BUF,X,NFLG)
      IF (NFLG) 390,390,40
  390 IF (BUF(1).EQ.BLANK) GO TO 670
C** WRITE ON OUTPUT FILE
      WRITE (KA,400) (BUF(I),I=1,63)
  400 FORMAT (10X,63A1)
      GO TO 380
C=====================================================================
C  FRAME TYPE: Q(UESTION)
C
C     SEE SUBROUTINE MCQFR1 FOR PARAMETERS
C
  410 CALL MCQFR1 (BUF,IP,FR,NPPX,NTERM)
      IF (MODE) 30,780,30
C=====================================================================
C  FRAME TYPE: M(ARKING) OR M(ULTIPLE CHOICE)
C
C     SEE SUBROUTINE MCMFRM FOR PARAMETERS
C
  420 CALL MCMFRM (BUF,IP,FR,NPPX,NTERM)
      IF (MODE) 30,780,30
C=====================================================================
C  FRAME TYPE: A(NSWER) - WRITES TEXT ON ANSWER FILE (KA)
C  *A  NFR  LDISP  SCR  N  FR
C     NFR - REFERENCE NUMBER OF THE FRAME
C     LDISP - DISPLAY CODE IN *A-FRAME IS USED AS FOLLOWS:
```

```
SUBROUTINE MACAID
CONTINUED

C                  0 = WRITE NEXT LINE(S) OF TEXT FILE ONTO ANSWER FILE
C                 >0 = WRITE FROM TEXT FILE LDISP LINES AFTER LAST LINE
C                      OF DIRECTORY (LADRS) ONTO ANSWER FILE
C      SCR - SCORE OR INSTRUCTION (SEE ABOVE UNDER FRAME 'T(EXT)')
C      N - IF NEGATIVE: -1 = WRITE SCORE ON ANSWER FILE,
C                       -2 = WRITE SUM ON ANSWER FILE
C          IF POSITIVE: (+)N = WRITE N LINES FROM THE TEXT FILE, STARTING
C                              AT ADDRESS (LADRS+LDISP), ON ANSWER FILE
C      FR - FRAME NUMBER OF THE NEXT FRAME
C
  430 CALL MACNUM (BUF,IP,FR,NFLG,R)
      N=IFIX(ADD)
      IF (LDISP) 440,440,490
  440 IF (N+1) 450,470,550
C** WRITE SUM OR SCORE ON ANSWER FILE (KA)
  450 WRITE (KA,460) SUM
  460 FORMAT (10X,'TOTAL=',F9.2)
      GO TO 30
C** WRITE ON OUTPUT FILE
  470 WRITE (KA,480) SCORE
  480 FORMAT (10X,'SCORE=',I4)
      GO TO 30
  490 NPP=LADRS+LDISP
      IF (NPP+N-NNEND) 520,520,500
  500 WRITE (KT,510) NFR
  510 FORMAT (1X,'*** FRAME *A',I5,' ATTEMPTS TO READ OFF END-OF-FILE')
      IF (MODE.EQ.1) GO TO 780
      STOP
  520 DO 530 IP = 1,N
      CALL MACRND (BUF,IERR)
C** WRITE FROM END-OF-TEXT (WORK AREA) ONTO OUTPUT FILE
  530 WRITE (KA,540) (BUF(I),I=1,72)
  540 FORMAT (1X,72A1)
      GO TO 30
C WRITE TEXT LINE(S) ONTO OUTPUT FILE
  550 CALL MACRND (BUF,IERR)
      IF (BUF(1).EQ.STAR) GO TO 30
C** WRITE ON OUTPUT FILE
      WRITE (KA,560) (BUF(I),I=1,65)
  560 FORMAT (8X,65A1)
      GO TO 550
C=========================================================================
C  FRAME TYPE: S(UBROUTINE)
C  *S  NFR  LDISP  SCR  NSUB  FR
C      NFR - REFERENCE NUMBER OF THE FRAME
C      LDISP - DISPLAY CODE (SEE ABOVE UNDER FRAME '*T(EXT)')
C      SCR -  SCORE OR INSTRUCTIONS (SEE ABOVE)
C      NSUB - IDENTIFICATION NUMBER FOR THE SUBROUTINE
C      FR - FRAME NUMBER OF THE NEXT FRAME
C
  570 NSUB=IFIX(ADD)
      CALL MCSUBR (NSUB,NTERM)
      CALL MACNUM (BUF,IP,FR,NFLG,R)
      IF (MODE) 30,780,30
C=========================================================================
C  FRAME TYPE: F(LAG)
C  *F  NFR  LDISP  SCR  FLAG  FR
C        NFR - REFERENCE NUMBER OF THE FRAME
C        LDISP - DISPLAY CODE (SEE ABOVE)
C        SCR - SCORE (SEE ABOVE)
C        FLAG - INTEGER CODE (INTEGER BETWEEN 0 AND 11)
C          SETS 'FLAG' TO THE SPECIFIED VALUE.  IF FLAG =  0, SETS
C          VALUE OF FLAG ACCORDING TO CURRENT SCORE
C        FR - FRAME NUMBER OF NEXT FRAME
C
  580 FLAG=IFIX(ADD)
      IF (FLAG) 590,590,600
C FLAG READ AS ZERO -
C IF SCORE=100, FLAG=1; IF S=90, FLAG=2; IF S=80, FLAG=3, ETC.
```

SUBROUTINE MACAID
CONTINUED

```
  590 FLAG=INT(11.5-FLOAT(SCORE)*.1)
  600 CALL MACNUM (BUF,IP,FR,NFLG,R)
      GO TO 30
C=========================================================================
C  FRAME TYPE : I(F)
C  *I NFR  LDISP  SCR  ADD  FR1  FR2  FR3  ..  ..  ..  ..  ETC.
C        NFR - REFERENCE NUMBER OF THE FRAME
C        LDISP - DISPLAY CODE (SEE ABOVE)
C        SCR - SCORE (SEE ABOVE)
C        ADD - SUM TO BE ADDED (SEE ABOVE)
C        FR(S) - ADDRESSES
C          CHECK THE CURRENT VALUE OF THE FLAG AND
C          BRANCH TO ONE OF THE FRAMES SPECIFIED IN THE LIST
C
  610 DO 620 I = 1,FLAG
      CALL MACNUM (BUF,IP,FR,NFLG,R)
      IF (NFLG) 630,620,620
  620 CONTINUE
      GO TO 350
  630 WRITE (KT,640) NFR,FLAG
  640 FORMAT (1X,'*** NOT ENOUGH ADDRESSES FOR *I',I5,' FRAME - PLEASE R
     XEPORT',/,5X,'FLAG =',I4)
      IF (MODE.EQ.1) GO TO 780
      STOP
C=========================================================================
C  FRAME TYPE: E(ND)
C  *E  NFR  (LDISP)
C     LAST FRAME - STOPS THE DRIVER, AFTER PRINTING TEXT;
C        NFR - REFERENCE NUMBER OF THE FRAME
C        LDISP - DISPLAY CODE (SEE ABOVE - OPTIONAL)
C
  650 RETURN
C=========================================================================
C  FRAME TYPE: Z - USER DEFINED, MAKE IT WHAT YOU LIKE
  660 CONTINUE
      GO TO 670
C=========================================================================
C  FRAME TYPE: R(ETURN TEXT) - CALLED WITHIN SUBROUTINE MCRETN
C                              IN ASSOCIATION WITH MCQFR1 AND MCMFRM
C                              OR DIRECTLY FROM MCQFR1
C  *R  NFR  (LDISP)  (SCR)  (ADD)
C        NFR - REFERENCE NUMBER OF THE FRAME
C        LDISP - DISPLAY CODE (SEE ABOVE) - DISPLAY POSITION NORMALLY
C              CONTROLLED WITHIN SUBROUTINES MCMFRM AND MCQFR1
C        SCR - SCORE (SEE ABOVE - OPTIONAL PARAMETER - BUT IF
C              IT IS TO BE USED, THEN 'LDISP' MUST ALSO BE SPECIFIED
C              TO PREVENT AMBIGUITY)
C        ADD - ADD (SEE ABOVE - OPTIONAL PARAMETER - BUT IF
C              IT IS TO BE USED, THEN 'LDISP' AND 'SCR' MUST ALSO BE
C              SPECIFIED TO PREVENT AMBIGUITY)
C
C        AS THERE IS NO EXIT ADDRESS, AN *R FRAME CALLED FROM
C        SUBROUTINE MCQFR1 WILL RETURN CONTROL TO THAT FRAME AGAIN
C        (AFTER PRINTING THE TEXT OF THE FRAME)
C=========================================================================
C UPDATE SUM BY ADDING 'ADD', AFTER CHECKING FOR CONTROL INSTRUCTIONS
  670 IXX=-IFIX(ADD)
      IF (IXX) 750,750,680
  680 IF (IXX.GT.7) IXX=7
C TO UNDERSTAND THIS BRANCHING SEE COMMENTS IN T-FRAME HANDLING
      GO TO (760,760,720,700,710,690,730), IXX
  690 SUM=0.
  700 AION=1.
      GO TO 760
  710 SUM=0.
      GO TO 760
  720 AION=0.
      GO TO 760
  730 WRITE (KT,740) SUM
```

```
SUBROUTINE MACAID
CONTINUED

  740 FORMAT (1X,'PRESENT TOTAL IS',F9.1)
      GO TO 760
  750 SUM=SUM+ADD
  760 ADD=0.
C IF *R(ETURN) FRAME CALLED, USE LAST FRAME NUMBER
      IF (N-6) 30,770,30
  770 IF (FR.GT.0.) GO TO 60
      WRITE (KT,370)
      CALL MACINP (BUF,X,NFLG)
      GO TO 60
C=========================================================================
C    'AUTHOR' WAS DETECTED ON INPUT -  CALL SUBROUTINE 'AUTHR2'
C (NOTE: THIS CALL CAN BE DELETED WITHOUT ANY ALTERATION TO THE
C  DRIVER, EXCEPT THE LOSS OF AUTHORING CAPABILITIES)
  780 FR=FLOAT(LASTF)
C NEXT ONLY NEEDED FOR AUTHORING FACILITIES
      CALL AUTHR2 (TRACE,FR)
C IF 'STOP' REQUESTED DURING AUTHORING, RETURN TO MAIN PROGRAM
      IF (ION) 650,790,790
  790 IF (FR) 30,10,30
      END
```

SUBROUTINE MACINL

```
      SUBROUTINE MACINL (NSTRT)
C
C  READS DIRECTORY CONTROL FRAME NUMBERS AND LOCATIONS OF CONTROL
C  FRAMES AND DICTIONARIES (IF ANY) INTO ARRAY 'KEY',
C  AND STORES GLOBAL KEY WORDS AND ADDRESSES
C*
C     CHARACTER BLANK,YY,QUOTE,BB,GG,STAR,BUF(72),KWDS
      INTEGER BLANK,YY,QUOTE,BB,GG,STAR,BUF(72)
      INTEGER FLAG,SCORE
      COMMON KT,KL,INI,NW1,NW2,JKL,NPRT,LDISP,KA,ITRIG(73),NEOF
      COMMON /FLS/ KF,LADRS,NPP,NNST,NNEND,MODE,FLAG,ION,SCORE,AION,SUM
      COMMON /TABLE/ NTOT,NKA,NFR,KYMAX,KEY(2,250),NDFR(14)
      COMMON /GLB/ NG,NGFR,KWDS(6,5),KNUM(6)
      DATA YY,BB,GG,QUOTE,BLANK,STAR/'Y','B','G',1H','  ','*'/
C
C LOCATE THE '*B-FRAME' - IT SHOULD BE AT ADDRESS NNST (USUALLY LINE 1,
C EXCEPT IN COMPOUND FILES).
C IF NOT, GIVE OPTION OF REMAKING FILE, IF S/R 'AUTHR1' AND 'NEWFIL'
C ARE ATTACHED.  LADRS=ADDRESS OF RECORD CONTAINING THE VALUE OF NTOT.
C THE TABLE OF ADDRESSES (KEY) IS STORED STARTING AT ADDRESS LADRS+1
C
      NFILE=0
   10 NPP=NNST
      CALL MACRND (BUF,IERR)
   20 FORMAT (72A1)
C IF FILE IS EMPTY GIVE OPTION OF CREATING A BLANK BUT FUNCTIONAL FILE
      IF (BUF(1).EQ.STAR.AND.BUF(2).EQ.BB) GO TO 30
      WRITE (KT,250)
      IF (MODE.NE.1) STOP
      NFILE=-1
      GO TO 40
C LOCATED *B-FRAME - GET STARTING FRAME NUMBER AND ADDRESS OF DIRECTORY
   30 IP=3
      CALL MACNUM (BUF,IP,X,NFLG,R)
      NSTRT=IFIX(X)
      CALL MACNUM (BUF,IP,X,NFLG,R)
      LADRS=IFIX(X)
      IF (MODE-1) 40,40,60
C*** LOCAL ARRANGEMENTS - NEXT ONLY NEEDED FOR AUTHORING FACILITIES
   40 CALL AUTHR1 (NSTRT,NFILE)
      IF (MODE-1) 50,130,130
C  READ THE DIRECTORY FROM THE TEXT FILE (STARTING AT 'LADRS')
   50 MODE=1
   60 NPP=LADRS
C*** LOCAL DIRECT ACCESS FILE ARRANGEMENTS
      READ (KF'NPP,70,ERR=240) NTOT
   70 FORMAT (8(I4,I5))
      N=(NTOT-1)/8+1
C DETECT INADEQUATE DIRECTORY SPACE ALLOCATION
      IF (LADRS+N+1-NNEND) 80,80,240
   80 DO 110 I = 1,N
      L2=I*8
      L1=L2-7
      IF (NTOT-L2) 90,100,100
   90 L2=NTOT
  100 LADRS=LADRS+1
      NPP=LADRS
C*** LOCAL DIRECT ACCESS FILE ARRANGEMENTS
      READ (KF'NPP,70,ERR=240) ((KEY(J,L),J=1,2),L=L1,L2)
  110 CONTINUE
      LADRS=LADRS+1
      NPP=LADRS
C*** LOCAL DIRECT ACCESS FILE ARRANGEMENTS
      READ (KF'NPP,120,ERR=240) (NDFR(I),I=1,14)
  120 FORMAT (14I5)
C  SET NTOT=NTOT+1 FOR USE IN BINARY SEARCH (SEE S/R MACLOC)
  130 NTOT=NTOT+1
C=======================================================================
C GLOBAL KEYWORDS - 'AUTHO(R)' IS ALWAYS A GLOBAL KEYWORD, CHECK OTHERS.
```

```
SUBROUTINE MACINL
CONTINUED

C IF *G FRAME IS PRESENT, EXTRACT GLOBAL KEYWORDS AND THE CORRESPONDING
C FRAME NUMBERS. (N.B. THE *G FRAME, IF PRESENT, MUST BE LOCATED
C IMMEDIATELY AFTER THE *B FRAME)
      NPP=NNST+1
      CALL MACRND (BUF,IERR)
      IF (BUF(1).NE.STAR.OR.BUF(2).NE.GG) GO TO 230
      IP=3
C EXTRACT GLOBAL KEYWORDS IN QUOTES AND ASSOCIATED FRAME NUMBERS
C EXAMPLE:  *G 'HELP'100   'STOP',1000   'SCORE' 1250
  140 DO 150 I = IP,72
      IF (BUF(I).EQ.QUOTE) GO TO 160
  150 CONTINUE
      GO TO 230
  160 NG=NG+1
C NOTE, UP TO 5 GLOBAL KEYS (EACH UP TO 5 CHARACTERS LONG) ARE ALLOWED,
C IN ADDITION TO 'AUTHO(R)', WHICH IS ALWAYS A GLOBAL KEYWORD
      IF (NG-6) 170,170,230
  170 DO 180 J = 1,5
  180 KWDS(NG,J)=BLANK
      IP=I+1
      J=0
      DO 200 I = IP,72
      IF (BUF(I).EQ.QUOTE) GO TO 220
      J=J+1
      IF (J-5) 190,190,200
  190 KWDS(NG,J)=BUF(I)
  200 CONTINUE
C CLOSING QUOTE MISSING, PRINT ERROR MESSAGE
      WRITE (KT,210)
  210 FORMAT(1X,'*** CLOSING QUOTE MISSING IN *G FRAME - PLEASE REPORT')

      RETURN
  220 IP=I+1
      CALL MACNUM (BUF,IP,X,NFLG,R)
      KNUM(NG)=IFIX(X)
      IF (IP-72) 140,230,230
  230 RETURN
  240 WRITE (KT,250)
  250 FORMAT (1X,'*** DIRECTORY OR FILE INADEQUATE - PLEASE REPORT')
      STOP
      END
```

SUBROUTINE MACINP

```
      SUBROUTINE MACINP (ANS,XANS,NFLG)
C
C PROMPT FOR AND ACCEPT INPUT FROM TERMINAL- STORE IMAGE IN ARRAY 'ANS'
C IF INPUT MATCHES ONE OF THE GLOBAL KEYWORDS, SET NFLG=1 AND 'NGFR' TO
C THE CORRESPONDING FRAME (TO WHICH A DIRECT BRANCH WILL BE MADE).
C OTHERWISE, SCAN THE INPUT STRING FOR A NUMBER. IF A NUMBER IS FOUND
C THEN STORE IT IN 'XANS' AND SET NFLG=0.
C IF NO NUMBER WAS FOUND THEN SET NFLG=-1 (BY S/R MACNUM) AND XANS=0.
C*
C     CHARACTER KWDS,ANS(72)
      INTEGER ANS(72)
      INTEGER FLAG,SCORE
      COMMON KT,KL,INI,NW1,NW2,JKL,NPRT,LDISP,KA,ITRIG(73),NEOF
      COMMON /FLS/ KF,LADRS,NPP,NNST,NNEND,MODE,FLAG,ION,SCORE,AION,SUM
      COMMON /TABLE/ NTOT,NKA,NFR,KYMAX,KEY(2,250),NDFR(14)
      COMMON /GLB/ NG,NGFR,KWDS(6,5),KNUM(6)
      XANS=0.
C*** OPTIONAL LOCAL ARRANGEMENTS FOR PROMPT
      WRITE (KT,10)
   10 FORMAT (1X,'? ')
      READ (INI,20) (ANS(I),I=1,72)
   20 FORMAT (72A1)
C*** LOWER-CASE INPUT COULD BE UPSHIFTED FOR MATCHING HERE
C
C CHECK FOR GLOBAL KEYWORDS IN INPUT STRING
      DO 50 I = 1,NG
      DO 30 J = 1,5
      IF (KWDS(I,J).NE.ANS(J)) GO TO 50
   30 CONTINUE
C GLOBAL KEYWORD MATCHED, PUT ITS FRAME IN NGFR AND SET NFLG TO 1
      NFLG=1
      NGFR=KNUM(I)
C PRINT ANY ACCEPTED GLOBAL KEYWORD ON ANSWER FILE
C** WRITE ON OUTPUT FILE
      WRITE (KA,40) (ANS(I),I=1,5)
   40 FORMAT (1X,5A1)
      GO TO 60
   50 CONTINUE
C NO GLOBAL KEYWORDS FOUND - SET NFLG=0
      NFLG=0
C EVALUATE THE FIRST NO.,IF ANY,IN THE INPUT - RETURN ITS VALUE IN XANS
      I=1
      CALL MACNUM (ANS,I,XANS,NFLG,R)
   60 RETURN
      END
```

SUBROUTINE MACLOC

```
      SUBROUTINE MACLOC (IADRS)
C
C THIS SUBROUTINE PERFORMS A BINARY SEARCH ON THE TABLE OF FRAMES
C KEY(1,K)  (STORED IN ASCENDING ORDER) TO FIND THE TARGET FRAME NUMBER
C 'NFR'.  IF A MATCH IS FOUND THEN ITS ADDRESS (I.E. KEY(2,K)) IS
C RETURNED AS THE VALUE OF 'IADRS'. IF NFR IS NOT FOUND THEN IADRS=0
C
      COMMON /TABLE/ NTOT,NKA,NFR,KYMAX,KEY(2,250),NDFR(14)
      I=0
      J=NTOT
      DO 30 N = 1,14
      K=(I+J+1)/2
      IF (KEY(1,K)-NFR) 10,40,20
   10 I=K
      GO TO 30
   20 J=K
   30 CONTINUE
C FRAME NOT LOCATED - RETURN IADRS=0
      IADRS=0
      RETURN
C  FRAME LOCATED
   40 IADRS=KEY(2,K)
   50 RETURN
      END
```

SUBROUTINE MACNUM

```
      SUBROUTINE MACNUM (BUF,IP,XX,NFLG,R)
C
C BUF = CHARACTER ARRAY (72), CONTAINING IMAGES IN 72A1 FORMAT.
C IP  = POINTER TO THE CURRENT LOCATION IN THIS ARRAY.
C THIS SUBROUTINE WIIL EVALUATE THE NEXT NUMBER IN 'BUF', SKIPPING
C OVER ANY LEADING NON-NUMERIC CHARACTERS. THE VALUE OF THE NUMBER
C IS RETURNED IN XX (REAL NO.) AND THE POINTER IS MOVED TO THE FIRST
C NON-BLANK CHARACTER AFTER THE NUMBER.
C IF A NUMBER IS FOUND, IT IS RETURNED IN 'XX' AND NFLG=0
C IF NOT, THEN XX=0. AND NFLG=-1
C IF AN ASTERISK (*) IS FOUND, STOP FURTHER READING OF THE LINE
C AND SET IP TO 72 (TO INDICATE END-OF-LINE)
C*
C     CHARACTER BLANK,STAR,BUF(72),NO(13),K
      INTEGER BLANK,STAR,BUF(72),NO(13)
      DATA NO/' ','0','1','2','3','4','5','6','7','8','9','.','-'/
      DATA BLANK,STAR/' ','*'/
      S=1.0
      F=1.0
      R=1.0
      X=0.
      NFLG=-1
      DO 90 I = IP,72
      K=BUF(I)
      DO 10 L = 1,13
      IF (K.EQ.NO(L)) GO TO 20
   10 CONTINUE
      IF (K.EQ.STAR) GO TO 100
      GO TO 50
   20 IF (L-1) 50,50,30
   30 IF (L-12) 40,60,60
C DIGIT
   40 X=X*10.+FLOAT(L-2)
      F=F*R
      NFLG=0
      GO TO 90
C SKIP LEADING BLANKS OR NON-NUMERIC CHARACTERS. TERMINATE ON FIRST
C NON-NUMERIC CHARACTER
   50 IF (NFLG) 90,110,110
   60 L=L-11
      GO TO (70,80,90), L
C DECIMAL PT (.)
   70 R=0.1
      GO TO 90
C MINUS SIGN (-)
   80 S=-1.0
   90 CONTINUE
  100 IP=72
      GO TO 140
C MOVE POINTER TO THE NEXT NON-BLANK CHARACTER AFTER THE NUMBER
  110 DO 120 J = I,72
      IF (BUF(J).NE.BLANK) GO TO 130
  120 CONTINUE
      J=72
  130 IP=J
  140 XX=X*F*S
      RETURN
      END
```

SUBROUTINE MACPRN

```
      SUBROUTINE MACPRN (IADRS)
C
C STACK ARGUMENTS TO NEXT S/R (MACPRT), THUS AVOIDING RECURSION
C
      DIMENSION IST(10)
      I=1
      LLL=IADRS
   10 CALL MACPRT (LLL,LLF)
      IF (LLF) 30,30,20
   20 IST(I)=LLL
      I=I+1
      LLL=LLF
      GO TO 10
   30 IF (I-1) 50,50,40
   40 I=I-1
      LLL=IST(I)
      GO TO 10
   50 RETURN
      END
```

SUBROUTINE MACPRT

```
      SUBROUTINE MACPRT (LLL,LLF)
C
C DISPLAY TEXT LINES STARTING AT # (IADRS+1) THROUGH TO THE NEXT FRAME.
C IF THE TEXT CONSISTS OF '/USE (FRAME NO.)' THEN DISPLAY THE
C TEXT FROM THE SPECIFIED FRAME (SAVES DUPLICATING TEXT)
C*
C     CHARACTER STAR,BLANK,SLASH,PLUS,UU,BUF1,BUF(72)
      INTEGER STAR,BLANK,SLASH,PLUS,UU,BUF1,BUF(72)
      INTEGER FLAG,SCORE
      COMMON KT,KL,INI,NW1,NW2,JKL,NPRT,LDISP,KA,ITRIG(73),NEOF
      COMMON /FLS/ KF,LADRS,NPP,NNST,NNEND,MODE,FLAG,ION,SCORE,AION,SUM
      COMMON /TABLE/ NTOT,NKA,NFR,KYMAX,KEY(2,250),NDFR(14)
      EQUIVALENCE (BUF1,BUF(1))
      DATA STAR,BLANK,SLASH,PLUS,UU/'*',' ','/','+','U'/
C*** OPTIONAL LINEFEED
C     WRITE (KT,5)
C   5 FORMAT (/)
      L=LLL
   10 L=L+1
      NPP=L
      CALL MACRND (BUF,IERR)
   20 FORMAT (72A1)
C IS THE FIRST CHAR. AN ASTERISK (*)? (= END OF TEXT FOR THIS FRAME)
      IF (BUF1.EQ.STAR) GO TO 120
C IS IT A SLASH (/)? - BRANCH OUT TO CHECK FOR '/USE (FRAME NO.)'
   30 IF (BUF1.EQ.SLASH) GO TO 90
C IS IT A PLUS (+)?
   40 IF (BUF1.EQ.PLUS) GO TO 10
C NO - PRINT TEXT (SUPRESS TRAILING BLANKS)
   50 DO 60 I = 1,72
      N=73-I
      IF (BUF(N).NE.BLANK) GO TO 70
   60 CONTINUE
   70 WRITE (KT,80) (BUF(I),I=1,N)
   80 FORMAT (1X,72A1)
      GO TO 10
C FOUND A SLASH - CHECK IF THE SECOND CHAR. IS 'U'
   90 IF (BUF(2).NE.UU) GO TO 40
C IF IT IS, PRINT TEXT FROM THE OTHER DESIGNATED FRAME
  100 IP=3
      CALL MACNUM (BUF,IP,X,NFLG,R)
      NFR=IFIX(X)
      CALL MACLOC (LN)
      IF (LN) 10,10,110
C EXIT TO STACK PARAMETERS AND AVOID RECURSIVE ENTRY
  110 LLF=LN
      LLL=L
      RETURN
  120 LLF=-1
      RETURN
  130 LLL=LLL+1
      LLF=LLF+1
      RETURN
      END
```

SUBROUTINE MACRND

```
      SUBROUTINE MACRND (BUF,IERR)
C
C THIS SUBROUTINE PERFORMS A RANDOM-ACCESS READ AT ADDRESS 'NPP' ON
C DISC FILE (LOGICAL UNIT 'LF') AND RETURNS THE RESULT IN ARRAY 'BUF'
C AS A CHARACTER BUFFER, READ UNDER FORMAT 72A1. IF AN ERROR OCCURS
C (OR EOF IS FOUND), IERR=1. ON SUCCESSFUL READS, IERR=0
C*
C     CHARACTER BUF(72)
      INTEGER BUF(72)
      INTEGER FLAG,SCORE
      COMMON /FLS/ KF,LADRS,NPP,NNST,NNEND,MODE,FLAG,ION,SCORE,AION,SUM
C
      IERR=0
C*** LOCAL DIRECT ACCESS ARRANGEMENTS.  *N.B. INCREMENT OF NPP
C    THAT FOLLOWS READ STATEMENT MAY NOT BE NEEDED ON SOME MACHINES.
C    'EOF=20' WOULD BE A DESIRABLE ADDITION TO THE READ STATEMENT
      READ (KF'NPP,10,ERR=20) (BUF(K),K=1,72)
C     NPP=NPP+1
   10 FORMAT (72A1)
      RETURN
   20 IERR=1
      RETURN
      END
```

SUBROUTINE MCDISP

```
      SUBROUTINE MCDISP (NTERM,NCODE)
C
C THIS SUBROUTINE CONTROLS THE HANDLING OF DISPLAY INSTRUCTIONS
C DERIVED FROM THE BLANK COMMON INTEGER VARIABLE 'LDISP'.
C THIS HAS (POTENTIALLY) 4 DIGITS - EACH CODES FOR A DIFFERENT
C INSTRUCTION FOR CURSOR POSITION, SCREEN CLEARING, ETC.
C INPUT PARAMETERS:
C   NTERM=TYPE OF TERMINAL
C   NCODE=INSTRUCTION WHICH OF THE 4 DIGITS OF LDISP TO USE
C DIGIT 1 - USED TO POSITION THE TEXT OF FRAMES READ FROM THE MAIN
C           DRIVER (S/R MACAID), BUT CAN ALSO BE USED WITHIN SUBROUTINES
C DIGIT 2 - USED TO POSITION QUESTIONS WITHIN SUBROUTINES MCMFRM,
C           MCRETN AND MCQFR1 (BUT CAN ALSO BE USED ELSEWHERE)
C DIGIT 3 - SPARE, EG. FOR CONTROL OF EXTERNAL DEVICES
C DIGIT 4 - SPARE, AS ABOVE
C
C FOR 1ST AND 2ND DIGITS, ONLY:
C      0 OR 1 = NO SPECIAL LOCATION; NO CHANGE IN CURSOR LOCATION
C      2 = TOP LEFT; CLEAR ENTIRE SCREEN
C      3 = GO TO ROW # 6; CLEAR ALL SCREEN BELOW THIS LINE
C      4 = GO TO ROW # 8; CLEAR ALL SCREEN BELOW THIS LINE
C      5 = GO TO ROW # 10; CLEAR ALL SCREEN BELOW THIS LINE
C      6 = GO TO ROW # 12; CLEAR ALL SCREEN BELOW THIS LINE
C      7 = GO TO ROW # 14; CLEAR ALL SCREEN BELOW THIS LINE
C      8 = GO TO ROW # 16; CLEAR ALL SCREEN BELOW THIS LINE
C      9 = GO TO ROW # 18; CLEAR ALL SCREEN BELOW THIS LINE
C ARGUMENT 'NTERM' GIVES THE TYPE OF TERMINAL.
C ARGUMENT 'NCODE' TELLS THE SUBROUTINE WHICH DIGIT TO ACT UPON
C  ( 1,2,3 OR 4 )
C
C**** LOCAL ARRANGEMENTS WILL DEPEND ON TERMINAL TYPES AND LOCAL CODES
C    APPROPRIATE FOR SCREEN CURSOR OR PROJECTOR CONTROLS, ETC.
C*
C     CHARACTER ESC,HH,JJ,RR,AA,ONE,TWO,FOUR,SIX,EIGHT,ZERO,AMP
      INTEGER ESC,HH,RR,AA,ONE,TWO,FOUR,SIX,EIGHT,ZERO,AMP
      COMMON KT,KL,INI,NW1,NW2,JKL,NPRT,LDISP,KA,ITRIG(73),NEOF
C**** LOCAL ARRANGEMENTS FOR DISPLAY CONTROL
      DATA ESC,HH,JJ,RR,AA,ONE,TWO,FOUR,SIX,EIGHT,ZERO,AMP/
     X 'E','H','J','R','A','1','2','4','6','8','0','&'/
C MAKE NDISP = 1ST DIGIT
      NDISP=LDISP/1000
      IF (NCODE.EQ.1) GO TO 10
C MAKE NDISP = 2ND DIGIT
      MDISP=LDISP-NDISP*1000
      NDISP=MDISP/100
      IF (NCODE.EQ.2.OR.NCODE.EQ.5.OR.NCODE.EQ.6) GO TO 10
C MAKE NDISP = 3RD DIGIT
      MDISP=MDISP-NDISP*100
      NDISP=MDISP/10
      IF (NCODE.EQ.3) GO TO 10
C MAKE NDISP = 4TH DIGIT
      NDISP=MDISP-NDISP*10
C IF NDISP INTEGER IS 0 OR 1, DO NOTHING TO THE SCREEN
   10 IF (NDISP.LE.0) RETURN
      IF (NCODE.EQ.5) NDISP=NDISP+1
      IF (NCODE.EQ.6) NDISP=NDISP+2
      GO TO (20,130), NTERM
C CURSOR CONTROLS FOR HP/2640 SERIES TERMINALS
   20 GO TO (30,40,60,70,80,90,100,110,120,120,120), NDISP
   30 RETURN
C IF NDISP INTEGER IS 2, CLEAR SCREEN; CURSOR MOVED TO TOP LEFT
   40 WRITE (KT,50) ESC,HH,ESC,JJ
   50 FORMAT (1X,4A1)
      RETURN
C IF NDISP INTEGER IS 3, CLEAR SCREEN FROM LINE 6 AND MOVE TO LINE 6
   60 WRITE (KT,140) ESC,AMP,AA,SIX,RR,ESC,JJ
      RETURN
C IF NDISP IS 4, CLEAR SCREEN FROM LINE 8 AND MOVE TO LINE 8
   70 WRITE (KT,140) ESC,AMP,AA,EIGHT,RR,ESC,JJ
```

SUBROUTINE MCDISP
CONTINUED

```
      RETURN
C IF NDISP IS 5, CLEAR SCREEN FROM LINE 10 AND MOVE TO LINE 10
   80 WRITE (KT,140) ESC,AMP,AA,ONE,ZERO,RR,ESC,JJ
      RETURN
C IF NDISP IS 6, CLEAR SCREEN FROM LINE 12 AND MOVE TO LINE 12
   90 WRITE (KT,140) ESC,AMP,AA,ONE,TWO,RR,ESC,JJ
      RETURN
C IF NDISP IS 7, CLEAR SCREEN FROM LINE 14 AND MOVE TO LINE 14
  100 WRITE (KT,140) ESC,AMP,AA,ONE,FOUR,RR,ESC,JJ
      RETURN
C IF NDISP IS 8, CLEAR SCREEN FROM LINE 16 AND MOVE TO LINE 16
  110 WRITE (KT,140) ESC,AMP,AA,ONE,SIX,RR,ESC,JJ
      RETURN
C IF NDISP IS 9, CLEAR SCREEN FROM LINE 18 AND MOVE TO LINE 18
  120 WRITE (KT,140) ESC,AMP,AA,ONE,EIGHT,RR,ESC,JJ
      RETURN
C****  CURSOR CONTROLS FOR OTHER TERMINALS CAN BE PUT IN HERE
  130 CONTINUE
  140 FORMAT (1X,8A1)
      RETURN
      END
```

SUBROUTINE MCMFRM

```
      SUBROUTINE MCMFRM (BUF,IP,FR,NPPX,NTERM)
C
C PROCESS A *M(ARKING) FRAME:
C ARGUMENTS:
C  BUF(72)=ARRAY CONTAINING M-FRAME CONTROL LINE
C  IP=CURRENT POSITION POINTER IN BUF
C  NPPX=ADDRESS OF THIS M-FRAME ON TEXT FILE
C  FR=NEXT FRAME NO. TO WHICH DRIVER WILL REFER OR TRANSFER CONTROL
C  NTERM=SCREEN CURSOR CONTROL IN OPERATION IF >0
C
C ALLOWS A SET OF 1 TO 9 QUESTIONS WITH NUMERICAL (OR NUMERICALLY
C EQUIVALENT) ANSWERS.   ACTION IS TAKEN AND/OR SCORES GIVEN
C ACCORDING TO THE ANSWERS.  POSSIBLE ANSWERS ARE
C Y(ES)(=1), N(O)(=0) OR ? (NOT 'Y' OR 'N', =2) IN THE CASE
C OF A SIMPLE MULTIPLE CHOICE QUESTION, OR 3 TO 5 GRADES ON A
C SCALE 0-2(0,1,2), 0-3(0,1,2,3) OR 0-4(0,1,2,3,4).
C ANY INDETERMINATE CHARACTER WILL BE TAKEN TO BE '2', EXCEPT FOR
C 'E' ('EXPLAIN') WHICH IS TAKEN TO HAVE A VALUE OF '3'.  (THIS IS USED
C IN SINGLE QUESTIONS WITH 4 POSSIBLE ANSWERS - NO,YES,DON'T KNOW, AND
C EXPLAIN)
C *M  NFR  LDISP  SCR  NN  EXIT  FR1  FR2  FR3  ... ... ...
C E.G.
C *M   100  1000   0   35   100,  0   -1   60   60   60, 70 -1 0 -1 80,
C +  40 40 40 40 0
C
C    LDISP = DISPLAY CODE (SEE SUBROUTINES MACAID AND MCDISP)
C     IF CURSOR CONTROL IS IN USE (NTERM>0) LDISP IS A 4-DIGIT
C     NUMBER.  1ST DIGIT CONTROLS POSITION OF *M FRAME TEXT
C     ON THE SCREEN, 2ND DIGIT THE POSITION OF QUESTIONS AND
C     CORRECTIVE RESPONSES.  3RD AND 4TH DIGITS ARE SPARE
C    SCR = SCORE (SEE ALSO S/R MACAID, UNDER T(EXT) FRAME)
C               N.B. OTHER AUTOMATIC SCORING IS MADE ANYWAY IN
C               THIS SUBROUTINE, ACCORDING TO WHETHER ANSWERS
C               ARE EXACT(0), CLOSE(-1) OR INCORRECT(-2), PROVIDING THAT
C               THE SCORER IS SWITCHED ON
C        =(+)1 - RECORD FRAME NUMBER ON OUTPUT FILE
C        =   2 - SAME, BUT ALSO RECORD ACCEPTED OUTPUT FILE ENTRY
C    NN = 2 DIGIT NUMBER (1ST DIGIT = NUMBER OF QUESTIONS,
C    FROM 1 TO 9 - '3' IN EXAMPLE ABOVE;
C     2ND DIGIT = NUMBER OF POSSIBLE GRADES OR REPLIES TO EACH
C     QUESTION - 2 MIN.,5 MAX. - '5' IN EXAMPLE ABOVE)
C    EXIT = EXIT ADDRESS TO GO TO AFTER FRAME EXECUTED
C    FR1..ETC. AND LATER PARAMETERS = TABLE OF ADDRESSES FOR ANSWERS
C     0=IDEAL ANSWER, -1=ACCEPTABLY CLOSE ANSWER, (+)FR=FRAME ADDRESS
C     OF TEXT TO BE PRINTED
C
C NOTE THAT ADDRESSES 60,70,80 AND 40 IN EXAMPLE ABOVE WILL USUALLY
C BE *R(ETURN) FRAMES,  BUT THEY CAN REFER TO ANY FRAME WITH TEXT.
C COMMAS ARE OPTIONAL, BUT ARE SIMPLY USED TO IMPROVE INTELLIGIBILITY.
C CONTROL IS NOT NORMALLY TRANSFERRED OUT OF AN *M FRAME EXCEPT TO THE
C EXIT ADDRESS, SINCE *R FRAMES ARE COMMONLY USED TO PROVIDE TEXT
C COMMENTS - BUT IF ANY ADDRESS IS NOT A *R(ETURN) FRAME, CONTROL WILL
C BE TRANSFERRED ALTOGETHER, OUT OF THE *M FRAME, AND NO FURTHER
C PROCESSING OF ANSWERS WILL BE DONE.
C
C IN THE EXAMPLE ABOVE, 0 -1 60 60 60 REFERS TO QUESTION 1,
C 70 -1 0 -1 80 TO QUESTION 2, ETC.  IF THE RESPONSE TO QUESTION 2 IS
C '0', THE TEXT OF FRAME # 70 WOULD BE PRINTED, AND IF IT IS '4' THE
C TEXT OF FRAME # 80.  THE ANSWER '2' IS THE ONLY COMPLETELY
C CORRECT ONE, WHICH GIVES NO MESSAGE.  THE RESPONSE '1' WOULD GIVE
C MESSAGE 'ACCEPTABLE - THOUGH MY GRADE WOULD BE SLIGHTLY HIGHER',
C WHILE REPONSE '3' WOULD GIVE A SIMILAR MESSAGE, SUGGESING THAT THE
C IDEAL RESPONSE SHOULD BE SLIGHTLY LOWER.
C NOTE THAT THE 3RD QUESTION IS CODED ON A CONTINUATION LINE
C BEGINNING WITH '+'  -  ANY NUMBER OF CONTINUATION LINES ARE
C ALLOWED
C*
C      CHARACTER BLANK,PLUS,QUERY,BUF(72),ANS(72),NO,NUM,INPUT
C      CHARACTER RR,HIGH(4),LOW(4)
```

SUBROUTINE MCMFRM
CONTINUED

```
      INTEGER BLANK,PLUS,QUERY,BUF(72),ANS(72),RR,HIGH(4),LOW(4)
      INTEGER FLAG,SCORE
      DIMENSION ADRES(5,9),NO(9),IANS(9),IDEAL(9),NUM(9)
      COMMON KT,KL,INI,NW1,NW2,JKL,NPRT,LDISP,KA,ITRIG(73),NEOF
      COMMON /FLS/ KF,LADRS,NPP,NNST,NNEND,MODE,FLAG,ION,SCORE,AION,SUM
      COMMON /TABLE/ NTOT,NKA,NFR,KYMAX,KEY(2,250),NDFR(14)
      DATA BLANK,PLUS,QUERY,RR/' ','+','?','R'/
      DATA NO/'O','1','2','3','4','N','Y','?','E'/
      DATA NUM/'1','2','3','4','5','6','7','8','9'/
      DATA HIGH/'H','I','G','H'/
      DATA LOW/' ','L','O','W'/
      CALL MACNUM (BUF,IP,X,NFLG,R)
      NN=IFIX(X)
C NN1=NUMBER OF QUESTIONS (1-9)
C NN2=NUMBER OF CHOICES FOR EACH QUESTION (2-5)
      NN1=NN/10
      NN2=NN-NN1*10
      N1=NN1-1
C GET FRAME NUMBER FOR EXIT
      CALL MACNUM (BUF,IP,EXIT,NFLG,R)
C STORE POINTER POSITION (IP) IN CASE IT IS NEEDED LATER AFTER
C UNACCEPTABLE ENTRY OF ANSWERS
      IPX=IP
C INITIALISE NUMBER OF TRIES
      NANS=0
C RESET FILE POINTER TO LINE IMMEDIATELY FOLLOWING CONTROL LINE
      NPP=NPPX
C UNACCEPTABLE ENTRY - RE-READ LINE AFTER RESETTING FILE POINTER
C (NPP) AND COLUMN POINTER(IP), UNLESS THERE HAVE ALREADY BEEN 2
C UNACCEPTABLE ANSWERS, AND CURSOR CONTROL IS NOT IN USE
   10 IF (NANS-1) 30,20,70
   20 IP=IPX
      NPP=NPPX-1
      CALL MACRND (BUF,IERR)
   30 K=NN2-1
C BYPASS NEXT TEXT IF THERE IS ONLY 1 QUESTION
      IF (N1) 60,60,40
C**** LOCAL ARRANGEMENTS TO POSITION CURSOR, IF POSSIBLE
C     (ACTS ON 2ND DIGIT OF PARAMETER LDISP)
   40 IF (NTERM.GT.0) CALL MCDISP (NTERM,2)
      WRITE (KT,50)
   50 FORMAT (1X,'TYPE RESPONSES FOR EACH QUESTION ALONG A LINE')
C GET INPUT AND CHECK IF A GLOBAL KEYWORD WAS ENTERED
   60 CALL MACINP (ANS,XANS,NFLG)
C INCREMENT COUNTER FOR NUMBER OF TRIES
      NANS=NANS+1
C CHECK FOR GLOBAL KEYWORD ENTRY
      IF (NFLG) 80,80,500
C**** LOCAL ARRANGEMENTS CONCERNED WITH CURSOR POSITION
C IF THE CURSOR IS BEING CONTROLLED, NO NEED TO RERUN THE QUESTION
   70 IF (NTERM) 480,480,20
C=========================================================================
C READ TABLE OF ADDRESSES AND OF IDEAL OR ACCEPTABLE ANSWERS
   80 DO 150 J = 1,NN1
      DO 150 K = 1,NN2
   90 CALL MACNUM (BUF,IP,FRADR,NFLG,R)
      IF (NFLG) 120,100,100
  100 ADRES(K,J)=FRADR
      IF (FRADR) 150,110,150
  110 IDEAL(J)=K-1
      GO TO 150
C READ NEXT LINE, CHECK THAT IT IS A CONTINUATION LINE, THEN GO
C ON READING ADDRESSES INTO ARRAY 'ADRES'
  120 CALL MACRND (BUF,IERR)
      IF (BUF(1).NE.PLUS) GO TO 130
      IP=2
      GO TO 90
  130 WRITE (KT,140) NFR
  140 FORMAT (1X,'*** NOT ENOUGH ADDRESSES FOR *M',I5,' FRAME - PLEASE R
```

SUBROUTINE MCMFRM
CONTINUED

```
     XEPORT')
      IF (MODE.EQ.2) STOP
      MODE=0
      RETURN
  150 CONTINUE
C==========================================================================
C PROCESS ANSWERS - CONFIRM BY DISPLAYING BACK ETC.
      K=0
      DO 180 I = 1,72
      IF (ANS(I).EQ.BLANK) GO TO 180
      DO 160 J = 1,9
      IF (ANS(I).EQ.NO(J)) GO TO 170
  160 CONTINUE
      J=8
C ANY UNRECOGNISED NUMBER OR CHARACTER IS TREATED AS '?'
      ANS(I)=QUERY
  170 K=K+1
      IANS(K)=J-1
      IF (K-NN1) 180,230,180
  180 CONTINUE
      WRITE (KT,190)
  190 FORMAT (1X,'INCOMPLETE ANSWER')
C**** CURSOR CONTROL (NTERM>0) WILL NECESSITATE ANOTHER 'WRITE'
  200 IF (NTERM) 10,10,210
  210 WRITE (KT,220)
C*** LOCAL ARRANGEMENTS FOR 'RETURN', 'ESCAPE', ETC.
  220 FORMAT (1X,'PRESS *RETURN*, THEN RE-ENTER ANSWER')
      CALL MACINP (ANS,XANS,NFLG)
      IF (NFLG) 10,10,500
C IF ONLY 1 QUESTION, SKIP TO RECORD ANSWER - NO DISPLAY OR CHECK
  230 IF (N1) 320,320,240
C**** LOCAL ARRANGEMENTS TO REPOSITION CURSOR
C      (ACCORDING TO VALUE OF 2ND DIGIT OF PARAMETER LDISP)
  240 IF (NTERM) 260,260,250
  250 CALL MCDISP (NTERM,2)
  260 WRITE (KT,270) (I,I=1,NN1)
  270 FORMAT (1X,' FOR QUESTIONS -> ',10(I1,1X))
C DISPLAY ANSWERS ON FORMATTED LINE
      DO 280 I = 1,NN1
      IBD=2*I+39
      ANS(IBD)=NO(IANS(I)+1)
      IBD=IBD+1
      ANS(IBD)=BLANK
  280 CONTINUE
      WRITE (KT,290) (ANS(I),I=41,IBD),QUERY
  290 FORMAT (1X,'IS THIS RIGHT? -> ',21A1)
      READ (INI,300) INPUT
  300 FORMAT (A1)
      IF (INPUT.EQ.NO(7)) GO TO 320
      WRITE (KT,310) NN1
  310 FORMAT (1X,'PLEASE ANSWER AGAIN FOR EACH OF THE',I2,' STATEMENTS O
     XR QUESTIONS')
      GO TO 200
C ANSWERS HAVE BEEN CONFIRMED - RECODE Y(ES)->1 AND N(O)->0
C                                - RECODE E(XPLAIN) ->3
C  -  OTHER CHARACTERS (INCLUDING '?') ->2
  320 DO 330 I = 1,NN1
      IF (IANS(I).LT.5) GO TO 330
      IANS(I)=IANS(I)-5
  330 CONTINUE
C IF NKA=1, RECORD  RAW ACCEPTED INPUT ON OUTPUT FILE
      IF (NKA-1) 360,340,360
C** WRITE ON OUTPUT FILE
  340 WRITE (KA,350) NFR,(ANS(I),I=41,IBD)
  350 FORMAT (1X,'M',I5,3X,63A1)
C==========================================================================
C CHECK ANSWERS FOR CORRECTNESS, AND PRINT CORRECTIVE MESSAGES
  360 NFSV=NFR
      DO 470 J = 1,NN1
```

```
SUBROUTINE MCMFRM
CONTINUED

      IDLJ=IDEAL(J)
C NO FURTHER ACTION ON IDEAL ANSWER
      IF (IANS(J).EQ.IDLJ) GO TO 470
C**** LOCAL ARRANGEMENTS FOR CLEARING SCREEN BELOW AND REPOSITIONING
C     CURSOR 2 LINES DOWM
      IF (NTERM.GT.0) CALL MCDISP (NTERM,5)
      K=IANS(J)+1
C IF ? ENTERED FOR Y/N TYPE QUESTION, PRINT CORRECTIVE MESSAGE
      IF (NN2.EQ.2.AND.K.GT.2) GO TO 420
C GET BRANCHING FRAME NO. OR -1 IF ANSWER ACCEPTABLE
      FR=ADRES(K,J)
C IF Y/N TYPE QUESTION OR UNACCEPTABLE ANSWER DEDUCT 2 & PROCEED
      IF (NN2.EQ.2.OR.FR.GT.0.) GO TO 390
C ANY OTHER MULTIPLE CHOICE ANSWER, DEDUCT 1 FROM SCORE
      SCORE=SCORE-ION
C TEST FOR ACCEPTABLE BUT HIGH/LOW GRADES
      IF (K.GE.(IDLJ+1)) GO TO 380
      WRITE (KT,370) J,HIGH
  370 FORMAT (1X,'Q.',I1,' ACCEPTABLE - THOUGH MY GRADE WOULD BE SLIGHTL
     XY ',4A1,'ER')
      GO TO 440
  380 WRITE (KT,370) J,LOW
      GO TO 440
C IF MORE THAN ONE QUESTION PRINT QUESTION NUMBER
  390 IF (NN1.LE.1) GO TO 410
      WRITE (KT,400) J
  400 FORMAT (1X,'Q.',I1)
C SUBTRACT 2 MARKS FOR AN INCORRECT ANSWER, IF SCORER IS ON
  410 SCORE=SCORE-2*ION
      GO TO 430
  420 WRITE (KT,400) J
C SUBTRACT 1 MARK FOR INDETERMINATE OR ILLEGAL ANSWER AND GO TO THE
C HIGHEST NUMBERED FRAME.  (IN BINARY Y/N TYPE QUESTIONS, THE CORRECT
C ANSWER WILL NORMALLY BE CODED BY A ZERO (I.E. "DO NOTHING") ADDRESS)
      SCORE=SCORE-ION
      FR=AMAX1(ADRES(1,J),ADRES(2,J))
  430 CALL MCRETN (BUF,IP,FR,NTERM,NANS,6)
      IF (MODE) 440,480,440
C*** LOCAL ARRANGEMENTS - 'RETURN', 'ESCAPE' ETC.
  440 IF ((NN1.EQ.1.OR.NTERM.LE.0).AND.NANS.EQ.0) GO TO 460
      WRITE (KT,450)
  450 FORMAT (1X,'PRESS *RETURN*')
      CALL MACINP (ANS,XANS,NFLG)
  460 IF (NANS.EQ.0) RETURN
      IF (NFLG) 470,470,490
  470 CONTINUE
      FR=EXIT
      NFR=NFSV
  480 RETURN
  490 NFR=NFSV
C GLOBAL KEYWORD IDENTIFIED
  500 FR=-1.
      RETURN
      END
```

SUBROUTINE MCQFR1

```
      SUBROUTINE MCQFR1 (BUF,IP,FR,NPPX,NTERM)
C
C PROCESS A *Q(UESTION) FRAME:
C MULTIPLE CHOICE MAY BE NUMERIC, NUMERIC RANGE OR CHARACTER
C PARAMETERS:
C  BUF(72)=ARRAY CONTAINING Q-FRAME CONTROL LINE
C  IP=CURRENT POSITION POINTER IN BUF
C  NPPX=ADDRESS OF THIS Q-FRAME ON TEXT-FILE
C  FR=NEXT FRAME NO. TO WHICH THE DRIVER WILL TRANSFER CONTROL
C  NTERM=SCREEN CURSOR CONTROL IN OPERAVION, IF >0
C
C EXAMPLE OF A STANDARD *Q FRAME
C *Q NFR LDISP SCR NDICT  (..)FR1  (..,..)FR2  '...',FR3 ....ETC.
C *Q 100 1000   0     0    (1)10  (3.5,4.5)20 'HELP',30  'GO',40
C + 'REPEAT',50 (),60 ''70
C   1ST PARAMETER (LDISP) = DISPLAY CODE (SEE S/R MACAID & MCDISP)
C             IF CURSOR CONTROL IS IN USE (NTERM>0) LDISP IS A
C             4-DIGIT NUMBER.  1ST DIGIT CONTROLS THE POSITION OF THE
C             TEXT OF THE *Q FRAME, 2ND DIGIT CONTROLS THE POSITION
C             OF ANY CORRECTIVE MESSAGES, ETC. DIGITS 3 AND 4 ARE SPARE
C   2ND PARAMETER (SCR) = SCORE (SEE S/R MACAID, T(EXT) FRAME)
C             =(+)1 - RECORD FRAME NUMBER ON OUTPUT FILE
C             =   2 - SAME, BUT ALSO RECORD ACCEPTABLE ANSWERS ON FILE
C   3RD PARAMETER (NDICT) = >0 - DICTIONARY REFERENCE NUMBER (0=NONE TO
C                                  BE USED);
C                               -1=TAKE NUMERICAL INPUT FROM
C                                  SCORE, WITHOUT PROMPT;
C                               -2=TAKE NUMERICAL INPUT FROM
C                                  SUM, WITHOUT PROMPT)
C   THEN ALTERNATIVES AS FOLLOWS -
C  ON ANSWER = 1 OR 1.0 - GO TO FRAME 10
C             = BETWEEN 3.5 AND 4.5 (INCLUSIVE) GO TO 20
C             = ANY NUMERICAL ANSWER AT ALL, GO TO 60  (NOTE THAT THIS
C               WAS ON A CONTINUATION LINE, STARTING WITH '+')
C             = 'HELP' GO TO 30
C             = 'GO' GO TO 40
C             = 'REPEAT' GO TO 50
C             = ANY ANSWER AT ALL, GO TO 70
C BLANK LINE ENTRY - ASK TO TRY AGAIN
C
C EXAMPLE OF A *Q FRAME USING A DICTIONARY.  N.B. THE DICTIONARY(S) CAN
C BE PLACED ANYWHERE, BUT THEY MUST BE IN SEQUENTIAL ORDER
C OF INDEX NUMBER;  IN THIS EXAMPLE DICTIONARY # 4 IS SPECIFIED
C *Q 100 1000 0 4 <1+2+3>10 <1+3+2>10 <2+3+1>10 <1+2>20 <2+1>20 <1+3>30
C  WHAT IS THE DIAGNOSIS?
C *D 4 'MITRAL'1 'STENOS'2 'INCOMPE'3 'REGURG'3
C
C ON ANSWER 'MITRAL STENOSIS AND INCOMPETENCE', 'MITRAL
C           INCOMPETENCE AND STENOSIS' OR 'STENOSIS AND
C           INCOMPETENCE OF THE MITRAL VALVE' GO TO 10
C ON ANSWER 'MITRAL STENOSIS' OR 'STENOSIS OF THE MITRAL VALVE' GO TO 20
C           'THE PATIENT HAD MITRAL INCOMPETENCE' OR 'IT WAS
C           MITRAL REGURGITATION' OR JUST 'MITRAL INCOMPETENCE' OR
C           'MITRAL REGURGITATION' GO TO 30
C ON ANY OTHER ANSWER, ASK TO 'PLEASE TRY AGAIN'
C
C EXAMPLE OF A *Q FRAME TO PROCESS THE SUM IN 'SUM'  -
C *Q 100 1000 0 -2 (0,4)10 (4,10),20 (10,100),30 (100,16000) 40  ()50
C AFTER PRINTING THE TEXT (IF ANY) CONTROL IS TRANSFERRED, WITHOUT ANY
C PROMPT FOR INPUT, TO THE SPECIFIED FRAME NUMBER, ACCORDING TO THE
C VALUE CURRENTLY IN 'SUM'.   E.G. IF SUM=0-4 GO TO 10
C                                        =4-10 GO TO 20
C                                        =10-100 GO TO 30
C                                        =100-16000 GO TO 40
C                                        =ANY OTHER VALUE, GO TO 50
C
C     N.B. IT IS ESSENTIAL THAT THE COMPLETE RANGE OF POSSIBLE
C     SUMS IN 'SUM' BE COVERED BY THE *Q FRAME OPTIONS, OTHERWISE
C     ERRORS WILL OCCUR. NOTE: () WILL MATCH ANY NUMERICAL VALUE.
```

```
 SUBROUTINE MCQFR1
 CONTINUED

C     IF THE 3RD PARAMETER IN THE EXAMPLE ABOVE WAS -1 INSTEAD OF
C     -2, THE SAME TYPE OF PROCESSING WOULD BE APPLIED TO THE VALUE
C     OF THE SCORE
C*
C      CHARACTER BUF(72),ANS(72),BLANK,PLUS,HYPHN,RR
       INTEGER BUF(72),ANS(72),BLANK,PLUS,HYPHN,RR
       INTEGER FLAG,SCORE
C IF MAXWD/MAXKW ARE CHANGED, REDIMENSION NCOLM(MAXWD) & KWD(MAXKW)
       DIMENSION NCOLM(10),KWD(6)
       COMMON KT,KL,INI,NW1,NW2,JKL,NPRT,LDISP,KA,ITRIG(73),NEOF
       COMMON /FLS/ KF,LADRS,NPP,NNST,NNEND,MODE,FLAG,ION,SCORE,AION,SUM
       COMMON /TABLE/ NTOT,NKA,NFR,KYMAX,KEY(2,250),NDFR(14)
C MAXWD=MAX NO. OF WORDS ON ANSWER THAT CAN BE PROCESSED
C MAXKW=MAX NO. OF KEYWORDS FROM DICTIONARY THAT CAN BE PROCESSED
       DATA MAXWD/10/, MAXKW/6/
       DATA BLANK,PLUS,HYPHN,RR/' ','+','-','R'/
C GET THE THIRD NUMBER FROM Q-LINE (NDICT)
       CALL MACNUM (BUF,IP,X,NFLG,R)
C NDICT>0: DICTIONARY NUMBER TO BE USED FOR MATCHING KEYWORD(S)
C NDICT=0: ONLY ONE LETTER, CHARACTER, KEYWORD OR NUMBER ON INPUT TO
C            MATCH AGAINST ALTERNATIVES ON CONTROL LINE OF *Q FRAME
C NDICT<0: NO INPUT NEEDED - BRANCH ON CURRENT VALUE OF 'SUM'
       NDICT=IFIX(X)
C SAVE POINTER ON Q-LINE FOR LATER USE
       IPX=IP
C INITIALIZE ANSWER COUNTER 'NANS'
       NANS=0
C STORE FRAME NUMBER IN CASE GLOBAL KEYWORD RECOGNISED
       NFREF=NFR
C BRANCH ON VALUE OF NDICT AS OUTLINED ABOVE
   10 IF (NDICT) 20,50,50
C NDICT<0 - USE SCORE OR SUM AND SKIP INPUT
   20 IF (NDICT+1) 30,40,40
   30 XANS=SUM
      GO TO 140
   40 XANS=FLOAT(SCORE)
      GO TO 140
C READ INPUT INTO ARRAY 'ANS'. XANS HAS NUMERIC VALUE, IF ENTERED
   50 NANS=NANS+1
C**** LOCAL ARRANGEMENTS TO POSITION CURSOR BELOW TEXT, AND CLEAR SCREEN
C      (ACCORDING TO VALUE OF 2ND DIGIT)
      IF (NTERM.GT.0) CALL MCDISP (NTERM,2)
      CALL MACINP (ANS,XANS,NFLG)
C WAS A GLOBAL KEYWORD DETECTED? IF SO, SET FR=-1 AND RETURN
      IF (NFLG) 70,70,60
   60 FR=-1.
C  RESTORE *Q-FRAME NUMBER BEFORE RETURN AFTER GLOBAL INPUT FOUND
      NFR=NFREF
      RETURN
C===================== WORD COUNT ==================================-
C COUNT WORDS IN INPUT(=J), STORE LOCATION OF EACH WORD IN NCOLM(J)
   70 NWORD=0
      DO 80 I = 1,MAXWD
   80 NCOLM(I)=72
      IF (ANS(1).EQ.BLANK) GO TO 90
      NWORD=1
      NCOLM(1)=1
   90 DO 100 I = 2,72
C SKIP UNLESS NEXT CHARACTER PRECEDED BY BLANK OR HYPHEN
      IF ((ANS(I-1).NE.BLANK.AND.ANS(I-1).NE.HYPHN).OR.ANS(I).EQ.BLANK.O
     XR.ANS(I).EQ.HYPHN) GO TO 100
      NWORD=NWORD+1
      NCOLM(NWORD)=I
      IF (NWORD-MAXWD) 100,110,110
  100 CONTINUE
C============ LOOK FOR KEYWORDS IN DICTIONARY ==========================
C IF DICTIONARY IS USED, DECODE INPUT WORDS USING DICTIONARY 'NDICT'
  110 NKWD=0
      IF (NDICT) 140,140,120
```

```
SUBROUTINE MCQFR1
CONTINUED

  120 CALL MCQFR3 (NDICT,ANS,NWORD,NCOLM,NKWD,KWD,MAXKW,BUF)
      IF (MODE.EQ.0) RETURN
      MATCH=1
C RE-READ Q-LINE (SINCE 'BUF' MAY HAVE BEEN OVERWRITTEN) AND RESTORE
C POINTER.
  130 NPP=NPPX-1
      CALL MACRND (BUF,IERR)
      IP=IPX
      IF (MATCH) 10,10,140
C================ PROCESS LINE AND CHECK FOR MATCH =====================
C PROCESS Q-LINE AND ITS CONTINUATION LINES, IF ANY
  140 CALL MCQFR2 (ANS,XANS,NFLG,NWORD,NCOLM,NKWD,KWD,BUF,IP,MATCH)
      IF (MODE.EQ.0) RETURN
C TEST OUTCOME (MATCH= 0/1 MEANS FAILED/SUCCESS)
      IF (MATCH) 150,150,240
C FAILED TO MATCH ANYTHING ON INPUT;  BUT NDICT<0 IS AN ERROR
  150 IF (NDICT) 160,180,180
  160 WRITE (KT,170) NFR,SCORE,SUM
  170 FORMAT(1X,'*** Q-FRAME',I5,' HAS NO EXIT (SCORE=',I3,' ADSUM=',
     XF8.1,') - PLEASE REPORT')
      IF (MODE.EQ.2) STOP
      MODE=0
      RETURN
C=============== TRY AGAIN WITH NEW INPUT ==============================
C**** CURSOR CONTROL INSTRUCPIONS - DELETE IF NOT TO BE USED
C CHECK IF CURSOR CONTROL IS IN USE (NTERM>0) - IF SO, NO NEED TO
C REPEAT THE QUESTION, BUT PROMPT WILL BE NEEDED TO RESTORE
C PREVIOUS SCREEN POSITION
  180 IF (NTERM) 190,190,220
C AFTER THIRD FAILURE, RETURN TO CALLING FRAME TO REPEAT QUESTION
  190 IF (NANS-2) 200,200,300
  200 WRITE (KT,210)
  210 FORMAT (1X,'PLEASE TRY AGAIN')
      GO TO 130
C**** NEXT 4 STATEMENTS COULD BE DELETED IF CURSOR CONTROL NOT IN USE
  220 WRITE (KT,230)
C*** LOCAL ARRANGEMENTS - 'ESCAPE', 'RETURN', ETC.
  230 FORMAT(1X,'PLEASE PRESS *RETURN* - THEN TRY AGAIN')
      CALL MACINP (ANS,XANS,NFLG)
      IF (NFLG) 130,130,60
C========================== SUCCESSFULLY MATCHED ========================
C DETERMINE THE FRAME NO. FOR NEXT BRANCH (FR)
  240 CALL MACNUM(BUF,IP,FR,NFLG,R)
C**** IF THE CURSOR IS BEING CONTROLLED, DO NOT EXIT FROM FRAME, BUT
C CALL SUBROUTINE MCRETN INSTEAD
      IF (NTERM) 270,270,250
  250 CALL MCRETN (BUF,IP,FR,NTERM,NANS,5)
      IF (MODE) 260,300,260
  260 IF (NANS.EQ.0) GO TO 270
C IF *R FRAME WAS CALLED, TREAT AS A MISMATCH
      MATCH=0
      GO TO 180
C RECORD ACCEPTED INPUT ON ANSWER FILE IF RECORDER FLAG IS ON (NKA=1)
  270 IF (NKA-1) 300,280,300
C** WRITE ON OUTPUT FILE
  280 WRITE (KA,290) NFR,(ANS(I),I=1,63)
  290 FORMAT (1X,'Q',I5,3X,63A1)
  300 RETURN
      END
```

SUBROUTINE MCQFR2

```
      SUBROUTINE MCQFR2(ANS,XANS,NFLG,NWORD,NCOLM,NKWD,KWD,BUF,IP,MATCH)
C
C  INTERPRETS CHARACTERS OR STRINGS FROM *Q FRAME OR *D(ICTIONARY)
C   (USED IN CONJUNCTION WITH S/R MCQFR1)
C INPUT PARAMETERS:
C  ANS(72)=INPUT LINE READ FROM TERMINAL, UNALTERED
C  XANS=THE FIRST NUMBER, IF ANY, ON INPUT LINE
C  NFLG: 0/-1 = A NUMBER WAS FOUND/NOT FOUND ON INPUT
C  NWORD=NO. OF WORDS ON INPUT (EACH STARTS WITH A NON-BLANK CHARACTER)
C  NCOLM(1 TO NWORD)=COLUMN POSITIONS OF THESE WORDS ON ANS
C  NKWD=NO. OF KEYWORDS FROM DICTIONARY MATCHED ON INPUT
C  KWD(1-NKWD)=CORRESPONDING DICTIONARY CODE OF EACH WORD MATCHED
C  BUF=THE ACTUAL Q-LINE IMAGE (FIRST IF THERE ARE CONTINUATION LINES)
C  IP=CURRENT POINTER ON Q-LINE
C OUTPUT PARAMETERS:
C  MATCH= 0/1 : MATCH FAILED/SUCCESSFUL
C*
C     CHARACTER LB,RB,LCB,BLANK,COMMA,QUOTE,PLUS,STAR,K
C     CHARACTER BUF(72),ANS(72)
      INTEGER RB,BLANK,COMMA,QUOTE,PLUS,STAR
      INTEGER BUF(72),ANS(72)
      INTEGER FLAG,SCORE,OK
      DIMENSION NCOLM(10),KWD(6)
      COMMON KT,KL,INI,NW1,NW2,JKL,NPRT,LDISP,KA,ITRIG(73),NEOF
      COMMON /FLS/ KF,LADRS,NPP,NNST,NNEND,MODE,FLAG,ION,SCORE,AION,SUM
      COMMON /TABLE/ NTOT,NKA,NFR,KYMAX,KEY(2,250),NDFR(14)
C*** LOCAL ARRANGEMENTS - IF '<' IS NOT AN ACCEPTABLE CHARACTER, ANY
C OTHER MAY BE SUBSTITUTED, IF NOT USED ELSEWHERE. ARRAY NO IN
C S/R RENUM1 WILL ALSO THEN NEED TO BE CHANGED
      DATA LB,RB,LCB,BLANK,COMMA,QUOTE,PLUS,STAR/'(',')','<',' ',',',
     X 1H', '+','*'/
C
C EXAMMPLE OF A GENERAL Q-LINE
C  *Q 100 0 1 'HELP' 110 (2.33) 20  (3.5,5.5)300 <1>310 <1+2>310 <2+1>,3
C SCAN FOR NEXT TARGET IN BUF: 'ALPHA', (NUMBER), (MIN,MAX) OR <KWD REF>
   10 DO 20 I = IP,72
      K=BUF(I)
C CHECK FOR LEFT BRACKET - START OF A NUMBER OR A RANGE OF NUMBERS
      IF (K.EQ.LB) GO TO 60
C CHECK FOR QUOTE - START OF A KEYWORD 'ALPHANUMERIC'
      IF (K.EQ.QUOTE) GO TO 100
C CHECK FOR A LEFT CONICAL BRACKET < - SEARCH FOR KEYWORD REFERENCE
C NUMBER(S)
      IF (K.EQ.LCB) GO TO 170
C CHECK FOR STAR(*) - ENDS USEFUL INFORMATION IN BUF
      IF (K.EQ.STAR) GO TO 30
   20 CONTINUE
C IF CONTINUATION LINE(S) PRESENT, READ INTO BUF, OVERWRITING PREVIOUS
C LINE
   30 CALL MACRND (BUF,IERR)
   40 IF (BUF(1).NE.PLUS) GO TO 50
      IP=2
      GO TO 10
C END OF BUF - NO MATCH FOUND. SET MATCH=0 AND RETURN
   50 MATCH=0
      GO TO 250
C=======================================================================
C FOUND A LEFT BRACKET - CHECK VALUE (..), OR RANGE OF VALUES (.. , ..)
   60 IP=I+1
C IF NO NUMERIC ANSWER WAS FOUND (NFLG<0) SKIP COMPARISON
      IF (NFLG) 10,70,70
C EMPTY NUMBER () MATCHES ANY NUMERIC ANSWER
   70 IF (BUF(IP).EQ.RB) GO TO 240
C EVALUATE FIRST NUMBER IN BRACKETS - XMIN
      CALL MACNUM (BUF,IP,XMIN,L,R)
C IS THE NEXT CHARACTER A COMMA?
      IF (BUF(IP).EQ.COMMA) GO TO 80
C COMPARE NUMBER WITH ANSWER - EXACT MATCH DESIRED
      IF (XANS-XMIN) 10,240,10
```

```
SUBROUTINE MCQFR2
CONTINUED

C COMMA IS PRESENT, EVALUATE SECOND NUMBER, RANGE: (XMIN,XMAX)
   80 CALL MACNUM (BUF,IP,XMAX,L,R)
C CHECK ANSWER FOR RANGE: XMIN.LE.XANS .AND. XANS.LE.XMAX ?
      IF (XMIN-XANS) 90,90,10
   90 IF (XANS-XMAX) 240,240,10
C=======================================================================
C FOUND A QUOTE - COMPARE THIS KEYWORD WITH ALL WORDS ON INPUT
  100 IP=I+1
      IPX=IP
      DO 160 L = 1,NWORD
      J=NCOLM(L)-1
      IP=IPX
      OK=1
C SCAN FOR CLOSING QUOTE AND COMPARE CHARACTERS WITH INPUT STRING
C EMPTY STRING ON Q-LINE '' MATCHES ANY ANSWER
C OK=1 THIS KEYWORD MATCHED, OK=0 NOT MATCHED
      DO 120 I = IP,72
      IF (BUF(I).EQ.QUOTE) GO TO 140
      J=J+1
      IF (J-72) 110,110,30
  110 IF (BUF(I).EQ.ANS(J)) GO TO 120
      OK=0
  120 CONTINUE
C END OF BUF - SECOND QUOTE NOT FOUND
      WRITE (KT,130) NFR
  130 FORMAT(1X,'*** QUOTE MISSING IN *Q',I4,' - PLEASE REPORT')
      IF (MODE.EQ.2) STOP
      MODE=0
      RETURN
  140 IP=I+1
  150 IF (OK) 160,160,240
  160 CONTINUE
      GO TO 10
C=======================================================================
C FOUND A LEFT CONICAL BRACKET < - CHECK FOR DICTIONARY REFERENCE
  170 IP=I+1
C IF NO DICTIONARY MATCH WAS FOUND SKIP COMPARISON
      IF (NKWD) 10,10,180
  180 DO 230 I = 1,NKWD
      L=0
      CALL MACNUM (BUF,IP,XX,J,R)
      J=IFIX(XX)
  190 IF (J-KWD(I+L)) 200,210,200
C IF ONE KEYWORD NOT MATCHED, TRY THE OTHERS, IN ORDER
  200 L=L+1
      IF (I+L-NKWD) 190,190,10
  210 IF (BUF(IP).EQ.PLUS) GO TO 220
      GO TO 240
  220 IP=IP+1
  230 CONTINUE
C DICTIONARY CODE(S) DID NOT MATCH
      GO TO 10
C=======================================================================
  240 MATCH=1
  250 RETURN
      END
```

SUBROUTINE MCQFR3

```
      SUBROUTINE MCQFR3 (NDICT,ANS,NWORD,NCOLM,NKWD,KWD,MAXKW,BUF)
C INPUT PARAMETERS:
C  NDICT=DICTIONARY NUMBER REFRENCED
C  ANS(72)=INPUT LINE UNALTERED
C OUTPUT PARAMETERS:
C  NWORD=NO. OF WORDS FOUND IN INPUT LINE
C  NCOLM(1-NWORD)=THEIR LOCATIONS ON THE INPUT LINE
C  NKWD=NO. OF KEYWORDS IN INPUT MATCHED IN DICTIONARY
C  KWD(1-NKWD)=THE CODES OF MATCHED KEYWORDS FROM DICTIONARY
C  MAXKW=MAX NUMBER OF KEYWORDS THAT CAN BE MATCHED
C  BUF(72) USED HERE SIMPLY AS A WORK ARRAY, ITS CONTENTS ARE DESTROYED
C
C CHECKS THE INPUT WORDS AGAINST THE SPECIFIED DICTIONARY AND IF ANY
C MATCHES ARE FOUND THEN THEIR CODES AND TOTAL NUMBER OF MATCHES ARE
C RETURNED
C*
C     CHARACTER QUOTE,PLUS,BUF(72),ANS(72),K
      INTEGER QUOTE,PLUS,BUF(72),ANS(72)
      INTEGER FLAG,SCORE,OK
      DIMENSION NCOLM(10),KWD(6),ILOC(6)
      COMMON KT,KL,INI,NW1,NW2,JKL,NPRT,LDISP,KA,ITRIG(73),NEOF
      COMMON /FLS/ KF,LADRS,NPP,NNST,NNEND,MODE,FLAG,ION,SCORE,AION,SUM
      COMMON /TABLE/ NTOT,NKA,NFR,KYMAX,KEY(2,250),NDFR(14)
      DATA QUOTE,PLUS/1H',1+'/
C LOCATE SPECIFIED DICTIONARY ON THE TEXTFILE
      NPP=NDFR(NDICT)
      IF (NPP) 10,10,30
   10 WRITE (KT,20) NDICT,NFR
   20 FORMAT(1X,'*** DICTIONARY #',I2,' CALLED FROM *Q',I4,' NOT FOUND -
     X PLEASE REPORT')
      IF (MODE.EQ.2) STOP
      MODE=0
      RETURN
C INITIALISE KWD AND ILOC REGISTERS
   30 DO 40 I = 1,MAXKW
      KWD(I)=0
   40 ILOC(I)=72
C============ COMPARE EACH DICTIONARY WORD WITH INPUT WORDS ============
C READ DICTIONARY INTO BUF
      CALL MACRND (BUF,IERR)
   50 IP=2
   60 DO 70 I = IP,72
C LOOK FOR A QUOTE - START OF NEXT KEYWORD ON DICTIONARY
      IF (BUF(I).EQ.QUOTE) GO TO 80
   70 CONTINUE
C END OF BUF - CHECK CONTINUATION LINES OF DICTIONARY
      CALL MACRND (BUF,IERR)
      IF (BUF(1).EQ.PLUS) GO TO 50
      GO TO 170
C======================================================================
   80 IPX=I+1
C COMPARE CURRENT KEYWORD ON DICTIONARY WITH EACH INPUT WORD
      DO 150 L = 1,NWORD
C J=LOCATION OF NEXT WORD ON INPUT-1,  OK=0/1 : FAIL/SUCCESS
      J=NCOLM(L)-1
      OK=1
      IP=IPX
C SCAN FOR CLOSING QUOTE AND COMPARE THE CHARACTERS WITH INPUT WORD
      DO 100 I = IP,72
      K=BUF(I)
      IF (K.EQ.QUOTE) GO TO 120
      J=J+1
      IF (J-72) 90,90,100
   90 IF (K.NE.ANS(J)) OK=0
  100 CONTINUE
C END OF BUF - SECOND QUOTE NOT FOUND
      WRITE (KT,110) NDICT
  110 FORMAT(1X,'*** QUOTE MISSING IN DICTIONARY #',I3,' - PLEASE REPORT
     X')
```

```
SUBROUTINE MCQFR3
CONTINUED

      IF (MODE.EQ.2) STOP
      MODE=0
      RETURN
C FOUND CLOSING QUOTE. WAS THERE A MATCH?
  120 IP=I+1
      IF (OK) 150,150,130
C MATCHED - CHECK LIMIT OF DICTIONARY MATCHES ALLOWED
  130 IF (NKWD-MAXKW) 140,160,160
  140 NKWD=NKWD+1
C DETERMINE CODE FOR KEYWORD JUST MATCHED
      CALL MACNUM (BUF,IP,XX,LL,R)
      KWD(NKWD)=IFIX(XX)
C SAVE LOCATION OF INPUT WORD FOR LEFT TO RIGHT PRECEDENCE INFORMATION
      ILOC(NKWD)=NCOLM(L)
C HAVING FOUND FIRST MATCH, PASS ON TO NEXT WORD
      KN=KN+1
      GO TO 60
  150 CONTINUE
      GO TO 60
C===== RE-ARRANGE MATCHED CODES IN CORRECT LEFT TO RIGHT SEQUENCE ======
  160 NKWD=MAXKW
  170 IF (NKWD) 200,200,180
  180 NM1=NKWD-1
      DO 190 I = 1,NM1
      IP1=I+1
      DO 190 J = IP1,NKWD
      IF (ILOC(I).LE.ILOC(J)) GO TO 190
      L=ILOC(I)
      ILOC(I)=ILOC(J)
      ILOC(J)=L
      L=KWD(I)
      KWD(I)=KWD(J)
      KWD(J)=L
  190 CONTINUE
  200 RETURN
      END
```

SUBROUTINE MCRETN

```
      SUBROUTINE MCRETN (BUF,IP,FR,NTERM,NANS,NCODE)
C
C ALLOWS CONTROL TO BE RETAINED WITHIN SUBROUTINES
C MCMFRM AND MCQFR1 WHILE THE TEXT OF *R(ETURN) FRAMES
C ARE READ.  THIS ALLOWS ALL QUESTIONS TO BE PROCESSED
C AND ANSWERED WITHIN A *M(ARKING) FRAME, AND, WHEN THE
C CURSOR SCREEN CONTROL IS IN ACTION, ALLOWS THE SAME
C FOR THE *Q(UESTION) FRAME, THUS PREVENTING THE SAME
C QUESTION BEING POSED REPETITIVELY
C INPUT PARAMETERS:
C  BUF(72)=ARRAY CONTAINING *R OR *T FRAME CONTROL LINE
C  IP=CURRENT POINTER POSITION IN BUF
C  NTERM=TYPE OF DISPLAY TERMINAL IN USE (>0=CURSOR CONTROL IN USE)
C  NCODE=CURSOR CONTROL INSTRUCTION TO MCDISP
C OUTPUT PARAMETER:
C  FR=NEXT FRAME NUMBER
C*
C     CHARACTER BUF(72),RR
      INTEGER BUF(72),RR
      INTEGER FLAG,SCORE
      COMMON KT,KL,INI,NW1,NW2,JKL,NPRT,LDISP,KA,ITRIG(73),NEOF
      COMMON /FLS/ KF,LADRS,NPP,NNST,NNEND,MODE,FLAG,ION,SCORE,AION,SUM
      COMMON /TABLE/ NTOT,NKA,NFR,KYMAX,KEY(2,250),NDFR(14)
      DATA RR/'R'/
C LOCATE FRAME AND PRINT TEXT FROM IT, THEN ADD ON SCORE (SHOULD BE 0
C OR NEGATIVE), AND ALSO SUM (SHOULD BE 0 OR POSITIVE), IF EITHER
C ARE PRESENT
      NFR=IFIX(FR)
      CALL MACLOC (IADRS)
      IF (IADRS) 10,10,30
   10 WRITE (KT,20) NFR
   20 FORMAT (1X,'*** FRAME #',I5,' NOT FOUND - PLEASE REPORT')
      IF (MODE.EQ.2) STOP
      MODE=0
      RETURN
   30 NPP=IADRS
      CALL MACRND (BUF,IERR)
      IP=3
C READ FRAME NUMBER
      CALL MACNUM (BUF,IP,FR,NFLG,R)
C CHECK THAT FRAME IS A *R(ETURN) TYPE - OTHERWISE TRANSFER CONTROL
      IF (BUF(2).EQ.RR) GO TO 40
      NANS=0
      RETURN
C BYPASS DISPLAY CODE
   40 CALL MACNUM (BUF,IP,X,NFLG,R)
C READ SCORE INSTRUCTION AND ADD PARAMETERS
      CALL MACNUM (BUF,IP,X,NFLG,R)
      SCORE=SCORE+IFIX(X)*ION
      CALL MACNUM (BUF,IP,X,NFLG,R)
      SUM=SUM+X*AION
C**** REPOSITION CURSOR (ACCORDING TO VALUE OF 2ND DIGIT OF LDISP)
C     EXACT POSITION WILL DEPEND ON VALUE OF NCODE = 5 OR 6
      IF (NTERM.GT.0) CALL MCDISP (NTERM,NCODE)
      CALL MACPRN (IADRS)
      RETURN
      END
```

SUBROUTINE MCSUBR

```
      SUBROUTINE MCSUBR (NSUB,NTERM)
C
C ALLOWS ACCESS OF ANY FORTRAN SUBROUTINE (SIMULATION MODEL,
C CALCULATION OR PLOTTING ROUTINE, ETC.) ACCORDING TO THE
C NUMBER (NSUB) SPECIFIED.
C NTERM BRINGS ACROSS CURSOR CONTROL INSTRUCTIONS, IN CASE THESE ARE
C NEEDED IN THE SUBROUTINE
C
C EACH SUBROUTINE TO BE CALLED MUST BE LINKABLE TO THE DRIVER
C AND IS NUMBERED 1,2,3,... ETC. FOR REFERENCE IN THE TEXTFILE.
C EXAMPLE OF AN *S-FRAME ON TEXTFILE:
C         *S   NFR LDISP SCR  NSUB  FR
C         *S   100   1    0    3    110
C THIS IS S-FRAME #100. DISPLAY CODE IS 1, A FIGURE WHICH CAN BE USED
C FOR DISPLAY OR STORAGE INSTRUCTIONS IN THE SUBROUTINE.
C NO CHANGE TO BE MADE IN SCORE (SCR=0)
C SUBROUTINE # 3 IS TO BE CALLED (NSUB=3). CONTROL NOW PASSES TO THE
C FORTRAN SUBROUTINE NAMED (BY MEANS OF BRANCHING INSTRUCTIONS) AND
C THE SUBROUTINE CAN, OF COURSE, PERFORM ANY
C REASONABLE MATHEMATICAL, GRAPHICAL OR TEXT-PROCESSING OPERATION.
C IT MAY ALSO READ PARAMETERS OR CODED INSTRUCTIONS FROM THE TEXTFILE
C ON RECORDS IMMEDIATELY FOLLOWING THE *S-FRAME.
C WHEN THE EXECUTION OF SUBROUTINE NO. 3 ENDS, CONTROL RETURNS TO MCSUBR
C AND IS SUBSEQUENTLY PASSED TO NEXT FRAME (110 IN THE ABOVE EXAMPLE)
C
C*
C     CHARACTER BUF(72)
      INTEGER BUF(72)
      INTEGER FLAG,SCORE
      COMMON /FLS/ KF,LADRS,NPP,NNST,NNEND,MODE,FLAG,ION,SCORE,AION,SUM
      COMMON KT,KL,INI,NW1,NW2,JKL,NPRT,LDISP,KA,ITRIG(72),I,NEOF
C*** LOCAL ARRANGEMENTS - SPECIFY MAXIMUM NUMBER OF SUBROUTINES
      DATA MAXSR/5/
C* CHARACTER TYPE USAGE CHANGES MAY BE NEEDED HERE
C PICK UP COMMAND STRING FROM NEXT RECORD IN FILE.
C IN CHARACTER MODE, S/R MACRND CANNOT BE USED FOR ITRIG, AND A SEPARATE
C 'READ (KF' INSTRUCTION IS NEEDED INSTEAD
      CALL MACRND (ITRIG,IERR)
C     READ (KF'NPP,10) ITRIG
C  10 FORMAT(72A1)
C ENTER MODELS OR SUBROUTINES
      IF (NSUB) 30,30,20
   20 IF (NSUB-MAXSR) 50,50,30
   30 WRITE (KT,40) NSUB
   40 FORMAT (1X,'*** ROUTINE #',I2,' NOT AVAILABLE - PLEASE REPORT')
      IF (MODE.EQ.2) STOP
      MODE=0
      RETURN
C*** LOCAL ARRANGEMENTS FOR SUBROUTINE CALLS
   50 GO TO (60,70,80,90,100), NSUB
   60 CALL SUB1
      GO TO 110
C EXAMPLE OF A SUBROUTINE CALL GIVING TERMINAL TYPE INFORMATION TO S/R
   70 CALL SUB2 (NTERM)
      GO TO 110
   80 CALL SUB3
      GO TO 110
   90 CALL SUB4
      GO TO 110
  100 CALL SUB5
      GO TO 110
  110 RETURN
      END
```

SUBROUTINE AUTHR1

```
      SUBROUTINE AUTHR1 (NSTRT,NFILE)
C
C  (NOTE: NOT ESSENTIAL FOR RUNNING, AND CAN BE DROPPED, BUT WITH
C   LOSS OF THE FACILITIES FOR MAKING A DIRECTORY AND RENUMBERING)
C*
C     CHARACTER YY,CC,DD,STAR,BUF(72),KWDS(6,5)
      INTEGER YY,CC,DD,STAR,BUF(72)
      INTEGER FLAG,SCORE
      COMMON KT,KL,INI,NW1,NW2,JKL,NPRT,LDISP,KA,ITRIG(73),NEOF
      COMMON /FLS/ KF,LADRS,NPP,NNST,NNEND,MODE,FLAG,ION,SCORE,AION,SUM
      COMMON /TABLE/ NTOT,NKA,NFR,KYMAX,KEY(2,250),NDFR(14)
      DATA YY,CC,DD,STAR/'Y','C','D','*'/
C
      IF (NFILE) 10,40,40
   10 WRITE (KT,20)
   20 FORMAT (1X,'*B(EGIN) FRAME MISSING - CREATE NEW FILE?')
      CALL MACINP (BUF,X,NFLG)
      IF (BUF(1).NE.YY) GO TO 90
      NSTRT=0
      CALL NEWFIL(NSTRT,NFILE)
      IF (NFILE) 330,30,30
   30 NSTRT=10
      GO TO 110
   40 WRITE (KT,50)
   50 FORMAT (1X,'RENUMBER AND CHECK TEXT FILE?')
      CALL MACINP (BUF,X,NFLG)
      IF (BUF(1).NE.YY) GO TO 70
      WRITE (KT,60)
   60 FORMAT (1X,'HAVE YOU GOT A COPY IN CASE OF ACCIDENTS?')
      CALL MACINP (BUF,X,NFLG)
      IF (BUF(1).NE.YY) GO TO 70
      CALL RENUM1
C SET POINTER TO 1ST LINE OF FILE (THE *B - BEGIN - FRAME)
      NPP=NNST
      CALL MACRND (BUF,IERR)
      IP=3
      CALL MACNUM (BUF,IP,X,NFLG,R)
C GET STARTING FRAME NUMBER FROM THE *B FRAME
      NSTRT=IFIX(X)
      GO TO 110
   70 WRITE (KT,80)
   80 FORMAT (1X,'NEW DIRECTORY?')
      CALL MACINP (BUF,X,NFLG)
      IF (BUF(1).EQ.YY) GO TO 110
      MODE=0
      RETURN
   90 NPP=NNST+1
C*** LOCAL DIRECT ACCESS FILE ARRANGEMENTS - INSERT DUMMY FRAME ON LINE
C     2 TO ALLOW SUBSEQUENT EDITING
      WRITE (KF'NPP,100)
  100 FORMAT ('*T1 0 0 0 2')
      NSTRT=1
  110 MODE=1
C IN THIS MODE THE DRIVER CREATES A NEW TABLE OF FRAME ADDRESSES
C BY READING THROUGH THE ENTIRE TEXT FILE. THE TABLE
C IS THEN STORED JUST BEFORE THE END OF THE FILE (FOLLOWING THE
C RECORD CONTAINING '**' IN THE FIRST TWO COLUMNS).
C INITIALISE DICTIONARY COUNT AND ALL DICTIONARY LINE NUMBERS
      NDIR=0
      DO 120 I = 1,14
  120 NDFR(I)=0
      NTOT=0
      L=NNST
  130 L=L+1
      NPP=L
      CALL MACRND (BUF,IERR)
      IF ((L+NTOT/8+5).GT.NNEND.OR.IERR.NE.0) GO TO 220
C IGNORE TEXT LINES AND COMMENT FRAMES. READ ONLY THE CONTROL
C RECORDS (IE. WITH '*' IN COLUMN 1)
```

SUBROUTINE AUTHR1
CONTINUED

```
  140 IF (BUF(1).NE.STAR.OR.BUF(2).EQ.CC) GO TO 130
      IF (BUF(2).EQ.STAR) GO TO 250
      IF (BUF(2).EQ.DD) GO TO 180
      NTOT=NTOT+1
C CHECK THAT NUMBER OF FRAMES NOT GREATER THAN KYMAX & KEY(..,KYMAX)
      IF (NTOT-KYMAX-1) 150,160,130
  150 IP=3
      CALL MACNUM (BUF,IP,X,NFLG,R)
      KEY(1,NTOT)=IFIX(X)
      KEY(2,NTOT)=L
      GO TO 130
  160 WRITE (KT,170) KYMAX,KEY(1,KYMAX)
  170 FORMAT (1X,'CURRENT VERSION OF THE DRIVER ALLOWS MAXIMUM OF',I5,
     X' FRAMES.',/,1X,'REMAINING FRAMES WILL NOT BE INDEXED IN THE DIREC
     XTORY.',/,1X,'LAST FRAME INCLUDED WAS # ',I5)
      GO TO 130
C RECORD LOCATION OF DICTIONARY
  180 NDIR=NDIR+1
      IF (NDIR-14) 210,210,190
  190 WRITE (KT,200)
  200 FORMAT (1X,'*** WARNING - MORE THAN 14 DICTIONARIES ARE IGNORED')
      NDIR=14
  210 NDFR(NDIR)=L
      GO TO 130
  220 NPP=L
C*** LOCAL DIRECT-ACCESS FILE ARRANGEMENTS
      WRITE (KF'NPP,230)
  230 FORMAT ('**')
      WRITE (KT,240)
  240 FORMAT (1X,'FILE WAS DEGRADED OR TOO SHORT - TEXT HAS BEEN CHANGED
     X AT ITS END')
  250 LADRS=L+1
      IF (NTOT.GT.KYMAX) NTOT=KYMAX
      WRITE (KT,260) NTOT,L
  260 FORMAT (1X,I4,' CONTROL FRAMES.    ',I5,'= LAST TEXT LINE NUMBER')
C UPDATE B FRAME AND STORE THE DIRECTORY STARTING AT ADDRESS 'LADRS'
      NPP=NNST
      N=(NTOT-1)/8+1
C*** LOCAL DIRECT ACCESS FILE ARRANGEMENTS
      WRITE (KF'NPP,270) NSTRT,LADRS
  270 FORMAT ('*B',2I6)
      NPP=LADRS
C*** LOCAL DIRECT ACCESS FILE ARRANGEMENTS
      WRITE (KF'NPP,280) NTOT,NDIR
  280 FORMAT (8(I4,I5))
      DO 310 I = 1,N
      L2=I*8
      L1=L2-7
      IF (NTOT-L2) 290,300,300
  290 L2=NTOT
  300 LADRS=LADRS+1
      NPP=LADRS
C*** LOCAL DIRECT ACCESS FILE ARRANGEMENTS
  310 WRITE (KF'NPP,280) ((KEY(J,L),J=1,2),L=L1,L2)
C WRITE RECORD AFTER FRAME DIRECTORY WITH DICTIONARY FRAME NUMBERS
      LADRS=LADRS+1
      NPP=LADRS
C*** LOCAL DIRECT ACCESS FILE ARRANGEMENTS
      WRITE (KF'NPP,320) (NDFR(I),I=1,14)
  320 FORMAT(14I5)
  330 RETURN
      END
```

SUBROUTINE AUTHR2

```
      SUBROUTINE AUTHR2 (TRACE,FR)
C
C (NOTE:  THIS SUBROUTINE IS NOT ESSENTIAL TO MACAID - IT CAN
C         BE DROPPED WITH THE LOSS OF SOME AUTHORING AND EDITING
C         CAPABILITIES DESCRIBED BELOW)
C
C WHENEVER THE DRIVER FINDS 'AUTHOR' ON INPUT, IT BRANCHES TO
C THIS SUBROUTINE AND PROMPTS WITH 'COMMAND:'
C ANY OF THE FOLLOWING COMMANDS CAN THEN BE ENTERED:
C   ED(IT) - ALLOWS EDITING OF TEXT FRAMES (PROMPT CHANGES TO '/')
C         N.B. 'EDIT' COMMANDS OTHER THAN 'T'(YPE), 'L'(IST) AND 'E'(ND)
C         ARE VALID ONLY IF MACAID HAS BEEN STARTED IN 'AUTHOR' MODE
C         WITH THE 'AUTHORING PASSWORD' HAVING BEEN GIVEN.
C      X FRAME NO.,(NUM)  PERFORMS OPERATION 'X' AT FRAME NUMBER
C              SPECIFIED, PLUS OR MINUS 'NUM' LINES.  FOR EXAMPLE,
C              X10,-2  WOULD ALLOW OPERATION 'X' TO START 2 LINES BEFORE
C              FRAME NUMBER 10.   IF UNSPECIFIED, NUM=0.
C              IF NO FRAME NUMBER IS GIVEN, THE OPERATION WILL START
C              ON THE LINE WHICH FOLLOWS THE LAST EDITED LINE. THUS, FOR
C              EXAMPLE, LINES CAN BE SUCCESSIVELY MODIFIED BY TYPING
C              'M' REPEATEDLY.
C      T(YPE) THE SPECIFIED FRAME AND ITS TEXT, STOPPING WHEN THE NEXT
C              LINE BEGINS WITH '*' (E.G. T, T20 OR T20,5)
C      L(IST) THE SPECIFIED LINE, AND THEN WHEN PROMPTED SPECIFY THE
C              NUMBER OF FURTHER LINES TO BE LISTED (E.G. L, L20 OR
C              L20,-5 ...'HOW MANY LINES?'...'200'...)
C      O(VERWRITE) THE SPECIFIED FRAME OR LINE, AND
C      M(ODIFY) THE SPECIFIED FRAME OR LINE.  THE SYSTEM FIRST PRINTS
C              THE CURRENT LINE.   CORRECTIONS ARE ENTERED BELOW.
C              (E.G. O, O20 OR O20,3;  M, M20, M20,-3)
C              THE CORRECTED LINE IS THEN DISPLAYED AGAIN, REPEATEDLY,
C              UNTIL A BLANK LINE IS ENTERED.
C              WITH 'OVERWRITE' THE NEXT LINE IS THEN DISPLAYED, AND
C              AVAILABLE FOR FURTHER MODIFICATION, UNTIL A DOUBLE SLASH
C              IS TYPED (SEE BELOW) TO TERMINATE THE OPERATION.
C              WITH M(ODIFY) THE OPERATION FINISHES AT THIS POINT.
C              FOR M(ODIFY) OPERATIONS, A FURTHER INSTRUCTION CHARACTER
C              MUST BE ENTERED AT THE PLACE ON THE LINE AT WHICH THE
C              OPERATION IS TO TAKE PLACE.  THIS IS 'D'(DELETE), ONE 'D'
C              FOR EACH CHARACTER TO BE DELETED; 'R'(REPLACE) REPLACES
C              PREVIOUS TEXT BY THE CHARACTERS FOLLOWING THE 'R'; 'I'
C              (INSERT) INSERTS TEXT BEFORE THE CHARACTER BELOW WHICH 'I'
C              IS TYPED. HASHES BLANK CHARACTERS AS IN 'OVERWRITE'.
C              I(NSERT) MAY FOLLOW IMMEDIATELY AFTER D(ELETE), ON THE
C              SAME LINE - E.G.  DDDDDITHE
C            N.B. TO 'BLANK' A CHARACTER DURING 'OVERWRITE' TYPE A HASH
C            ( # ) UNLESS THE BLANK IS EMBRACED BY TEXT.
C            TO INSERT TRAILING BLANKS DURING 'MODIFY' USE HASHES
C            INSTEAD. 'REPLACE' DOES NOT REPLACE TRAILING BLANKS.
C      //      DOUBLE-SLASH ENTERED DURING 'MODIFY' OR 'OVERWRITE'
C              TERMINATES THE CURRENT OPERATION AND RETAINS PREVIOUS LINE
C              UNCHANGED
C      D(ELETE) GIVES INVITATION TO DELETE ANY NUMBER OF LINES STARTING
C              AT LINE SPECIFIED, AND CLOSES UP FILE (VERY SLOW!)
C      A(DD) GIVES INVITATION TO ADD ANY NUMBER OF LINES IMMEDIATELY
C              BEFORE SPECIFIED LINE, AND EXPANDS FILE (VERY SLOW!)
C      C(ONDENSE) THE FILE, STARTING FROM THE SPECIFIED LINE, AND REMOVE
C              ALL BLANK '...' LINES THROUGHOUT, TO THE END (VERY SLOW!)
C      S(PACED LIST OF ALL) - LISTS ENTIRE TEXT FILE ON LOGICAL UNIT
C              KT (OR ALTERNATIVELY, ON LINEPRINTER)
C      R(ESTART) - SEE BELOW
C      E(ND) - END EDIT MODE
C   TR(ACE) - TRACE THE SEQUENCE OF BRANCHING AT EACH NEW FRAME, AND
C     ALSO PRINT VALUES OF FLAG, SCORE AND SUM
C   UN(TRACE) - TURN TRACING OFF
C   RE(START) - RESTARTS THE PROGRAM, TO ALLOW REMAKING DIRECTORY,
C     RENUMBERING, OR EXTENDING THE TEXT FILE (ALSO ALLOWED IN 'EDIT')
C   GO (FRAME NO) - EXIT AUTHOR MODE AND BRANCH TO THE SPECIFIED FRAME.
C          IF NONE IS SPECIFIED, GO BACK TO THE CALLING FRAME
```

SUBROUTINE AUTHR2
CONTINUED

```
C   ST(OP) - STOP THE PROGRAM (COMPLETELY).
C*
C       CHARACTER BLANK,HASH,DOT,STAR,SLASH,BUF(72),ANS(73),COMDS(2,6),
C      X EDCOM(10),CC,YY,RR,DD,II,BUF1,BUF2,BUF3,LTYPE
        INTEGER BLANK,HASH,DOT,STAR,SLASH,BUF(72),ANS(73),COMDS(2,6),
      X EDCOM(10),CC,YY,RR,DD,BUF1,BUF2,BUF3
        INTEGER FLAG,SCORE,TRACE
        COMMON KT,KL,INI,NW1,NW2,JKL,NPRT,LDISP,KA,ITRIG(73),NEOF
        COMMON /FLS/ KF,LADRS,NPP,NNST,NNEND,MODE,FLAG,ION,SCORE,AION,SUM
        COMMON /TABLE/ NTOT,NKA,NFR,KYMAX,KEY(2,250),NDFR(14)
        EQUIVALENCE (BUF(1),BUF1),(BUF(2),BUF2),(BUF(3),BUF3),
      X (ANS(1),LTYPE)
        DATA BLANK,HASH,DOT,STAR,SLASH/' ','#','.','*','/' /
        DATA COMDS/'E','D',  'G','O',  'S','T',  'T','R',  'U','N',
      X  'R','E'/
        DATA EDCOM/'T','L','E','O','M','A','D','C','S','R'/
        DATA CC,YY,RR,DD,II/'C','Y','R','D','I'/
        IF (MODE.EQ.0) MODE=1
   10 WRITE (KT,20)
   20 FORMAT (1X,'COMMAND: ')
        READ (INI,30) BUF
   30 FORMAT (73A1)
        DO 50 N = 1,6
        DO 40 J = 1,2
        IF (BUF(J).NE.COMDS(J,N)) GO TO 50
   40 CONTINUE
C   VALID COMMANDS: ED(IT), GO(TO), ST(OP), TR(ACE), UN(TRACE), RE(START)
        GO TO (100,800,900,870,880,890), N
   50 CONTINUE
        WRITE (KT,140)
   60 WRITE (KT,70)
   70 FORMAT (1X,'*INVALID*')
        GO TO 10
   80 WRITE (KT,90)
   90 FORMAT (1X,'NOT ENOUGH ROOM IN FILE')
        GO TO 150
C=========================================================================
C 'ED(IT)' - ASK FOR AND PROCESS EDIT SUB-COMMANDS (T,L,E,O,M,A,D,C,S,R)
C KEEP CHECK ON LINE ADDITIONS TO PREVENT REMOVAL OF END-OF-FILE LINE
  100 NADDE=0
        NPP=NNST
        L=NPP+1
        CALL MACRND (BUF,IERR)
        IP=3
        CALL MACNUM (BUF,IP,X,NFLG,R)
        CALL MACNUM (BUF,IP,X,NFLG,R)
        NENDF=IFIX(X)
  110 WRITE (KT,30) BLANK,SLASH
        READ (INI,30) BUF
        NREF=NENDF+NADDE
        DO 120 IEC = 1,10
        IF (BUF1.EQ.EDCOM(IEC)) GO TO 180
  120 CONTINUE
  130 WRITE (KT,140)
  140 FORMAT (1X,'NON-EXISTENT COMMAND')
  150 WRITE (KT,70)
        GO TO 110
  160 WRITE (KT,170)
  170 FORMAT (1X,'EXCEPT IN AUTHOR MODE')
        GO TO 150
  180 IF (IEC.GT.3.AND.MODE.NE.1) GO TO 160
        GO TO (220,220,190,220,220,220,220,220,610,890), IEC
C-------------------------------------------------------------------------
C END EDITING - IF LINES ALTERED, WARN TO REMAKE DIRECTORY
  190 IF (NADDE) 200,10,200
  200 WRITE (KT,210)
  210 FORMAT (1X,'*** WARNING - NEW DIRECTORY IS NOW ESSENTIAL ***')
        GO TO 890
C-------------------------------------------------------------------------
```

```
SUBROUTINE AUTHR2
CONTINUED

C T(YPE), L(IST), O(VERWRITE), M(ODIFY), A(DD), D(ELETE) OR C(ONDENSE)
  220 IP=2
      CALL MACNUM (BUF,IP,X,NFLG,R)
      IF (NFLG.EQ.-1) GO TO 260
      NFR=IFIX(X)
      CALL MACLOC (IADRS)
      IF (IADRS) 230,230,250
  230 WRITE (KT,240)
  240 FORMAT (1X,'NON-EXISTENT FRAME NUMBER')
      GO TO 150
  250 CALL MACNUM (BUF,IP,X,I,R)
      L=IADRS+IFIX(X)
      NPP=L
  260 IF (NPP.LT.NNST.OR.(NPP.GT.(NREF-2).AND.IEC.NE.2.AND.IEC.NE.4.AND.
     XIEC.NE.5).OR.(NPP.GT.(NNEND-2))) GO TO 270
      CALL MACRND (BUF,IERR)
      IF (IERR) 270,290,270
  270 WRITE (KT,280)
  280 FORMAT (1X,'LINE(S) OUTSIDE LIMITS OF FILE')
      GO TO 150
  290 WRITE (KT,300) BUF
C*** LOCAL ARRANGEMENTS - TO ALIGN CORRECTIONS WITH TEXT IT MAY BE
C NECESSARY TO SUBSTITUTE '1X' FOR '2X' IN NEXT FORMAT STATEMENT
  300 FORMAT (2X,72A1)
      IF (IEC.EQ.1) GO TO 550
      IF (IEC.EQ.2) GO TO 570
      IF (IEC.GT.5) GO TO 650
C.....................................................................
C O(VERWRITE) OR M(ODIFY)
  310 WRITE (KT,320)
  320 FORMAT (1X)
      READ (INI,30) ANS
      IF (LTYPE.EQ.SLASH.AND.ANS(2).EQ.SLASH) GO TO 110
C LOCATE LAST NON-BLANK CHARACTER IN INPUT BUFFER (POSITION K)
      DO 330 I = 1,72
      K=73-I
      IF (ANS(K).NE.BLANK) GO TO 340
  330 CONTINUE
C ALL BLANK INPUT - STORE MODIFIED LINE
      GO TO 530
C SET REFERENCE VALUE FOR END OF INPUT
  340 KREF=K
      DO 360 J = 1,72
C REPLACE '#' BY BLANKS
      IF (ANS(J).NE.HASH) GO TO 350
      ANS(J)=BLANK
      IF (J.LE.72) BUF(J)=BLANK
C LOCATE FIRST NON-BLANK CHARACTER IN INPUT BUFFER (POSITION J)
  350 IF (ANS(J).NE.BLANK) GO TO 370
  360 CONTINUE
      GO TO 390
  370 IF (IEC.EQ.5) GO TO 400
      DO 380 I = J,K
  380 BUF(I)=ANS(I)
  390 WRITE (KT,300) BUF
      GO TO 310
C SET REFERENCE VALUE FOR BEGINNING OF INPUT
  400 JREF=J
      IF (ANS(J).EQ.RR) GO TO 420
      IF (ANS(J).EQ.DD) GO TO 440
      IF (ANS(J).EQ.II) GO TO 490
      WRITE (KT,410)
  410 FORMAT (1X,'MODIFY COMMAND MUST BEGIN WITH R,D,I OR #')
      GO TO 290
C 'R'EPLACE CHARACTERS
  420 M=K-1
      DO 430 I = J,M
  430 BUF(I)=ANS(I+1)
      GO TO 390
```

SUBROUTINE AUTHR2
CONTINUED

```
C 'D'ELETE CHARACTERS
  440 M=J+1
      DO 450 I = M,K
      IF (ANS(I).EQ.DD) GO TO 450
      KREF=I-1
      JREF=I
      GO TO 460
  450 CONTINUE
  460 N=KREF-J+1
      M=72-N
      DO 470 I = J,M
  470 BUF(I)=BUF(I+N)
      M=73-N
      DO 480 I = M,72
  480 BUF(I)=BLANK
      IF (ANS(KREF+1).NE.II) GO TO 390
C 'I'NSERT CHARACTER STRING
  490 K1=K-JREF
C MOVE EXISTING TEXT TO RIGHT TO MAKE ROOM FOR INSERT
      K2=J+K1
      DO 500 I = K2,72
      K3=K2+72-I
  500 BUF(K3)=BUF(K3-K1)
C FILL UP OLD REDUNDANT TEXT WITH NEW TEXT
  510 M=J+K1-1
      DO 520 I = J,M
      K1=JREF-J+I+1
      IF (ANS(K1).EQ.HASH) ANS(K1)=BLANK
  520 BUF(I)=ANS(K1)
      GO TO 390
  530 NPP=L
C*** LOCAL DIRECT ACCESS FILE ARRANGEMENTS
  540 WRITE (KF'NPP,30) BUF
C.......................................................................
C T(YPE)
  550 L=L+1
      NPP=L
      IF (IEC.EQ.5) GO TO 110
      CALL MACRND (BUF,IERR)
      IF (IERR) 270,560,270
  560 IF (BUF1.NE.STAR.OR.IEC.NE.1) GO TO 290
      NPP=L
      GO TO 110
C.......................................................................
C L(IST)
  570 WRITE (KT,670)
      CALL MACINP (ANS,XANS,NFLG)
      N=IFIX(XANS)
      IF (L+N-NNEND-1) 580,580,270
  580 NPP=L
      DO 590 J = 1,N
      CALL MACRND (BUF,IERR)
  590 WRITE (KT,300) BUF
      L=NPP
      GO TO 110
C.......................................................................
C S(PACED LIST)
C LIST THE WHOLE FILE ON THE LINEPRINTER (OR UNIT KT), WITH
C ALL *-FRAMES SEPARATED FROM EACH OTHER BY BLANK LINES (FOR
C EASIER INTELLIGIBILITY)
  610 KN=KT
C*** LOCAL ARRANGEMENTS FOR LINEPRINTER LISTING OF THE FILE - DELETE
C     IF A LINEPRINTER IS NOT AVAILABLE.   LINEPRINTER=LOGICAL DEVICE # 7
      WRITE (KT,620)
  620 FORMAT (1X,'LINEPRINTER LISTING?')
      CALL MACINP (ANS,XANS,NFLG)
      IF (LTYPE.EQ.YY.AND.MODE.EQ.1) KN=7
      NPP=NNST
      DO 640 I = NNST,NNEND
```

SUBROUTINE AUTHR2
CONTINUED

```
      CALL MACRND (BUF,IERR)
      IF (BUF1.NE.STAR) GO TO 630
      IF (BUF2.EQ.STAR) GO TO 110
      IF (LTYPE.NE.CC) WRITE (KN,320)
      LTYPE=BUF2
  630 WRITE (KN,300) BUF
  640 CONTINUE
      GO TO 110
C.......................................................................
C DELETE, ADD OR CONDENSE (N.B. THESE OPERATIONS ARE VERY SLOW,
C ESPECIALLY AT THE START OF A LARGE FILE)        ----
  650 NREF=NENDF+NADDE
      NPP=L+1
      IF (IEC.NE.8) GO TO 660
      N=0
      GO TO 680
  660 WRITE (KT,670)
  670 FORMAT (1X,'HOW MANY LINES?')
      CALL MACINP (ANS,XANS,NFLG)
      N=IFIX(XANS)
      IF (IEC.EQ.6) GO TO 740
C.......................................................................
C D(ELETE) OR C(ONDENSE)
  680 NPP=NPP-1+N
  690 CALL MACRND (BUF,IERR)
      IF (IERR) 700,720,700
  700 WRITE (KT,710) N
  710 FORMAT (1X,I3,' LINE(S) DELETED')
      NADDE=NADDE-N
      GO TO 110
  720 IF (IEC.NE.8.OR.BUF1.NE.DOT.OR.BUF2.NE.DOT.OR.BUF3.NE.DOT) GO TO
     X730
      N=N+1
      GO TO 690
  730 NPP=NPP-1-N
C*** LOCAL DIRECT ACCESS FILE ARRANGEMENTS ?INCREMENT NPP AFTERWARDS?
      WRITE (KF'NPP,30) BUF
C     NPP=NPP+1
      NPP=NPP+N
      IF (NPP.GT.NREF) GO TO 700
      GO TO 690
C.......................................................................
C A(DD)
  740 NREF=NREF-1
      IF (NREF+N-NNEND+(NTOT-1)/8+2) 750,80,80
  750 NPP=NREF
      CALL MACRND (BUF,IERR)
      NPP=NREF+N
C*** LOCAL DIRECT ACCESS FILE ARRANGEMENTS ?INCREMENT NPP AFTERWARDS?
      WRITE (KF'NPP,30) BUF
C     NPP=NPP+1
      NREF=NREF-1
      IF (NPP.GT.(L+1).AND.NREF.GT.NNST) GO TO 750
  760 NPP=L
      DO 780 I = 1,N
C*** LOCAL DIRECT ACCESS FILE ARRANGEMENTS ?INCREMENT NPP AFTERWARDS?
      WRITE (KF'NPP,770)
  770 FORMAT ('...')
C     NPP=NPP+1
  780 CONTINUE
      WRITE (KT,790) N
  790 FORMAT (1X,I3,' LINE(S) ADDED')
      NADDE=NADDE+N
      GO TO 110
C=======================================================================
C 'GO (TO)' COMMAND
  800 IP=3
      CALL MACNUM (BUF,IP,X,I,R)
C IF A FRAME NO. WAS SPECIFIED BRANCH TO IT, OTHERWISE RETURN
```

SUBROUTINE AUTHR2
CONTINUED

```
      IF (X) 860,860,810
C CHECK THAT ADDRESS EXISTS, AND IS NOT AN *R (RETURN) FRAME
  810 NFR=IFIX(X)
      CALL MACLOC (I)
      IF (I.GT.0) GO TO 830
      WRITE (KT,820) NFR
  820 FORMAT (1X,'FRAME # ',I4,' NON-EXISTENT, OR NOT IN THE DIRECTORY')
      GO TO 60
  830 NPP=I
      CALL MACRND (BUF,I)
      IF (BUF2.NE.RR) GO TO 850
      WRITE (KT,840)
  840 FORMAT (1X,'FRAME IS *R(ETURN) TYPE')
      GO TO 60
  850 FR=X
  860 RETURN
C=========================================================================
C 'TR(ACE)' AND 'UN(TRACE)'  - TURN TRACE FLAG ON OR OFF, RESPECTIVELY
  870 TRACE=1
      GO TO 10
  880 TRACE=0
      GO TO 10
C=========================================================================
C 'RE(START)' - RE-INITIALIZE DIRECTORY AND START OVER AGAIN
  890 FR=0.
      RETURN
C=========================================================================
C 'ST(OP)' COMMAND
  900 ION=-1
      RETURN
      END
```

SUBROUTINE RENUM1

```
      SUBROUTINE RENUM1
C
C  (NOTE: THIS S/R IS NOT ESSENTIAL AND CAN BE DROPPED WITH THE LOSS
C   OF THE CHECKING AND RENUMBERING FACILITY)
C
C RENUMBER AND CHECK ALL CONTROL FRAMES
C*
C     CHARACTER BUF1,BUF2,BUF(72),BUFNU(125),NO(5),ALPH(4),LEGAL(10)
C     CHARACTER BB,CC,GG,RR,STAR,BLANK,RB,RCB,QUOTE,COMMA,ZERO,DD,II,MM,
C    X  PLUS,MINUS,SLASH,UU,SS,EE,YY,K,KK,KKK,KKKK
      INTEGER BUF1,BUF2,BUF(72),BUFNU(125),NO(5),ALPH(4),LEGAL(10)
      INTEGER BB,CC,GG,RR,STAR,BLANK,RB,RCB,QUOTE,COMMA,ZERO,DD,PLUS,
     X SLASH,UU,SS,EE,YY
      INTEGER FLAG,SCORE
C*** LOCAL ARRANGEMENTS - SIZE OF THE ARRAY KEY(..,250) CONTROLS MAXIMUM
C    NUMBER OF CONTROL FRAMES WHICH CAN BE RENUMBERED (KYMAX=250)
      COMMON KT,KL,INI,NW1,NW2,JKL,NPRT,LDISP,KA,ITRIG(73),NEOF
      COMMON /FLS/ KF,LADRS,NPP,NNST,NNEND,MODE,FLAG,ION,SCORE,AION,SUM
      COMMON /TABLE/ NTOT,NKA,NFR,KYMAX,KEY(2,250),NDFR(14)
      EQUIVALENCE (BUF1,BUF(1)), (BUF2,BUF(2))
      DATA BB,CC,GG,RR,STAR,BLANK,RB,RCB,QUOTE,COMMA,ZERO,DD,II,MM,
     X PLUS,MINUS,SLASH,UU,SS,EE,YY/'B','C','G','R','*',' ',')','>',1H',
     X ',','O','D','I','M','+','-','/','U','S','E','Y'/
      DATA NO/'(','<',1H','>',')'/
      DATA LEGAL/'T','R','S','E','Q','M','I','F','A','Z'/
      NPP=NNST
      L=1
      IA=0
C=======================================================================
C FIRST PASS - READ ALL LINES, SELECTING ALL NUMBERED FRAMES - THUS
C EXCLUDING *B, *G, *D AND *C -
C THEN INSERT NUMBERS OF OLD FRAMES INTO KEY(1,...)
   10 IA=IA+1
C CHECK THAT FILE LENGTH IS ENOUGH - IF NOT, INSERT TEXT TERMINATOR
      IF ((IA+L/8+5).GT.NNEND) GO TO 60
      CALL MACRND (BUF,IERR)
      IF (IERR-1) 20,90,20
   20 IF (BUF1.NE.STAR.OR.BUF2.EQ.BB.OR.BUF2.EQ.CC.OR.BUF2.EQ.GG.OR.BUF2
     X.EQ.DD) GO TO 10
      IF (BUF2.EQ.STAR) GO TO 90
      IP=3
      CALL MACNUM (BUF,IP,XX,NFLG,R)
      KEY(1,L)=IFIX(XX)
      KEY(2,L)=0
      DO 30 I = 1,10
      IF (BUF2.EQ.LEGAL(I)) GO TO 50
   30 CONTINUE
      WRITE (KT,40) KEY(1,L)
   40 FORMAT (1X,'OLD FRAME #',I5,' ILLEGAL, OR TYPE LETTER NOT IN COLUM
     XN 2')
   50 L=L+1
C CHECK THAT NUMBER OF WORKING FRAMES DOES NOT EXCEED ARRAY CAPACITY
C*** LOCAL ARRANGEMENTS - SEE REMARKS ABOVE ABOUT ARRAY 'KEY'
      IF (L-KYMAX) 10,10,620
   60 NPP=IA+NNST
      WRITE (KF'NPP,70)
   70 FORMAT ('**')
      WRITE (KT,80)
   80 FORMAT (1X,'TEXT TERMINATOR ** MISSING - NEW ONE INSERTED')
   90 L=L-1
C RECORD NUMBER OF CONTROL FRAMES
      IXX=L
C CHECK ASCENDING ORDER & DUPLICATE FRAMES
      DO 120 I = 2,L
      IF (KEY(1,I)-KEY(1,I-1)) 100,100,120
  100 WRITE (KT,110) KEY(1,I)
  110 FORMAT (1X,'OLD FRAME ',I4,' WAS DUPLICATE OR OUT OF SEQUENCE & WI
     XLL BE RECODED')
  120 CONTINUE
```

SUBROUTINE RENUM1
CONTINUED

```
      NPP=NNST
C PRINT TABLE OF OLD FRAME NUMBERS
      WRITE (KT,130) (KEY(1,I),I=1,L)
  130 FORMAT (1X,'OLD CONTROL FRAMES WERE..',/,25(10I6,/))
C COUNT OF LINES PROCESSED
      M1=0
      M2=1
C INITIALISE COUNT OF CONTROL FRAMES
      NL=0
C==========================================================================
C SECOND PASS - RENUMBER ALL WORKING FRAMES IN 10'S, THEN RECODE
      IK=IA-1
      DO 550 IB = 1,IK
      CALL MACRND (BUF,IERR)
C DETECT *, + AND /, AND ELIMINATE *C FRAMES - DETECT + AFTER *D
      IF (BUF1.EQ.PLUS) GO TO 140
C FRAME IS NOT A *D(ICTIONARY)
      NDICT=0
      IF ((BUF1.NE.STAR.AND.BUF1.NE.SLASH).OR.BUF2.EQ.CC) GO TO 520
      IF (BUF2.NE.DD) GO TO 150
C FRAME IS A *D(ICTIONARY) - STOP FURTHER PROCESSING
      NDICT=1
      GO TO 520
C IF CONTINUATION LINE BELONGS TO A DICTIONARY, STOP PROCESSING
  140 IF (NDICT-1) 150,520,150
C FILL NEW LINE BUFFER WITH BLANKS
  150 DO 160 I = 3,125
  160 BUFNU(I)=BLANK
      NN1=3
C IF 1ST CHARACTER = /, INSERT '/USE'
      IF (BUF1.NE.SLASH) GO TO 170
      BUFNU(1)=SLASH
      BUFNU(2)=UU
      BUFNU(3)=SS
      BUFNU(4)=EE
      IP=5
      NN1=6
      GO TO 270
  170 BUFNU(1)=BUF1
      BUFNU(2)=BUF2
      IP=3
C DETECT A CONTINUATION LINE
      IF (BUF1.NE.PLUS) GO TO 180
C PUNCTUATE A CONTINUATION LINE FOR EASIER READING
      BUFNU(2)=BLANK
C MOVE POINTER BACK ONE SPACE TO MAKE SURE NO SIGNIFICANT CHARACTER
C IS LOST
      IP=2
      GO TO 270
C *B(EGIN) AND *G(LOBAL) FRAMES HAVE NO IDENTIFYING NUMBER TO BE
C RENUMBERED
  180 IF (BUF2.EQ.BB.OR.BUF2.EQ.GG) GO TO 270
      CALL MACNUM (BUF,IP,XX,NFLG,R)
C INCREMENT CONTROL FRAME COUNTER
      NL=NL+1
C IC= NEW FRAME NUMBER, IN ASCENDING ORDER OF TENS
      IC=NL*10
      I=IC
      CALL RENUM2 (ALPH,I)
C INSERT FRAME #
      DO 190 I = 1,4
  190 BUFNU(I+3)=ALPH(I)
C INSERT DISPLAY CODE (4-DIGIT INTEGER)
      CALL MACNUM (BUF,IP,XX,NFLG,R)
      I=IFIX(XX)
      CALL RENUM2 (ALPH,I)
      DO 200 I = 1,4
  200 BUFNU(I+8)=ALPH(I)
C *E(ND) FRAME DETECTED - NO FURTHER NUMBERS ARE SIGNIFICANT
```

```
SUBROUTINE RENUM1
CONTINUED

      IF (BUF2.EQ.EE) GO TO 410
      CALL MACNUM (BUF,IP,XX,NFLG,R)
      I=IFIX(XX)
      CALL RENUM2 (ALPH,I)
C INSERT SCORE OR OUTPUT INSTRUCTION NUMBER
      DO 210 I = 1,4
  210 BUFNU(I+13)=ALPH(I)
      IPX=IP
      CALL MACNUM (BUF,IP,XX,NFLG,R)
C INSERT ADD OR PROMPT INSTRUCTION NUMBER
      I=IFIX(XX)
C CHECK IF ADD PARAMETER HAS A DECIMAL POINT - IF SO, COPY UNCHANGED
      IF (R-.5) 220,240,240
  220 NN1=IP-IPX
      IF (NN1.GT.4) NN1=4
      DO 230 I = 1,NN1
  230 BUFNU(I+18)=BUF(IPX-1+I)
      GO TO 260
  240 CALL RENUM2 (ALPH,I)
      DO 250 I = 1,4
  250 BUFNU(I+18)=ALPH(I)
C *R(ETURN) FRAME DETECTED - NO MORE NUMBERS AFTER 'ADD' PARAMETER
  260 IF (BUF2.EQ.RR) GO TO 410
      NN1=24
C=======================================================================
C PROCESS REMAINDER OF LINE
  270 INC=0
C L=1 - OUTSIDE BRACKETS OR QUOTES, L=-1 - INSIDE BRACKETS OR QUOTES
      L=1
      DO 400 IT = NN1,125
C DETECT END-OF-LINE OR BUFFER, OR ASTERISK = PROCESSING COMPLETE
      IF (IT+INC-125) 280,280,410
  280 IF (IP.GE.72) GO TO 410
      K=BUF(IP)
      IF (K.EQ.STAR) GO TO 410
C TRANSCRIBE ALL COMMAS AND BLANKS WITHOUT CHANGE
      IF (K.EQ.COMMA.OR.K.EQ.BLANK) GO TO 310
C DETECT BRACKETS, OR INVERTED COMMAS
      DO 290 I = 1,5
      IF (K.EQ.NO(I)) GO TO 300
  290 CONTINUE
      IF (L) 310,310,320
  300 L=-L
  310 BUFNU(IT+INC)=K
      GO TO 400
  320 CALL MACNUM (BUF,IP,XX,NFLG,R)
C MOVE POINTER BACK 1 SPACE, BECAUSE IT WILL BE MOVED ON AT END OF LOOP
      IP=IP-1
      I=IFIX(XX)
C IGNORE ZERO OR NEGATIVE FRAME NUMBERS
      IF (I) 330,330,340
  330 N=I
      GO TO 380
  340 DO 350 N = 1,IXX
C CHECK KEY(1,...) TO MAKE SURE FRAME EXISTS
      IF (KEY(1,N)-I) 350,370,350
  350 CONTINUE
      WRITE (KT,360) IC
  360 FORMAT (1X,'NEW FRAME # ',I5,' ACCESSES NON-EXISTENT OLD FRAME - S
     XET TO 9999')
      N=9999
      GO TO 380
  370 KEY(2,N)=I
      N=N*10
  380 CALL RENUM2 (ALPH,N)
      DO 390 I = 1,4
      N=IT+INC+I
  390 BUFNU(N)=ALPH(I)
C *B FRAME ONLY HAS A SINGLE (STARTING FRAME) ADDRESS
```

SUBROUTINE RENUM1
CONTINUED

```
      IF (BUF2.EQ.BB) GO TO 490
      INC=INC+5
  400 IP=IP+1
  410 IF (L) 420,420,450
C IF BRACKETS OR QUOTES UNPAIRED, DELETE MOST OF LINE TO PREVENT
C AMBIGUOUS ADDRESSES
  420 WRITE (KT,430) IC
  430 FORMAT (1X,'NEW FRAME # ',I4,' HAD UNPAIRED BRACKETS OR QUOTES AND
     X WAS TRUNCATED')
      DO 440 I = 24,125
  440 BUFNU(I)=BLANK
      GO TO 490
  450 ML=0
C TIDY UP BY REMOVING REDUNDANT SPACES, AND LEADING ZEROS - THEN FILL
C REMAINING LINE WITH ASTERISKS
      K=STAR
      IF (BUF1.EQ.SLASH) K=BLANK
      DO 480 IT = 3,123
      I=IT-ML
      KK=BUFNU(I)
C CHECK THAT NEXT CHARACTER IS NOT BLANK, COMMA, R HAND BRACKET,
C MINUS, OR ASTERISK
      IF (KK.NE.BLANK.AND.KK.NE.COMMA.AND.KK.NE.RB.AND.KK.NE.MINUS.AND.K
     XK.NE.RCB.AND.KK.NE.STAR) GO TO 480
C CLOSE UP IF NEXT CHAR. IS BLANK
      KKK=BUFNU(I+1)
      IF (KKK.EQ.BLANK) GO TO 460
C CHECK THAT NEXT CHAR. IS =0, AND THERE IS NO SPACE OR COMMA BEYOND
      KKKK=BUFNU(I+2)
      IF (KKK.NE.ZERO.OR.KKKK.EQ.BLANK.OR.KKKK.EQ.COMMA) GO TO 480
  460 DO 470 N = I,123
  470 BUFNU(N+1)=BUFNU(N+2)
      ML=ML+1
C FILL FROM THE RIGHT END WITH ASTERISKS
      BUFNU(125)=K
  480 CONTINUE
  490 NPP=NPP-1
C*** LOCAL DIRECT ACCESS FILE ARRANGEMENTS - OVERWRITE WITH RECODED LINE
      WRITE (KF'NPP,500) (BUFNU(I),I=1,72)
C*** LOCAL - NEXT STATEMENT NEEDED IF 'WRITE' DOES NOT INCREMENT NPP
C     NPP=NPP+1
  500 FORMAT (72A1)
      IF (BUFNU(72).NE.STAR.AND.BUFNU(1).NE.SLASH.AND.IB.NE.1)
     X WRITE (KT,510) IC
  510 FORMAT (1X,'CHECK FRAME # ',I5,' - MAY HAVE BEEN TRUNCATED')
  520 M1=M1+1
      IF (M1-50) 550,530,530
  530 N=M1*M2
      WRITE (KT,540) N
  540 FORMAT (1X,I5,' TEXT LINES PROCESSED')
      M1=0
      M2=M2+1
  550 CONTINUE
C NPP IS NOW SET AT THE '**' LINE NUMBER
C CHECK FOR NON-ACCESSIBLE FRAMES
      DO 580 IB = 2,NL
      IF (KEY(2,IB)) 580,560,580
  560 IA=IB*10
      WRITE (KT,570) IA,KEY(1,IB)
  570 FORMAT (1X,'FRAME #',I5,' (OLD FRAME',I5,') NOT ACCESSED ANYWHERE'
     X )
  580 CONTINUE
      WRITE (KT,590)
  590 FORMAT (1X,'ADD MORE FRAMES?')
      CALL MACINP (BUF,X,NFLG)
C NFILE=1 TELLS S/R NEWFIL THAT THERE IS ALREADY A WORKING FILE
      NFILE=1
C 'NL' CONTAINS TOTAL NUMBER OF WORKING FRAMES SO FAR - S/R NEWFIL
C WILL CODE ANY ADDITIONAL FRAMES APPROPRIATELY.
```

SUBROUTINE RENUM1
CONTINUED

```
      IF (BUF(1).EQ.YY) CALL NEWFIL(NL,NFILE)
  600 WRITE (KT,610)
  610 FORMAT (1X,'NEW DIRECTORY WILL BE MADE')
      RETURN
  620 WRITE (KT,630) KYMAX
  630 FORMAT (1X,'MORE THAN',I4,' *-FRAMES - RENUMBERING IMPOSSIBLE')
      GO TO 600
      END
```

SUBROUTINE RENUM2

```
      SUBROUTINE RENUM2 (ALPH,N)
C
C  (NOT ESSENTIAL - USED IN CONJUNCTION WITH RENUM1)
C
C DOES VIRTUALLY OPPOSITE OF S/R MACNUM - I.E. THIS CONVERTS AN
C INTEGER (N) INTO A 4-CHARACTER STRING IN A1 FORMAT (ALPH)
C*
C     CHARACTER ALPH(4),DIGIT(10),MINUS
      INTEGER ALPH(4),DIGIT(10)
      DATA DIGIT/'1','2','3','4','5','6','7','8','9','0'/
      DATA MINUS/'-'/
      IF (N) 10,20,20
   10 ALPH(1)=MINUS
      N=-N
      GO TO 50
   20 I=N/1000
      N=N-I*1000
      IF (I) 40,30,40
   30 I=10
   40 ALPH(1)=DIGIT(I)
   50 I=N/100
      N=N-I*100
      IF (I) 70,60,70
   60 I=10
   70 ALPH(2)=DIGIT(I)
      I=N/10
      N=N-I*10
      IF (I) 90,80,90
   80 I=10
   90 ALPH(3)=DIGIT(I)
      IF (N) 110,100,110
  100 N=10
  110 ALPH(4)=DIGIT(N)
      RETURN
      END
```

SUBROUTINE NEWFIL

```
      SUBROUTINE NEWFIL (NSTRT,NFILE)
C
C    (NOT ESSENTIAL - USED WITH S/R AUTHR1 AND RENUM1)
C
C CREATES A FRAME SEQUENCE OF *T FRAMES, EACH ACCESSING THE NEXT
C E.G. *T10 1000 0 0 20
C       ...
C       *T20 1000 0 0 30
C       ...          ETC.
C OR ALLOWS SUCH A SEQUENCE TO BE TACKED ON TO AN EXISTING FILE
C*
C     CHARACTER BUF(72),YY
      INTEGER BUF(72),YY
      INTEGER FLAG,SCORE
      COMMON KT,KL,INI,NW1,NW2,JKL,NPRT,LDISP,KA,ITRIG(73),NEOF
      COMMON /FLS/ KF,LADRS,NPP,NNST,NNEND,MODE,FLAG,ION,SCORE,AION,SUM
      COMMON /TABLE/ NTOT,NKA,NFR,KYMAX,KEY(2,250),NDFR(14)
      DATA YY/'Y'/
      IF (NFILE) 10,40,40
   10 NPP=NNST
C======================================================================
C*** LOCAL ARRANGEMENTS FOR DIRECT ACCESS - ALL 'WRITE (KF' INSTRUCTIONS
C IN THIS SHORT SUBROUTINE NEED TO BE STANDARDISED
C N.B. THE 'NPP=NPP+1' STATEMENTS ARE NEEDED IF A DIRECT ACCESS
C 'WRITE' DOES NOT MOVE THE POINTER ON AUTOMATICALLY, OTHERWISE DELETE
      WRITE (KF'NPP,20)
   20 FORMAT ('*B')
C     NPP=NPP+1
      WRITE (KF'NPP,30)
   30 FORMAT ('*G')
C     NPP=NPP+1
   40 WRITE (KT,50)
   50 FORMAT (1X,'HOW MANY FRAMES?')
      CALL MACINP (BUF,X,NFLG)
      NADD=IFIX(X)
      WRITE (KT,60)
   60 FORMAT (1X,'HOW MANY LINES PER FRAME?')
      CALL MACINP (BUF,X,NFLG)
      NTEXT=IFIX(X)
      IF (NADD*(NTEXT+1)-NNEND+NNST+(NADD+NTOT-1)/8+4) 110,110,70
   70 WRITE (KT,80)
   80 FORMAT (1X,'FILE TOO SHORT - TRY AGAIN?')
      CALL MACINP (BUF,X,NFLG)
      IF (BUF(1).EQ.YY) GO TO 40
C IF NO NEW FILE CREATED, OVERWRITE *B FRAME WITH *G, TO PREVENT
C FILE BEING RECOGNISED ON SUBSEQUENT RUN
      IF (NFILE) 90,100,100
   90 NPP=NNST
      WRITE (KF'NPP,30)
  100 RETURN
  110 NSTRT=NSTRT*10
      DO 140 I = 1,NADD
      NSTRT=NSTRT+10
      L=NSTRT+10
      WRITE (KF'NPP,120) NSTRT,L
C     NPP=NPP+1
  120 FORMAT ('*T',I4,' 1000 0 0 ',I4)
      DO 140 K = 1,NTEXT
      WRITE (KF'NPP,130)
  130 FORMAT ('...')
C     NPP=NPP+1
  140 CONTINUE
      WRITE (KF'NPP,150)
  150 FORMAT ('**')
      NFILE=0
      RETURN
      END
```

# Appendix II

## TABLE OF THE MAIN FORTRAN SYMBOLS USED IN THE MACAID DRIVER

---

*COMMON store integers compatible with the 'MAC' series of physiological and clinical models*

The BLANK COMMON store of all our physiological models and of MACAID begins with the following integer variables:
KT, KL, INI, NW1, NW2, JKL, NPRT, LDISP, KA, ITRIG (73), NEOF.
Most of these are described in detail in the published account of a computer simulation of human respiration (Dickinson, 1977). The MACAID Driver only uses KT, INI, LDISP, KA and, in subroutine MCSUBR only, array ITRIG. However, for reference purposes all are listed below. The way in which the other integer variables are used in subroutines is exemplified by the two subroutines SUB4 and SUB5 (together with their associated input subroutine NXTWD). These subroutines, which are used in conjunction with the illustrative text exercise of Chapter 3, are given in full in Appendix III, p. 170. The complete list of BLANK COMMON integer variables is as follows:

KT – Logical number of the output device most suitable for operator interaction (will usually be a visual display unit console).

KL – Logical number of the lineprinter if in use (unit KL is not used by MACAID itself, but may be needed by associated subroutines).

INI – Logical number of the input unit, which for MACAID will be the console teletype or equivalent.

NW1 – Maintains a pointer in the 73 integer (or character) array ITRIG, which is read from left to right.

NW2 – Initialized at zero before any call by a simulation model to subroutine NXTWD (e.g. see Appendix III). If greater than zero, calls to NXTWD use information already stored in array ITRIG, instead of requesting user input.

JKL – Index governing processing by NXTWD of sequences of numbers separated by blanks (e.g. see Appendix III).

NPRT – Index controlling suppression of printing output by a MACAID subroutine (0 = suppress output; 1 = print output normally).

LDISP – Integer of up to 4 digits giving cursor control instructions (in MACAID to subroutine MCDISP, and in associated subroutines for special purposes).

KA – Logical number of the output or 'answer' file, recording selected entries by a user.

ITRIG (73) – Integer (or character) array used for communication between simulation models and the input subroutine NXTWD.

NEOF – Specifies the maximum number of numerical entries expected in the next call to subroutine NXTWD.

*Other integer variables* (those which could be of character type are marked with an asterisk)

*ANS (72) – Buffer for input of up to 72 characters in sequential keyboard entry.

*BUF (72) – General purpose buffer for storing 72-character strings, in most cases read from the text file by subroutine MACRND.

FLAG – Value of integer flag, which should be between 1 and 11 (default = 1).

IADRS – Line number of a specified frame (found by subroutine MACLOC).

IERR – Error index (1 = some error found in reading the random-access text file. 0=no error).

ION – Score switch (0 = scorer off; 1 = scorer on; default = 0).

IP – Maintains a pointer in the integer (or character) array BUF.

IPX – Store of pointer location IP for back reference later.

KEY (2, KYMAX) Table giving the line address of each control line or frame.

KF – Logical number of direct or random-access file containing uncompiled text and control lines (fixed 72-character length).

KNUM(NG) – Frame number for exit when global keyword #NG is entered.

*KWDS(NG, 5) 5-character string defining keyword #NG.

KYMAX – Maximum number of control frames allowed within any single text file (initialized in the main Driver program of Appendix I at 250, but this, and the 2nd dimension of array KEY can in principle be made any size which the computer can handle).

LADRS – Last line number address (at the end of the file), at which the frame directory is stored.

LASTF – Last frame number to have been accessed.

| | |
|---|---|
| MATCH | – Index of success (= 1) or failure (= 0) in matching input with a keyword in a *Q frame. |
| MODE | – 2 = 'authoring' password given, full range of editing commands allowed; 1 = normal use, editing restricted; 0 = logical error found in a control line of the text file. |
| NANS | – Number of lines (in a *Q or *M frame). |
| NCODE | – Cursor position control index (between 1 and 6), telling subroutine MCDISP which digit of LDISP to act on. |
| NCOLM(N) | – Location of keyword #N in an answer line. |
| NDFR(N) | – Line location of dictionary #N. |
| NDICT | – Code number of a dictionary (used with a *Q-frame). |
| NDIR | – Total number of dictionaries in the text file. |
| NDISP | – Cursor control instruction number (in subroutine MCDISP). |
| NFILE | – Index of adequacy of a text file (=0); inadequate file missing a *B line (= −1). |
| NFLG | – Index to record if subroutine MACNUM locates a number (= 0) or not (= −1). |
| NFR | – Next frame number to be located and processed. |
| NFSV | – Next frame number, to be saved for future reference. |
| NG | – Number of global keywords (including 'AUTHOR') to be tested at each user input. |
| NGFR | – Frame number for transfer of control when a global keyword is successfully matched. |
| NKA | – Output file record switch (0 = off; 1 = output file recorder switched on; default = 0). |
| NKWD | – Number of keywords entered in the answer to a *Q-frame. |
| NNEND | – Last line number of the random access text file (not to exceed 5 digits). |
| NNST | – First line number of the random access text file (not to exceed 5 digits). |
| NPP | – Line number (of the random access text file) used in a READ or WRITE statement. |
| NPPX | – Store of line number NPP for future reference. |
| NSTRT | – Frame number of 1st frame of the text file to be read, as specified by the *B-line. |
| NSUB | – Code number of the subroutine called by a *S-frame. |
| NTERM | – Identifies any special type of terminal to be used (>0); 0 = no cursor positioning or special display instructions to be used. |
| NTOT | – Number of control frames in a text file. |
| SCORE | – Value of a ranking score (integer between 100 and 0; default = 100). |
| TRACE | – 1 = tracing information to be printed at every frame; 0 = no trace (default = 0). |
| *TPLST | – Array of frame type letters. |
| *TYPE | – Frame type letter in use. |

*Floating point variables*

| | |
|---|---|
| ADD | – Floating point value of the 3rd ('add') parameter of a control line. |
| ADRES(N,M) | – Table of frame addresses (for *M frames only). |
| AION | – Sum (total) switch (0 = adder off; 1 = adder on; default = 0). |
| EXIT | – Frame exit address (number of next frame to be accessed). |
| FR | – Frame number. |
| R | – Identifies a decimal point in a number (R = .1) or no decimal point (R = 1). |
| SCR | – Value of the 2nd ('score') parameter of a control line. |
| SUM | – Value of a running total (minimal value = 0; default = 0). |
| XANS | – Floating point number entered as keyboard input. |

# Appendix III

## COMPLETE FORTRAN SUBROUTINES SUB4, SUB5 AND NXTWD AS USED WITH THE MACAID DRIVER (APPENDIX I) TO RUN THE ILLUSTRATIVE TEXT EXERCISE LISTED IN CHAPTER 3

```
      SUBROUTINE SUB4
C SUBROUTINE TO RECORD TODAY'S DATE AND DATE OF BIRTH, AND THEN
C TO WORK OUT AGE IN YEARS, ENTERING THE RESULT AS
C 'AGE ..' ON THE WORK-SPACE AT THE END OF THE TEXT FILE,
C SO THAT IT CAN LATER BE COLLECTED AND ENTERED INTO THE ANSWER FILE
C
C*
C     CHARACTER BUF(72)
      INTEGER BUF(72)
      INTEGER FLAG,SCORE
      COMMON KT,KL,INI,NW1,NW2,JKL,NPRT,LDISP,KA,ITRIG(73),NEOF
      COMMON /FLS/ KF,LADRS,NPP,NNST,NNEND,MODE,FLAG,ION,SCORE,AION,SUM
      NPP=LADRS+LDISP
   10 WRITE (KT,20)
   20 FORMAT (1X,'PLEASE TYPE TODAY*S DATE LIKE THIS.. 12/10/79 ..THEN P
     XRESS *RETURN*')
      CALL MACINP (BUF,X,NFLG)
      IP=1
      CALL MACNUM (BUF,IP,D1,NFLG,R)
      CALL MACNUM (BUF,IP,D2,NFLG,R)
      CALL MACNUM (BUF,IP,D3,NFLG,R)
      IF ((D1*D2*D3).LT..5.OR.D1.GT.31..OR.D2.GT.12..OR.D3.GT.99.) GO TO
     X 10
C*** LOCAL ARRANGEMENTS FOR DIRECT ACCESS
      WRITE (KF'NPP,30) (BUF(I),I=1,63)
   30 FORMAT (9X,63A1)
   40 WRITE (KT,50)
   50 FORMAT (1X,'NOW YOUR DATE OF BIRTH, IN SIMILAR FORMAT, PLEASE')
      CALL MACINP (BUF,X,NFLG)
      IP=1
      CALL MACNUM (BUF,IP,B1,NFLG,R)
      CALL MACNUM (BUF,IP,B2,NFLG,R)
      CALL MACNUM (BUF,IP,B3,NFLG,R)
      IF ((B1*B2*B3).LT..5.OR.B1.GT.31..OR.B2.GT.12..OR.B3.GT.99.) GO TO
     X 40
      NAGE=IFIX(D3-B3)
      IF (D2.LT.B2.OR.(D2.EQ.B2.AND.D1.LT.B1)) NAGE=NAGE-1
      IF (NAGE.LT.15.OR.NAGE.GT.80) GO TO 10
C*** LOCAL ARRANGEMENTS FOR DIRECT ACCESS
      WRITE (KF'NPP,60) NAGE
   60 FORMAT (9X,'AGE',I3)
      RETURN
      END
```

SUBROUTINE SUB5

```
      SUBROUTINE SUB5
C SUBROUTINE TO PLOT GRAPHS OF QUADRATIC EQUATIONS TO ORDER
C
C*
C     CHARACTER CROSS(1),BLANK,ZERO,MARK,BAR,ONE,FIVE,BUF(70)
      INTEGER CROSS(1),BLANK,ZERO,BAR,ONE,FIVE,BUF(70)
      INTEGER FLAG,SCORE
      DIMENSION KEY(20),IANS(4),T(4)
      COMMON KT,KL,INI,NW1,NW2,JKL,NPRT,LDISP,KA,ITRIG(72),NUM,NEOF
      COMMON /FLS/ KF,LADRS,NPP,NNST,NNEND,MODE,FLAG,ION,SCORE,AION,SUM
      DATA CROSS,BLANK,ZERO,MARK,BAR,ONE,FIVE/'X',' ','0','I','-','1','5
     X'/
      DATA IZERO/1H0/
      COMP(D,C,A,B,X)=IFIX((A*X**B+C*X+D)*.2)
      DO 10 I = 1,4
   10 T(I)=0.
      IF (ITRIG(1).NE.IZERO) GO TO 20
      NW2=20
      NW1=3
   20 IF (NW2.GT.19) GO TO 40
      WRITE (KT,30)
   30 FORMAT (1X,'DO YOU WANT TO..1.CHANGE, 2.PLOT THE GRAPH, 3.STORE TH
     XE GRAPH, 4.STOP')
   40 CALL NXTWD (NQ,XXX,NNN,1,4)
      NFLAG=0
      GO TO (60,160,50,320), NNN
   50 NFLAG=1
      NPP=LDISP+LADRS
      GO TO 160
   60 IF (NW2.GT.19) GO TO 80
      WRITE (KT,70)
   70 FORMAT (1X,'TYPE FACTOR NUMBERS (1-4) TO CHANGE')
      NW2=0
   80 NEOF=5
      NL=0
      KYY=-1
      JKL=1
   90 CALL NXTWD (NQ,XXX,NNN,1,4)
      KYY=KYY+1
      NW2=NW2+1
      NL=NL+1
      IF (JKL.EQ.0) GO TO 100
      IF (NEOF.EQ.0) GO TO 110
      IANS(NL)=NNN
      GO TO 90
  100 IANS(NL)=NNN
      KYY=KYY+1
  110 IF (NW2.GT.19) GO TO 120
      NW2=0
  120 DO 150 IJ = 1,KYY
      I=IANS(IJ)
      IF (NW2.GT.19) GO TO 140
      WRITE (KT,130) I,T(I)
  130 FORMAT (1X,'FACTOR ',I1,' (CURRENT VALUE=',F7.1,'), SPECIFY NEW VA
     XLUE')
  140 CALL NXTWD (NQ,XXX,NNN,-100,100)
      T(I)=XXX
  150 CONTINUE
      GO TO 20
  160 DO 260 N = 1,21
      K=21-N
      DO 170 I = 1,70
  170 BUF(I)=BLANK
      BUF(13)=MARK
      IF (K.NE.20) GO TO 180
      BUF(9)=ONE
      BUF(10)=ZERO
      GO TO 200
  180 IF (K.NE.10) GO TO 190
```

SUBROUTINE SUB5
CONTINUED

```
      BUF(10)=FIVE
      GO TO 200
  190 IF (K.NE.0) GO TO 210
  200 BUF(11)=ZERO
      BUF(12)=BAR
  210 DO 220 I = 13,70,3
      X=FLOAT((I-13)/3)
      IF ((COMP(T(1),T(2),T(3),T(4),X)).EQ.K) BUF(I)=CROSS(1)
  220 CONTINUE
      IF (NFLAG) 230,230,250
  230 WRITE (KT,240) BUF
  240 FORMAT (1X,70A1)
      GO TO 260
C** LOCAL ARRANGEMENTS FOR OUTPUT
  250 WRITE (KA,240) BUF
  260 CONTINUE
      DO 270 I = 9,70
  270 BUF(I)=BAR
      IF (NFLAG.GT.0) GO TO 280
      WRITE (KT,240) BUF
      GO TO 300
C** LOCAL ARRANGEMENTS FOR OUTPUT, NEXT 2 LINES
  280 WRITE (KA,240) BUF
      WRITE (KA,310)
      WRITE (KT,290)
  290 FORMAT (1X,'*** GRAPH NOW STORED')
      GO TO 20
  300 WRITE (KT,310)
  310 FORMAT (13X,'0        2        4        6        8        10        12
     X 14')
      GO TO 20
  320 NW2=0
      RETURN
      END
```

SUBROUTINE NXTWD (LL3,XXX,NNN,IMIN,IMAX)

```
      SUBROUTINE NXTWD (LL3,XXX,NNN,IMIN,IMAX)
C THIS SR ALLOWS NUMBERS TO BE ENTERED IN FREE FORMAT
C AND RETRIEVED IN STANDARD REAL OR INTEGER FORM, OR FED INTO
C ARRAYS, IF NEEDED
C*
C     CHARACTER ITRIG,BLANK,SLASH
      INTEGER BLANK,SLASH
      COMMON KT,KL,INI,NW1,NW2,JKL,NPRT,LDISP,KA,ITRIG(73),NEOF
      DATA BLANK,SLASH/' ','/'/
      XMIN=IMIN
      XMAX=IMAX
      IF (NW2.GE.1) GO TO 40
      NW2=0
   10 CONTINUE
C*** LOCAL ARRANGEMENTS, FOR PROMPT ?
      WRITE (KT,20)
   20 FORMAT(1X,'?')
      READ (INI,30) (ITRIG(IM),IM=1,72)
   30 FORMAT (72A1)
      IF (ITRIG(1).EQ.BLANK.AND.LL3.EQ.14) GO TO 140
      NW1=1
   40 IF (NW1.NE.72) GO TO 50
      IF (NEOF.GT.0) GO TO 80
      GO TO 10
   50 CALL MACNUM (ITRIG,NW1,XXX,NFLG,R)
      IF (NW1.EQ.72) NW2=0
      IF (NFLG) 120,60,70
   60 IF ((XXX-XMIN)*(XMAX-XXX).LT.0) GO TO 100
      NNN=XXX
C NUMERIC VALUE ENTERED WITHIN RANGE
   70 IF (ITRIG(NW1).NE.SLASH) GO TO 90
      NW2=20
      JKL=0
      NW1=NW1+1
   80 NEOF=0
      RETURN
   90 NEOF=NEOF-1
      RETURN
  100 WRITE (KT,110) IMIN,IMAX
  110 FORMAT (1X,'IT HAS TO BE BETWEEN',I7,' AND',I7)
  120 WRITE (KT,130)
  130 FORMAT (1X,'PLEASE TRY AGAIN')
      NW2=0
      GO TO 10
  140 XXX=-999.
      NNN=-999
      NW2=0
      JKL=0
      RETURN
      END
```

# Appendix IV

## EXAMPLE OF INITIAL LINE NUMBERS OF A SET OF TEACHING EXERCISES STORED CONSECUTIVELY ON A 10 000 LINE DIRECT-ACCESS FILE. THIS INDEX IS STORED AT THE START OF THE TEXT FILE, AND IS USED BY THE MACAID SUPERVISOR LISTED IN APPENDIX V

```
 1  00051   CHILDHOOD ASTHMA
 2  00405   ABDOMINAL PAIN, NAUSEA AND VOMITING
 3  00838   HYPERTENSION
 4  01292   CHRONIC BRONCHITIS
 5  01738   EPILEPSY
 6  02110   KIDNEY INFECTION
 7  02476   PULMONARY OEDEMA
 8  02912   DIABETES MELLITUS
 9  03325   PERNICIOUS ANAEMIA
10  03763   ENURESIS
11  04158   A DEPRIVED CHILD
12  04592   SLIPPED DISC
MNTX 5000   ELEMENTARY PRINCIPLES OF HAEMODYNAMICS
CPRT 5754   CARDIO-PULMONARY RESUSCITATION
PUFT 6854   CLINICAL ASPECTS OF RESPIRATION
MULT 7615   MULTIPLE CHOICE QUESTIONS IN MEDICINE
SILL 8816
SPAR 9267
++++10000
```

# Appendix V

## EXAMPLE OF A FORTRAN SUPERVISORY MAIN PROGRAM TO SET INITIAL AND FINAL LINE NUMBERS (NNST AND NNEND) ACCORDING TO A USER'S INSTRUCTIONS, USING A TEXT FILE OF 10 000 LINES, STARTING WITH THE INDEX LISTED IN APPENDIX IV

---

```
C MAIN 'SUPERVISORY' PROGRAM FOR RUNNING GENERAL PRACTICE PROBLEMS,
C CPR AND MANAGEMENT PROBLEMS, AND SIMULATION MODELS
C     AUTHORS:  DR. D.INGRAM AND PROF. C.J. DICKINSON,
C               DEPT. OF MEDICINE, ST. BARTHOLOMEW'S HOSPITAL,
C               LONDON, ENGLAND;
C               DR. K. AHMED,
C               COMPUTATION SERVICES UNIT, HEALTH SCIENCES CENTRE,
C               MCMASTER UNIVERSITY, HAMILTON, ONTARIO, CANADA.
C
C               VERSION 12    1 FEBRUARY 1980
C*
C      CHARACTER BUF(72)
       INTEGER BUF(72)
       INTEGER FLAG,SCORE
       COMMON KT,KL,INI,NW1,NW2,JKL,NPRT,LDISP,KA,ITRIG(73),NEOF
       COMMON /FLS/ KF,LADRS,NPP,NNST,NNEND,MODE,FLAG,ION,SCORE,AION,SUM
C
C*** LOCAL ARRANGEMENTS FOR FILE DEFINITION, ETC.
       DEFINE FILE 3(12000,72,E,NPP)
C
C*** SET LOGICAL UNITS
       INI=5
       KT=6
       KF=3
       KA=4
   10 WRITE(KT,20)
   20 FORMAT(//,1X,'TUTORIAL AND SELF-ASSESSMENT EXERCISES IN CLINICAL M
     XEDICINE',/,1X,'AND GENERAL PRACTICE',
     X/,1X,'TYPE  1  FOR PROBLEMS IN CLINICAL PHYSIOLOGY',/,1X,
     X     '      2  FOR CASE STUDIES IN GENERAL PRACTICE',/,1X,
     X     '      3  FOR CLINICAL MANAGEMENT PROBLEMS AND TESTS',/,1X,
     X     '      0  TO STOP ALTOGETHER')
   30 CALL MACINP (BUF,X,NFLG)
      IF (NFLG) 10,40,10
   40 IT=IFIX(X)
      IF (IT.LE.0) STOP
      IF (IT.LE.3) GO TO 60
      WRITE (KT,50)
   50 FORMAT(1X,'INVALID OPTION - PLEASE TRY AGAIN')
      GO TO 30
C** WRITE ON OUTPUT FILE
   60 WRITE (KA,70) IT
   70 FORMAT(1X,'EXERCISE TYPE ',I1)
      CALL INIT (IT)
      IF (IT) 10,80,80
   80 CALL MACRUN
      GO TO 10
      END
```

SUBROUTINE INIT (IT)

```
      SUBROUTINE INIT (IT)
C*
C     CHARACTER BUF(60),NAME(4),IQ,IS,PLUS
      INTEGER BUF(60),PLUS
      DIMENSION NAME(4),IREF(3),INDEX(50),MAX(3)
      COMMON KT,KL,INI,NW1,NW2,JKL,NPRT,LDISP,KA,ITRIG(73),NEOF
      COMMON /FLS/ KF,LADRS,NPP,NNST,NNEND,MODE,FLAG,ION,SCORE,AION,SUM
      DATA IQ,IS,PLUS/'Q','S','+'/
      DATA IREF,MAX/1,6,31,5,25,20/
      DATA INDEX/13,15,3*0,1,2,3,4,5,6,7,8,9,10,11,12,13*0,
     X 14,16,17,18,16*0/
   10 WRITE (KT,20)
   20 FORMAT(/,1X,'ENTER THE NUMBER OF THE EXERCISE YOU WISH TO STUDY. T
     XYPE L  FOR',/,1X,'A LIST OF EXERCISES AVAILABLE, Q FOR INTRODUCTOR
     XY COMMENTS, S TO STOP')
      CALL MACINP (ITRIG,XANS,NFLG)
      IP=1
      CALL MACNUM (ITRIG,IP,XX,NRET,R)
      IF (NRET) 90,30,90
   30 IEX=IFIX(XX)
C** WRITE ON OUTPUT FILE
      WRITE (KA,40) IEX
   40 FORMAT(1X,'EXERCISE #  =',I3)
      IOF=IREF(IT)
      IF (IEX*(MAX(IT)-IEX+1)) 50,50,70
   50 WRITE (KT,60)
   60 FORMAT (1X,'NO SUCH EXERCISE AVAILABLE. PLEASE TRY AGAIN')
      GO TO 10
   70 NPP=INDEX(IOF+IEX-1)
      IF (NPP.LE.0) GO TO 50
C*** DIRECT ACCESS, READ STARTING LINE # - ?INCREMENT NPP AFTERWARDS?
      READ (KF'NPP,80) NAME,NNST
C     NPP=NPP+1
C*** DIRECT ACCESS, READ LAST LINE (1ST OF NEXT EXERCISE)
      READ (KF'NPP,80) NAME,NNEND
   80 FORMAT (4A1,I5)
      NPP=NNST
      RETURN
   90 IF (ITRIG(1).EQ.IQ) GO TO 180
      IF (ITRIG(1).EQ.IS) GO TO 200
      IOF=IREF(IT)-1
      IL=MAX(IT)
  100 DO 130 I=1,IL
      NPP=INDEX(IOF+I)
      IF (NPP) 130,130,110
C*** DIRECT ACCESS FILE READ
  110 READ (KF'NPP,140) NAME,N,BUF
      IF (NAME(1).EQ.PLUS) GO TO 50
      N=NPP
  120 WRITE (KT,150) I,BUF
  130 CONTINUE
      GO TO 10
  140 FORMAT (4A1,I5,60A1)
  150 FORMAT (1X,'STUDY ',I4,3X,60A1)
      WRITE (KT,160)
C*** LOCAL ARRANGEMENTS FOR PROMPT
  160 FORMAT(1X,'PRESS *RETURN* TO CONTINUE LIST')
      READ (INI,170) I
  170 FORMAT (I1)
      GO TO 100
  180 IF (ITRIG(1).NE.IQ) GO TO 190
      CALL MCQUER (1,IT)
      GO TO 10
  190 IF (ITRIG(1).EQ.IS) RETURN
      GO TO 10
  200 IT=-1
      RETURN
      END
```

SUBROUTINE MCQUER (LL,IT)

```
      SUBROUTINE MCQUER (LL,IT)
C
C*** DESCRIPTIONS OF LOCALLY-AVAILABLE TEACHING EXERCISES
C
      INTEGER FLAG,SCORE
      COMMON KT,KL,INI,NW1,NW2,JKL,NPRT,LDISP,KA,ITRIG(73),NEOF
      COMMON/ FLS/ KF,LADRS,NPP,NNST,NNEND,MODE,FLAG,ION,SCORE,AION,SUM
      GO TO (50,10,70),IT
   10 WRITE (KT,20)
   20 FORMAT(1X,'THESE CASE STUDIES WERE DEVELOPED BY DR. MURRAY AND COL
     XLEAGUES',/,1X,'AT GLASGOW UNIVERSITY AND HAVE BEEN RE-WRITTEN USIN
     XG',/,1X,'THE *MACAID* COMPUTER-AIDED INSTRUCTION SYSTEM BY',/
     X,1X,'DR.D.INGRAM, PROF. C.J.DICKINSON AND DR.K.AHMED.')
      WRITE (KT,30)
   30 FORMAT(1X,'WHEN YOU HAVE SELECTED A CASE TO STUDY YOU WILL BE SHOW
     XN THE CASE',/,1X,'DETAILS FROM INITIAL CONSULTATION, THROUGH DIAGN
     XOSIS, TREATMENT',/1X,'AND LONG TERM MANAGEMENT AS APPROPRIATE.',/,
     X1X,'AT EACH STAGE YOU WILL BE ASKED TO ASSESS ALTERNATIVE DECISION
     XS',/,1X,'AND COURSES OF ACTION.  YOU ARE ASKED TO MARK THESE ON A
     XSCALE', /,1X,'0 TO 4, WHERE YOU SHOULD THINK OF THE MARKS AS FOLLO
     XWS:',/,1X,'0 = MUST NOT DO',/,1X,'1 = SHOULD NOT DO, AS A RULE',/
     X,1X,'2 = COULD DO, OR MIGHT DO',/,1X,'3 = SHOULD DO, AS A RULE',/
     X,1X,'4 = MUST DO')
      WRITE (KT,40)
   40 FORMAT (1X,'YOUR ANSWERS ARE THEN COMPARED WITH THE ASSESSMENT OF
     XA PANEL',/,1X,'OF EXPERIENCED PRACTITIONERS AND GUIDANCE GIVEN'
     X,' ACCORDINGLY.',/,1X,'YOU WILL ALSO BE GIVEN MARKS SO THAT YOU CA
     XN COMPARE YOUR',/,1X,'PERFORMANCE WITH THE IDEAL.')
      RETURN
   50 WRITE (KT,60)
   60 FORMAT (1X,'THESE EXERCISES ARE BASED ON THE CIRCULATORY MODELS DE
     XVELOPED',/,1X,'OVER THE PAST 8 YEARS AT ST. BARTHOLOMEW*S HOSPITAL
     X',/,1X,'MEDICAL COLLEGE BY PROF. C.J.DICKINSON AND DR. D.INGRAM AN
     XD BY',/,1X,'COLLEAGUES AT MCMASTER UNIVERSITY.',/,1X,'THEY HAVE BE
     XEN DESIGNED TO SIMPLIFY THE USE OF THE MODELS AND',/,1X,'AT THE SA
     XME TIME ADD NEW FEATURES FOR COMPUTER-ASSISTED LEARNING',/,1X,'AND
     X ASSESSMENT.')
      RETURN
 70   WRITE (KT,80)
   80 FORMAT (1X,'THESE EXERCISES HAVE BEEN DEVELOPED AT ST.BARTHOLOMEW*
     XS HOSPITAL MEDICAL',/,1X,'COLLEGE OR HAVE BEEN ADAPTED THERE TO TH
     XE BARTS/MCMASTER',/,1X,'COMPUTER-ASSISTED LEARNING SYSTEM (MACAID)
     X.',/,1X,'THEY COVER GENERAL PROBLEMS IN CLINICAL MEDICINE AND MULT
     XIPLE CHOICE',/,1X,'EXAMINATIONS')
      RETURN
      END
```

# Appendix VI

## AVAILABILITY OF THE PROGRAMS

The authors of this book have published it in the hope that MACAID may achieve recognition as a standard way to store interrogative text and simultaneously run FORTRAN subroutines for more sophisticated purposes. It appeared to us that the potential benefits to those using, or proposing to use, interrogative programs for computer-aided instruction or interviews would be much diminished if we restricted the distribution of the programs in any way. Therefore we have described MACAID in the fullest possible detail in this book.

However, there have already been many people who have asked us to supply the master Driver program, a test text file, and actual examples of teaching exercises in the field of medical education. No doubt there will be more in the future. We shall therefore continue to make such programs available on magnetic tape at nominal cost, to those who will write, from U.K. and Europe, to:

Dr D. Ingram,
Department of Medicine,
St Bartholomew's Hospital Medical College,
West Smithfield,
London EC1A 7BE
England. (Tel. 01-600 9000 (Ext. 3431 or 2248))

or, from North America and elsewhere, to:

Dr K. Ahmed,
Systems Manager,
Computation Services Unit,
McMaster University Medical Centre,
Main Street West,
Hamilton,
Ontario, Canada. (Tel. 416-525-9140 (Ext. 2676))

We hope to be able to maintain current and, if necessary, corrected and up-to-date versions of all programs and teaching exercises at these addresses.

# Index